ASSESSING PERSONALITY

ASSESSING PERSONALITY

Robert R. Holt

New York University

Irving L. Janis, *Editor*

HARCOURT BRACE JOVANOVICH, INC.

New York   *Chicago*   *San Francisco*   *Atlanta*

ISBN: 0-15-503982-2

Library of Congress Catalog Card Number: 79-152579

Printed in the United States of America

ACKNOWLEDGMENTS AND COPYRIGHTS

The author wishes to thank the companies and persons listed below
for permission to use material in this book.

Textual Material

Chapter 1 Opening quote: From *Of Human Bondage*, by W. Somerset
Maugham. Copyright 1915, by Doubleday & Company, Inc. Reprinted by permission of Doubleday & Company, Inc., William
Heinemann Ltd., and the Literary Executors of the late W. Somerset Maugham.

3 Test items from Siegel (1956) courtesy of the American Psychological Association.

4 Sample test item from Kuder (1948) reprinted by permission of
Science Research Associates, Inc. All rights reserved.

6 Test items from G. W. and F. H. Allport, *A-S Reaction Study*,
Houghton Mifflin, 1928.

Test items from G. W. Allport, P. E. Vernon, & G. Lindzey, *The
Study of Values*, Houghton Mifflin, 1951.

7 Opening quote: From *A Portrait of the Artist as a Young Man* by
James Joyce. Copyright 1916 by B. W. Huebsch, Inc.; renewed
1944 by Nora Joyce. Copyright © 1964 by the Estate of James
Joyce. All rights reserved. Reprinted by permission of the Viking
Press, Inc., Jonathan Cape Ltd., and the Executors of the James
Joyce Estate.

9 Opening quote: From *Book of French Quotations*, translated and
edited by Norbert Guterman. By permission of Norbert Guterman.

Illustrative Material

Figure 2-1   Feleky, A. M. The expression of the emotions. *Psychological Review*, 1914, *21*, 33–44. Courtesy of the American Psychological Association.

2-2   Permission S.P.A.D.E.M. 1969 by French Reproduction Rights, Inc. Courtesy of Musée Rodin. Photo by Andrieu d'Andres.

2-4   Harlow, H. F. The heterosexual affectional system in monkeys. *American Psychologist*, 1962, *17*, 1–19. Copyright 1962 by the American Psychological Association, and used by permission. Photo courtesy of Dr. Harry F. Harlow.

2-5   Machover, K. *Personality projection in the drawing of the human figure*, 1949. Courtesy of Charles C Thomas, Publisher, Springfield, Ill.

4-1   Sheldon, W. H., et al. *The varieties of human physique*. New York: Harper & Row, 1940.

4-2   Glueck, S., & Glueck, E. Unraveling juvenile delinquency. New York: Commonwealth Fund; Cambridge, Mass.: Harvard University Press, 1950.

4-3   Photo by David Linton.

4-4   Witkin, H. A., et al. *Personality through perception*, pp. 534, 545. New York: Harper & Row, 1954.

6-1   Allport, G. W., & Vernon, P. E. *The study of values*. Boston: Houghton Mifflin, 1931.

6-2a   Permission S.P.A.D.E.M. 1969 by French Reproduction Rights, Inc. Courtesy of The Cleveland Museum of Art.

8-1   Reproduced by permission. Copyright 1943, The Psychological Corporation, New York, N.Y. All rights reserved.

8-2   Allport, G. W., Vernon, P. E., & Lindzey, G. *The study of values*. Boston: Houghton Mifflin, 1951.

8-4   From Hidden Figures Test-cf-1. Copyright © 1962 by Educational Testing Service. All rights reserved. Developed under NIMH Contract M-4186. Reprinted by permission.

Table 4-1   Star, S. A. The screening of psychoneurotics. In S. A. Stouffer et al., *Measurement and prediction*. Princeton, N.J.: Princeton University Press, 1950. Used by permission of the publisher.

4-2   Strong, E. K., Jr. *Vocational interests of men and women*. Palo Alto, Calif.: Stanford University Press, 1943. Used by permission of the publisher.

4-3   Bellak, L., & Holt, R. R. Somatotypes in relation to dementia praecox. *American Journal of Psychiatry*, 1948, *104*, 713–24, by permission of *American Journal of Psychiatry* and the authors.

4-4   Norman, W. T. Toward an adequate taxonomy of personality attributes: Replicated factor structure in peer nomination personality ratings, *Journal of Abnormal and Social Psychology*, 1963, 66, p. 577, Table 1. Copyright 1963 by the American Psychological Association, and reproduced by permission of the American Psychological Association and the author.

Table 8-3   Block, J. *The Q-sort method in personality assessment and psychiatric research*. Springfield, Ill.: Charles C Thomas, Publisher, 1961. Used by permission of the author.

10-1   Gough, H. G. Clinical versus statistical prediction in psychology. In L. Postman (Ed.), *Psychology in the making: Histories of selected research problems*. New York: Knopf, 1962. Used by permission of the publisher.

PREFACE

Personality assessment has come into being as a distinct branch of psychology during the years since the Second World War, a period that coincides with the years during which I have been studying, practicing, teaching, and doing research on various aspects of personality and its assessment. Thirty years ago the now united components of this discipline were relatively independent: diagnostic testing of psychiatric patients was mostly in the hands of professional clinical psychologists practicing in hospitals and clinics; a group of academic psychologists and psychometricians were developing questionnaires, inventories, and other tests of personality traits; within social psychology a number of workers were starting to focus on social perception—the study of ways people get impressions and form conceptions of one another as persons; and another group of academics calling themselves personality psychologists were doing experiments and writing theories about personality. The process of integration is not yet complete, nor has it been smooth and steady; but this book is in part an expression of my conviction that these somewhat disparate streams have been converging and can be made to flow together to the advantage of all.

On just about any level, the answer to the question, "What is this book's orientation?" must include a striving for integration. Thus the book includes elements of theory, practice, empirical research, and clinical case study, but tries to view each issue from all these perspectives. The theoretical orientation is largely psychoanalytic, but with an eclectic and skeptical flavor, and with an effort to use insights and concepts from many other schools of personality theory (from the biological to the sociocultural) to avoid the narrowness of one outlook. The approach to measuring variables of personality urged here is pluralistic. I have not hesitated to enter controversial areas, nor have I tried to conceal my biases; but if there is special pleading, it is for compromise and balance. For example, I have tried to be fair in my presentation of both the clinical and the objective approaches to personality assessment, though this is an area of intense controversy and I have been in the thick of it—as an advocate not so much of the clinical tradition, in which I received most of my training, as of the view that the contributions of both traditions are indispensable to the discipline that is emerging.

The goal of the book is to supply a solid introduction to personality assessment on a fairly sophisticated but not specialized level. It has been used successfully with both undergraduate and graduate students, in general courses on personality and clinical psychology as well as in courses on assessment. I have tried to keep the presentation clear and interesting enough to get the less highly prepared student over the more intellectually demanding spots, without oversimplifying complex issues. Wherever possible I have approached each problem by setting it in a historical and theoretical context, summarizing relevant research, and illustrating it in the case history of William Morris Brown. The book, like the discipline it presents, is of potential interest to anyone who is curious about himself and others, but especially to anyone who needs to use interviewing, testing, or the analysis of "personal documents" in his professional activities.

A word about what this book is *not*. It is not a text on "tests and measurements" or psychometrics, nor is it a comprehensive survey of available methods of studying and measuring personality (though it discusses and exemplifies many of the most widely used methods as well as some that have not attained as much use as they deserve). The student or teacher who wants a book on clinical psychodiagnosis should look elsewhere, for this one concentrates on the general problems of assessing personalities to the exclusion of differential diagnosis, and more on normal subjects than on psychiatric patients.

The first four chapters lay out the general problems and issues of personality assessment, going from informal, everyday processes of sizing people up, to formal assessment and its two traditions, here called clinical and objective. The next five chapters treat the issues and methods concretely, as applied to and embodied in an intensive and extensive case study. The student will get to know the principal events in the first 52 years of one man's life, and can study in detail the kinds of data supplied by many methods of studying him in two multiform assessments separated by an interval of 26 years.

This book was first published as Part IV of *Personality: Dynamics, Development, and Assessment* (Harcourt Brace Jovanovich, 1969) by Irving L. Janis, George F. Mahl, Jerome Kagan, and Robert R. Holt, under the editorship of Irving L. Janis. Many people helped me in preparing it. In addition to thanking the individuals, publishers, and organizations mentioned in the list of acknowledgments for permission to use textual and illustrative material, I want to add a few words of special gratitude. My loyal and highly competent secretary, Dorothy Gorham, typed the various drafts and helped in countless other ways. Suzette H. Annin contributed an expert editorial reading, supplementing the somewhat different kinds of valuable advice I received from my colleagues Drs. Janis, Kagan, and Mahl. Special mention should be made of "William Morris Brown," who permitted the account of the interviews and personality tests administered to him in 1940 and 1966 to be published in this book. His extraordinary generosity, trust, and candor won him my deep gratitude and admiration. I also owe a considerable debt of gratitude to Robert Freed Bales of Harvard University, who was my collaborator on the original case study of "Morris Brown" in 1940 and who permitted the joint report to be drawn on freely here.

Robert R. Holt

CONTENTS

7

The Synthesis of Diverse Data on Personality, 150

8

Recent Developments in Nonprojective Assessment, 164

9

The Maturing of a Personality, 190

10

The Evaluation of Personality Assessment, 201

References, 231

Index, 239

ASSESSING PERSONALITY

As the weaver elaborated his pattern for no end but the pleasure of his aesthetic sense, so might a man live his life, or if one was forced to believe that his actions were outside his choosing, so might a man look at his life, that it made a pattern. . . . Out of the manifold events of his life, his deeds, his feelings, his thoughts, he might make a design, regular, elaborate, complicated, or beautiful. . . . In the vast warp of life . . . a man might get a personal satisfaction in selecting the various strands that worked out the pattern.

W. SOMERSET MAUGHAM. Of Human Bondage

CHAPTER 1
THE WHAT
AND WHY
OF PERSONALITY
ASSESSMENT

E verybody routinely spends a great deal of time assessing the personalities of others, for in its first and basic sense, personality assessment means an informal process of getting to know and understand people and describing them. This same term also refers to a scientific and professional specialty, which applies a formal discipline of analyzing and measuring personalities. Both kinds of assessment will interest us here. Although the formal assessment of personality is young both as a science and as a profession—still very much a skill or even an art—studying it can help sharpen anyone's capacity to size people up informally. And the professional psychologist can improve his own results by investigating how the good natural judge of men operates. In the chapters that follow, therefore, the term "assessment" will be used broadly to refer to all the complex processes of perceiving and observing personalities, analyzing them, measuring their components with tests and other instruments, and understanding them.

The Nature of Personality
and Its Assessment

BEHAVIOR PATTERNS

People behave in organized, recognizable ways. That is the basic fact on which the whole psychology of personality is founded. At least two levels of organization, or patterning, can be distinguished: the *trait* and the *personality*. As soon as we begin to use adjectives to describe someone's behavior, we are talking trait language. To say someone is clever implies not just a single clever remark on his part, for almost anyone may occasionally say something delightfully witty; rather, it implies some regularity: Clever acts and sayings must be a recurrent feature of the clever person's behavior. Since recurrence is the paramount property of recognizable pattern, a trait is a simple behavioral pattern—a disposition to behave in a describable way. And a first approximation to a working definition of personality, for the purposes of the assessor, is that it is a pattern of traits.

What is meant by the phrase "a pattern of traits"? Surely more than just a list. Indeed, the pattern of deeds, feelings, and thoughts in a person's life makes up a design far richer and more complex than that of the Persian rug to which Maugham's hero compared his own life. Just as two weavers may take identical batches of threads but make from them markedly different designs, so too the uniqueness we always associate with personality is mainly to be found in the pattern rather than in the elements.

The uniqueness of pattern arises in part because the same traits have different strengths in two people. Both Henry and Herbert are to some degree strong, friendly, tidy, anxious, and effeminate; but Henry's friends notice in particular that he is both very strong and markedly effeminate, less friendly than average, and neither very tidy nor very anxious, while Herbert's friendliness and anxiety stand out, his effeminacy is near average, and the amount of strength and tidiness he possesses are slight. These hypothetical examples can illustrate another type of patterning, the *causal*. Because of his effeminacy, Henry has concentrated on keeping down anxiety by building up his muscles, at the expense of cultivating friendships. Though Herbert's effeminacy is slightly above average, it is unrelated to his anxiety—a fear of being rejected that leads him to be unusually friendly to others. Traits may conflict with one another; ambition, for instance, sometimes gets in the way of friendliness. Sometimes the traits alternate in their manifestation. Traits differ not only in strength but in the degree to which the person is conscious of them. Out of these relations (and others) is the unique pattern of a personality made.

Even the hypothetical examples given above clearly imply that the patterning of behavior in a personality must take place over time. Murray (1938) has said that the psychology of personality is the study of human lives, implying that the full pattern of a person's behavior becomes manifest only across the span of his entire life. The *genetic method* of studying life histories is therefore centrally important to personality. Getting a person to tell his life story is a basic method of formal assessment. It is the most natural way of intensifying informal assessment in pursuit of deeper understanding.

Most of the time when we talk about personality, however, we use the term in a cross-sectional, or contemporaneous, rather than a genetic sense. Fortunately, at any one time a person does have a complexly patterned set of dispositions to behave in particular ways, which can be assessed by tests and interviews; otherwise personality assessment would be limited to developmental studies over unmanageably long periods of time. A formal assessment of personality may include some direct observation of behavior patterns, but the observation is generally done in such a brief period of hours as to be like a stop-action snapshot. Nevertheless, it is good to be reminded that the ultimate subject matter of a science of personality is entire lives.

A DESCRIPTIVE DISCIPLINE

The key terms *personality* and *trait* have been defined in two apparently different ways: in terms of observable patterns of ongoing behavior and in terms of inferred dispositions to behave in patterned ways. Though dispositions refer to future actions and sound somehow more intrinsic to a person than do behavior patterns, the difference is only verbal. To say that a person is disposed to be punctual or that he has been observed to show up promptly time after time amounts to the same thing. A trait, therefore, is a descriptive, not an explanatory, concept. The failure to grasp this point exposes us to the dangers of two fallacies—that of *tautology*, or thinking in circles, and that of *reification*, taking an abstraction as if it referred to something concrete. To say that a person is prompt because he has the trait of punctuality is an excellent example of a tautology in which what looks like an explanation adds nothing to the original observation. The attempt to give the concept more solidity by thinking of traits as real structures somewhere inside the person is a clear reification.

To be sure, there *are* real structures inside people that determine their behavior in lawful ways. Two main classes of such structural determinants may usefully be distinguished. First, the kind of gross structure we call *physique* has some causal influence on behavior; for example, a man may be a good athlete partly because he has a sturdy skeleton and well-developed muscles. Second, a finer but more pervasively important type of structure is the *organization of the central nervous system.* The good bodily coordination that the athlete needs seems to be to some extent an inborn capacity, which in some unknown way is "wired in" as a property of his brain.

Most psychologists believe, however, that the brain influences behavior primarily because it contains an ever-changing record of the modifications of its innate programs produced by *learning.* A person is characteristically generous not so much because he was born that way but because a complex pattern of experience taught him how to be generous and how to get gratification from generosity. In ways that are only beginning to be understood, learning causes submicroscopic structural changes in the brain, probably in the organization of its biochemical substance.

If such structural determinants of behavior patterns exist and if they constitute causal, not merely descriptive, concepts, why should we be concerned with traits? In part, it is a matter of necessity. Eventually, psychologists may be able to find out which characteristics of the body—especially in the fine structure of the brain and its electrical and biochemical processes—determine specific aspects of behavior. At present, that is only an interesting possibility; even if it becomes an actuality, we shall never escape from the need to identify recurrent patterns of behavior, so that we may specify the personality traits of interest to us and for many other reasons. Furthermore, behavior is an interesting and significant kind of reality worthy of being studied on its own level without attempting to reduce it to something presumably more basic. Sometimes psychology is criticized on the grounds that behavior is too evanescent and impalpable to be objectively studied; such criticism often comes from those who wish to replace behavior patterns with physiological concepts, which they feel to be more substantial. To be sure, it is not as simple and objective a matter to assess traits of behavior as it is to make many kinds of physical measurements. Nevertheless, we can measure the extent to which different people agree on their ratings of a personality trait after independently studying a person, and the agreement is often quite good. Moreover, when this kind of reliability proves poor, we know a number of ways to improve it. There is nothing more mysterious about the ability to perceive consistency, or patterning, in behavior than there is about the ability of a person with a trained ear to listen to a few minutes of music and describe its musical form.

There is a final, more important, reason to retain and respect the descriptive concepts of personality assessment. They perform a necessary task, for which they were designed; and even when a causal theory can explain such a phenomenon as hesitancy, the explanation cannot be substituted for the description of trait. Suppose we knew that impulses from brain area x to area y caused indecisiveness; suppose also that we could measure them. The personality assessor would have a splendid way of assessing an important aspect of behavior that would be vital in, for example, selecting executives, but he would report his findings not in terms of the frequency of impulses but as an estimate of how decisive the man would be.

For the reasons given above, personality assessment is almost entirely a descriptive discipline. Nevertheless, good description can yield a great deal of understanding and can enable us to predict and—to some extent—control behavior.

An analogy with metallurgy will illustrate how a descriptive discipline can make possible a great deal of practical application. During the middle ages, alchemists and more practical men learned much about metals by working with them. In time, they learned to make precise measurements of a metal's melting point, its density, hardness, and other descriptive properties—long before there was an explanatory theory to show how these properties were interrelated. As it became possible to classify metals and measure their descriptive properties, a complex technology of working with metals grew up; indeed, much of the Industrial Revolution was based on it. Today, metallurgists know that the "traits" of metals are determined by their crystalline molecular structure, which in turn depends on the structure of the metallic atom. Yet measurements of a given metal's ductility, hardness, conductivity, and the like, have not been replaced by statements about free electrons in its atomic shell, nor could they be.

PERSON VERSUS PERSONALITY

Notice that person and personality are not identical terms; the second is more restricted. A person is an individual human organism. He has not only a personality (a distinctive and characteristic pattern of traits) but also a physique, an anatomy, a physiology, a social role, and a status; he expresses and transmits a culture, performs such operations as spending and investing to keep an economy going, and, in short, is the concrete embodiment of that grand generalization, man. The psychology of personality is only one of the sciences relevant to persons, the principal subject matter of all the behavioral, social, and medical sciences. A person is so complex and many-layered that many disciplines can be brought to bear on the physiochemical, fleshly, ideological, spiritual, or other aspects of his being. The student of personality must know something about all these aspects of persons, for they affect the patterns of behavior, which are his special concern.

What Are the Uses
of Informal Assessment?

In order to interact with people, even in the simplest ways, we have to be able to understand them and to predict what they will do. Most of the time it is relatively easy to do so because much behavior is conforming and a great deal of the patterning in personalities is contributed by society and culture. Nevertheless, it is a happy fact that no one conforms completely to social norms (including laws, customs, and other standards for conduct). If we are to know what to expect from a specific person, one of the first things we must learn is the extent of his conformity and conventionality.

ASSESSMENT OF NONCONFORMITY

There are three principal types of nonconformity to major social norms: criminal, psychotic, and creative nonconformity. Each type has quite different implications for action toward the deviant person.

Criminals, psychopaths, or, more generally, people who are poorly socialized and narrowly self-seeking often break laws and other norms because they think they can do what they want and get away with it. Of course, everyone has *some* minor antisocial trends, but people differ tremendously in this respect. Clearly, honesty or integrity is one of the first qualities we look for, consciously or not, in sizing a person up.

If we saw someone driving down the wrong side of the street or taking a short cut across a busy airfield, we might be tempted to yell, "What's the matter, are you crazy?" Sometimes such a nonconformist is, for it is a hallmark of psychosis that the affected person loses touch with the social reality of norms; his deviant behavior may endanger himself or others. Hence the degree of *contact with reality* is another absolutely basic dimension of assessment. These two fundamental decisions about other people—the degree to which they are reasonably ethical and sane—are usually tacit. We are not aware of making them and probably could not explain how we do so, but someone has only to raise the issue for us to be quite emphatic in our judgments.

Creative nonconformity is the kind we have in mind as needed when we deplore the conformity of modern life. It represents a questioning of norms and an attempt to improve on them. Sometimes the questioning is more negativistic and rebellious than constructive, and violent disagreement can arise about what constitutes improvement. For example, many persons would be reluctant to classify social and political rebellion as creative. Sometimes, however, progress requires revolutionary change. In the long run, society's most valuable members are those who contribute new ways of doing things; we must, therefore, be able to distinguish creative nonconformists from destructive types in assessing personalities. In some cases the three forms of nonconformity may be intricately combined. Raskolnikov, the protagonist in Dostoevsky's *Crime and Punishment*, was a psychotic who committed a crime that he thought of as an act of creative nonconformity.

ASSESSMENT
OF OTHER INDIVIDUAL DIFFERENCES

In most everyday situations, you want to know a good deal more about a person than the extent to which he can be counted on to behave like most other people. There is a great deal of latitude for individual variation *within* the general framework of the norms in many areas of life, and people do differ from one another in interesting and important ways. One reason we are concerned with such differences is simply that they are inherently fascinating—perhaps because of the universal tendency to assume that everyone else is essentially like us, which makes each discovery that someone else can behave or view things differently something of a surprise. Indeed, personal idiosyncrasies are the favorite topic of gossip, if not of most conversation.

Another reason to assess these differences is the need to know how others will respond to things, for all kinds of decisions at every level of human enterprise hinge directly on this knowledge. For example, your strategy against an opponent in any kind of competitive situation (love, war, business, play) will be determined by your evaluation of him and his probable aggressiveness, courage, wiliness, tractability, or intelligence. Or if you are looking for someone to marry, it is not much help to know that, on the average, the men or women you encounter in your everyday social life would probably be satisfactory: You want to find the *best* combination of qualities. The same reasoning holds for finding a good adviser, choosing a secretary, or seeking a compatible business partner or professional collaborator. Although everyone is subject to the same general laws of behavior, there is a great range in ability, disposition, emotional make-up, and other behavioral tendencies. One would be crippled in interpersonal relationships without some ability to assess individual differences in personality.

In these few examples, it should be apparent that informal assessment is the rule. Even though computer-arranged dating is proving acceptable on many college campuses, it would be highly inappropriate to try to use formal procedures of assessment in serious courtship or in business competition (although there would be no objection to a person's sharpening his native wits by the extracurricular application of scientific principles). In choosing an employee, however, most organizations of any size have found that it is good business to replace or supplement informal assessment by such formal means as tests of stenographic and typing skills.

SELF-ASSESSMENT

Perhaps the most important, and surely the most interesting, subject for a person's informal assessment is himself. As soon as self-awareness is possible, a child begins to evaluate himself and to form expectations about what he can do compared to others. The self-assessing process is closely connected with ambitions, ideals, and levels of aspiration, as well as with feelings of self-respect, inferiority, shame, guilt, or pride. Learning more about both informal and formal methods of assessing personality *can* help a person to know himself better, though it cannot be guaranteed to do so.

THE MECHANISMS OF INFORMAL ASSESSMENT

Once we realize that informal assessment begins as soon as a child starts to form expectations and conceptions about himself, his parents, playmates, and the other people in his world, it is apparent how involuntary and essentially nonverbal an operation it is. Informal assessment is one of the best examples of what the eminent philosopher Polanyi (1964) calls *tacit knowing.* That is, informal assessment does not generally operate by means of a highly conscious, rational, explicit drawing of inferences; it typically happens outside the spotlight of our fullest (or *focal*) awareness. A child knows far more about his mother—her moods and impulses, how to get around her, how far he can trust her, how much she will do for him— than he can begin to put into words.

Expectations Based on Experience

In part, informal assessment is the building up of expectations on the basis of experience. There is little basic difference between learning to recognize a mother's face and learning to recognize her quick temper: Both are abstractions, or concepts, formed gradually. The process involved may be illustrated by an experiment in concept formation conducted by Rommetveit and Kvale (1965). They taught their subjects to recognize complex geometrical patterns indicating "good luck" and "bad luck" on a wheel of fortune; the payoff was in fact controlled by the experimenter. After repeated trials with the wheel, the subjects began to learn the types of patterns that paid off—long before they could correctly verbalize the difference between the "lucky" and "unlucky" designs. For example, certain subjects were told that they would be tested on their ability to tell the lucky from the unlucky patterns by choosing the correct verbal description of this difference from among various formulations. As their ability to recognize the lucky and unlucky patterns improved, as shown by increasing "success" on the wheel, they selected the correct description *less* often. Such a capacity to perform better than one can verbalize is part of what we mean by tacit knowing. Even though the abstractive process of forming concepts or expectations usually takes place automatically and without any necessary involvement of deliberate intent, it nevertheless can be shown to have a logical structure.

Empathy

A process of tacit knowing of people that is less rational than building up expectations, but is nevertheless fundamental to informal assessment, is *empathy*. As usually defined, empathy is a process of feeling what another person feels, but exactly how it happens is still unclear. It has been repeatedly observed, however, that a very young baby will grow tense and restless if the mother holding him is herself anxious; this process has been called emotional contagion. In an experimental demonstration, Campbell (1957) studied two groups of mothers and babies at a well-baby clinic, where the children are brought for routine injections. Some of the mothers were given preliminary instructions that emphasized the possible dangers and difficulties surrounding the injection; the others were given neutral instructions. Significantly more mothers in the first group became noticeably anxious, and significantly more of their babies cried *before* getting their shots.

Empathy, the mature version of emotional contagion, makes it possible for one person to know some things about another on rather brief acquaintance. Like all other capacities, it is not present in everyone to the same extent, nor is it infallible. The main information empathy gives us is emotional; it can tell us nothing about how intelligent a person is and can give no specific facts about his background or history (though we may sense such general events as that he has been deeply disappointed at some time in the past) and little information about the way his thinking is organized. But through empathy it is possible to tell how friendly or hostile, tense or relaxed, interested or bored, open or defensive, hopeful or bitter, self-confident or doubtful a person feels; how much he enjoys life; and even how sick he is. Empathy cannot always provide this information; nor does it work for everybody with complete accuracy; but the fact that so much information *can* be picked up by this effortless opening of oneself to impressions of another person means that it is important to consider how empathy becomes impaired and what can be done to improve it. It seems to be at the center of what is commonly called intuition, though that ill-defined term probably refers to all the processes of tacit knowing. Further discussion of empathy may be found in Chapter 2.

The Basic Steps   Effective informal assessing presupposes that you *care* about people. It is likely that the more interested you are in other human beings as individuals, the better you will be at assessing them. The objective ideal of a completely mechanized assessment will be impossible until computers can be taught to feel, to judge, and to care about people. Having an interest in a person and a desire to get to know him is, then, the first step in informal assessment; next we obtain immediate impressions through empathy; and finally we continue to observe his behavior until we notice invariances in it—persistent, recognizable trends. There is more to the process, as will be seen in the next chapter, but these are the basic steps.

THE PLACE OF INFORMAL ASSESSMENT
IN MODERN PSYCHOLOGY

There has been a curiously antipsychological tradition within the discipline of psychology, which makes a kind of fetish of skepticism and iconoclasm so far as the main processes of informal assessing are concerned. According to this view, intuition, empathy, judging personality from facial or bodily expression, are all unscientific mysticism. So eager were generations of leading psychologists to separate themselves from quacks and charlatans that they indoctrinated their students with the belief that the processes by which we directly come to know and understand one another are completely untrustworthy and sources of self-deception. Moreover, they produced a sheaf of apparently good experimental demonstrations of their indictments. In study after study it was shown that judges could not recognize emotions from photographs, could not distinguish geniuses from idiots by their portraits or their handwriting, and so forth. The proponents of this view held that psychologists should be laboratory scientists, not skillful gypsies, and that they should be concerned not with understanding individual people but with seeking the general laws of behavior. Once you had learned enough of these laws, you might then be able to apply that basic knowledge to everyday affairs; but since psychology was a young science, it could not yet be expected to have wide applications.

A few psychologists held out against the tide. Most psychoanalysts were unaffected by this "know-nothing" orientation, which chiefly charac- terized behaviorism, though many of them were a little too impressed with Freud's theories as a short cut to understanding by means of formulas and not aware enough of his own practice, which relied on his intuitive feelings about people, enriched by a deep literary culture. Within academic psy- chology, G. W. Allport (1937) was expounding a different but equally humanistic approach. In one of the experiments Allport stimulated, Estes (1938) studied various people's ability to judge personality from watching a brief movie of subjects doing such things as taking off a shirt and putting it on again. Unhappily, he found that psychologists were poorer judges than artists, thus unintentionally providing evidence that studying the psychology of the 1930's had apparently produced a "trained incapacity" to size peo- ple up.

In recent years, however, the tide has begun to turn. As part of the study of "social perception," social psychologists have begun to elucidate the processes by which people form impressions of one another. And within the philosophy of science, the superobjectivists have simmered down as it has become apparent that no scientist actually worked in the ways they had described. There is a large element of skill or art (know-how) in scientific theorizing and experimenting, which must be recognized and respected be- fore we can begin the laborious job of studying scientific inquiry and formu- lating parts of it in explicit rules. All psychologists can agree that a science of human behavior must eventually establish lawful relationships by objec- tive methods, but in *discovering* psychological principles (as opposed to nailing them down in scientific laws) and in applying them to everyday life, we should not hesitate to make use of empathy and to rely on our own feelings.

What Are the Uses
of Formal Assessment?

Those who are involved in formal assessment must supplement the tacit processes of informal assessment by a number of technical procedures for obtaining data about people and reaching conclusions about them. Even within the field of personality assessment there are those who strive to eliminate all human judgment and other nonmechanical processes from their work; typically they rely upon "objective" tests. They often deny that they make any use of the intuitive methods of the ordinary man. But they do continue to rely on them, anyway, because they must, if only to recognize when a mechanically-arrived-at assessment is so implausible as to indicate that the system has broken down.

The techniques of gathering data in formal assessment include interviewing, testing, obtaining personal documents (such as autobiographies and letters), and making observations in specially controlled situations. The technical procedures for reaching conclusions may be summarized as clinical and statistical inference, processes that will be explained in Chapter 3.

Formal assessment is undertaken for the most part by five types of professional people: psychologists of several specialized kinds, psychiatrists, personnel workers, social workers, and guidance counselors. (To a lesser degree, anthropologists, criminologists, and sociologists also assess personalities.) The settings in which the work goes on also can be classified into five groupings, though these do not precisely correspond to the five types of professions.

CLINICAL SETTINGS

Clinical settings include hospitals, mental-health clinics, and private offices of psychodiagnosticians and psychotherapists of various kinds (including psychoanalysts). People being assessed in these settings suffer from the personal problems and difficulties in living that are often called mental illnesses, emotional disorders, or types of psychopathology. The tradition of regarding these as "health problems" is understandable because until recently most psychotherapists have been psychiatrists, who have received full medical training and who use medical treatments as well as psychotherapy. (Nonmedical therapists, such as clinical psychologists, use only psychological methods of treatment such as psychoanalysis, psychotherapy, and behavior therapy.) Because of the traditional conception of mental health and mental disease (see Szasz, 1961), the suffering individual often takes himself to medical institutions or practitioners and is called a patient. In this context assessment goes by the name of diagnosis. The focus of assessment in clinical settings is to find out just what is wrong with the person and to measure the strengths or assets that are relevant to helping him, so that the most effective plan of treatment may be devised. A private practitioner of psychotherapy or psychoanalysis may conduct a diagnostic assessment by means of a single, unstructured interview, relying on his empathic impressions and the other methods of informal assessment.

In institutional clinical settings, such as hospitals for severely disturbed people, the task of assessment is often divided up between clinical psychologists, social workers, and psychiatrists. The psychologist concentrates on administering and interpreting tests; the social worker conducts interviews, obtaining a *social history* from the person and from members of his family; and the psychiatrist may supplement his own interviewing by such physical procedures as testing reflexes in a neurological examination or by such laboratory procedures as X-rays or studies of blood biochemistry or of brain waves (the electroencephalograph). All this information is brought together in case conferences where the participating members of the clinical team construct a picture of the personality pattern—how the person got that way, his assets and liabilities, and his future prospects. They then plan what to do to help him. A similarly elaborate assessment is sometimes used to gauge the effects of a course of treatment, although more usually the patient is merely reinterviewed by one person and retested.

LEGAL SETTINGS

Professionals of the types described above often assist judges, prison officials, and other legal authorities in assessing the personalities of people accused of crimes. To some extent—especially in the most enlightened legal systems—the purpose of the assessment is to decide on a plan for treating, rehabilitating, or otherwise helping the prisoner change his behavior. Often, however, this forensic assessment is conducted for the scientifically less meaningful purpose of deciding whether the accused is "sane" and may thus be held legally responsible for his acts. At times the assessment may be used to help the judge decide on the nature of punishment or duration of imprisonment. Also, when it is necessary to decide on a person's eligibility for parole, the resources of formal assessment are sometimes called upon to help predict the man's behavior.

EDUCATIONAL AND VOCATIONAL GUIDANCE

The people who offer themselves (or who are referred by teachers or administrators) for assessment at schools, colleges, or vocational-guidance centers are looking for advice in deciding what to do with themselves educationally or vocationally. Should this young woman go to a junior college or to a university? Does this young man have what it takes to become a linotyper, or a lawyer, or a laundromat operator? Perhaps the person is confused about his own abilities and interests or knows too little about the spectrum of possible jobs to make up his own mind about a career. Vocational counselors are usually psychologists, but they are sometimes social workers. Educational counselors generally have had training in education or psychology. Interviewing and testing are the most common methods of assessing personality for purposes of advisement.

EDUCATIONAL AND VOCATIONAL SELECTION

The prospective student or employee is not the only one concerned with the question of who is to fill which slot in schools, businesses, and government: Whenever they can, educational institutions and employers *select* from among applicants those most likely to succeed. Thus, students who have been carefully tested and advised to apply to, let us say, medical schools find themselves subjected to a further assessment by application form, credentials (transcripts of grades and letters of recommendation), and often more tests and personal interviews before they are admitted. An employer too may have a personnel department where specialized workers (who are sometimes industrial psychologists) screen and evaluate applicants for each job.

Sometimes such selection is for special assignments in the government —as, for example, Peace Corps projects and, during World War II, the undercover operations of the OSS; in these cases elaborate programs of assessment may be employed. By extension of this logic, the armed forces are also employers trying to select the most suitable workers, even when the latter "apply" only after receiving a notice from a draft board. The medical and psychiatric examining and the psychological testing of recruits have constituted the largest personality-assessment programs in history.

RESEARCH SETTINGS

Research on assessment is conducted in university, government, and commercial laboratories or research centers. Psychologists do most of this work, but psychiatrists and other behavioral scientists are also involved. Whether the research has a primarily applied and practical or a purely scientific emphasis, assessment has to be sufficiently formalized to make it possible to collect data about the personalities of adequate numbers of subjects and to relate facts about characteristic patterns of behavior to some other aspect of a person.

For example, suppose you were interested in the problem of high school drop-outs who are intelligent enough to handle the academic work. It would be reasonable to study the possibility that—among other causes— something about their personalities was related to dropping out. If you happened to know a drop-out personally, you would already have some ideas about what he was like from your informal assessment of him, which would probably suggest leads for systematic study. Perhaps you knew that your friend had constant battles with his parents and you suspected that in some way this struggle interfered with his schoolwork. You might be right, and yet there are others who make the grade despite similar family crises. To settle the question you would have to get good information on performance in school and relationships with parents from a large enough sample of both failures and successes in high school. For this purpose you would probably use a focused interview or a test, or both. Groups of students who are alike in intelligence but who differed on dropping out could then be compared on the quantitative measures or scores obtained from the systematic assessment. Thus you could check on the validity of the initial inference about the effect of the family struggle on schoolwork.

Formal assessment in these different settings, carried out for different purposes, focuses on different aspects of personality. Just as no set of abilities is relevant to any and all jobs, there can be no single scheme of personality variables that should be measured in every formal assessment. Nevertheless, the general principles that are presented in the chapters that follow are useful, no matter what specific facets of personality may be appropriate for a particular assessment enterprise.

This initial survey of the field of assessment has necessarily been just a quick introduction. In the next three chapters, we shall take a closer look first at informal assessment and then at clinical and "objective" formal assessment. In Chapters 5–9, we shall see the various methods and approaches at work on a concrete example, a man whom we shall study in some depth. Finally, in Chapter 10, we shall appraise the field of assessment and some of its controversies.

I do not love thee, Dr. Fell;
The reason why I cannot tell,
But this alone I know full well:
I do not love thee, Dr. Fell.

THOMAS BROWN

CHAPTER 2
MAJOR
PROCESSES
OF INFORMAL
ASSESSMENT

The process of informally assessing personality begins the moment one person claps eyes on another, in the formation of a first impression. Much of what can go right and wrong in informal assessment can be seen operating during this initial phase. Insights or misconceptions acquired during a first meeting can have a lasting effect on a relationship and may heavily weight a person's final assessment of another. An important part of initial impressions is the perception of affects, or emotions; empathy plays a large role in the assessment of these states. This chapter surveys the present state of knowledge about all these matters, concluding with a discussion of the methods by which informal understanding of personalities is deepened and systematized.

First Impressions of Personality

A large proportion of the systematic psychological research on informal assessment has dealt with the formation of first impressions, since these are relatively easy to investigate. We are therefore beginning to learn something about the subtle and complicated processes involved in what is rather misleadingly called "social perception" or "person perception." True, a first impression of a personality is largely a perceptual event, but it also involves judgment, inference, and various other processes, among which emotion plays a surprisingly large role.

Recent research on forming impressions of personality has confirmed a fact we know from direct experience: The process begins with a vague but total impression (a *Gestalt*), which has a strongly evaluative or affective character. This impression later takes on greater clarity and specificity as well as increased organization, always remaining the percept of a *person*. We never form an impression by perceiving a few isolated traits, nor do we build up an overall concept of someone the way a child builds a block tower, piece by separate piece. Typically, a first impression of a stranger—a "Dr. Fell"—is poorly differentiated and hard to put into words; yet it often yields a distinct emotional flavor of liking or dislike. This affective reaction may be a source of both useful information and error. Yet remarkably enough, most people learn to pick up a modicum of truth about one another on very brief acquaintance. As it happens, however, most of the research on forming impressions of personality has focused on uncovering ways in which first impressions are faulty. Such informal assessments may be erroneous because the observer gets mistaken impressions (for any of a number of reasons shortly to be surveyed) or because the person being judged is inscrutable.

SOURCES OF ERROR IN THE OBSERVER

Hearsay   Very frequently, we form impressions of people from *hearsay*. Even a brief description may affect our expectations about someone so markedly that when we do meet him our perception and judgment of what he actually does and says is selective and biased. In a controlled experiment on this topic, Kelley (1950) met a class after arranging for their usual instructor to be absent. He gave the students a brief note describing a stranger who was to be their substitute teacher. This description included the following information: "He is 26 years old, a veteran, and married. People who know him consider him a rather cold person, industrious, critical, practical, and determined." On half the notes, the words "rather cold" were replaced by "very warm." After the substitute instructor had conducted a 20-minute discussion and left, the students rated him on 15 traits. On related variables (consideration of others, informality, sociability, popularity, humor) students who had been told the teacher was warm gave him significantly higher ratings than did those whose notes had described him as cold; on unrelated traits like intelligence the difference was negligible. This experiment also showed that the hearsay effect could affect overt behavior, for students in the "warm" group were noticeably more likely to participate in the discussion than were students in the "cold" group.

The Halo Effect Kelley's experiment demonstrates not only the power of hearsay and the organized nature of first impressions but also the power of a generally positive or negative impression to affect more specific judgments about a person. This spread is usually called the *halo effect.* If you like a person, you will probably consider him "a good guy" in most respects, and if he rubs you the wrong way, you are likely to rate him low on any trait that is evaluatively tinged.

One result of the halo effect is to wash out most of the potential differentiation, or particularity, in a first impression, leaving just a general feeling of liking or dislike. Even in a formal assessment situation, when professional people are trying to make relatively specific behavioral ratings after extensive contact with a subject, they may be unable to come up with anything more meaningful than a general sense of how good a man they are dealing with. In an experimental attempt to find ways of selecting young physicians for psychiatric training (Holt & Luborsky, 1958), supervisors were given careful instruction on evaluating the performance of psychiatric residents on 20 aspects of work; they also rated each resident on how well they liked him after guiding his work for several months. A factor analysis of these ratings showed that liking and *all other* variables were highly loaded on one general factor. The impression of general competence pervaded every rating and was closely related to the supervisors' affective feelings about the residents.

The halo effect tends to produce an unnaturally consistent impression of a person, which is most marked when the contact is brief and not focused on a particular aspect of behavior. Yet the halo effect is not necessarily all error; because it is the outgrowth of a complex emotional and empathic response to a person, it may contain valuable information.

The Leniency Effect Another emotional effect on first impressions is called the *leniency effect*; it also primarily concerns evaluative aspects of personality. When a person adopts the policy of always giving the other fellow the benefit of the doubt in order to maintain a picture of himself as a benign and decent person, the leniency effect is operating. The converse error is the sour or suspicious assumption that "people are no good unless proved otherwise," an orientation that implies a deeply injured, often paranoid, person.

Stereotypes *Stereotypes* and folk theories about personality tend to give a bias to first impressions. For instance, if the stranger differs from the perceiver in any immediately obvious way, that difference is likely to be noticed first and to bring to mind the set of standard notions the perceiver has about "that kind" of person. Such foci of stereotypes include, of course, ethnic-group membership with all the prejudicial clichés that entails; nationality; unusual or perceptually salient physical characteristics, such as marked beauty or ugliness, height or weight, prominent facial features ("weak chin," "intellectual forehead," and so on), physical deformity, or handicaps of any sort; and anything out of the ordinary about a person's voice or expressive movements. Most cultures are full of such misinformation, and though we may become aware of prejudices and try to disregard them, their effects are insidious. Even members of minority groups often cannot escape from prejudice against their own kind.

A stereotype or folk theory has the logical structure of an inferential rule and can be translated into one, as in these examples: "If anyone is a Negro, infer that he loves rhythmic music and loud colors"; "if a person has red hair, infer that he has a hot temper." Signs of irritation that would not be noticed in a brunette are more readily noticed in a redhead because the prejudiced person is set to perceive them; such a person can then protest that it's not just a theory because he has actually seen it work out most of the time. Such theories also operate, in R. K. Merton's words, like "self-fulfilling prophecies" in that they lead us to act toward people in a way that brings out the traits we expect them to have. Thus, if a person believes that those who come from a higher socioeconomic class than he does are generally haughty and condescending, he may very well approach such people with a chip on his shoulder and provoke rejection.

The obvious unfairness of prejudice and such oversimplifications as expecting all fat people to be jolly should not blind us to the fact that folk theories often do contain a germ of usable truth. As long as we do not fall into the trap of assuming that "all Jews are alike," we can make cautious use of a set of expectations that arise from cultural uniformities: Jewish traditions of hospitality are such that it is safe more often than not to assume that a middle-aged Jewish hostess will be pleased by a guest's overeating. (See also the discussion of constitutional psychology in Chapter 4.)

Stereotypes exert their biasing effects on formal as well as on informal assessment. Recent research (summarized by Masling, 1966) shows that clinical psychologists are influenced in their formal assessments by such variables as ethnic-group membership and socioeconomic status whether they realize it or not. A similar effect showed up in a study of the attempts of psychiatrists to select people for psychiatric training on the basis of a brief interview (Holt & Luborsky, 1958). It turned out that a particular interviewer's impression of poor voice quality was completely unrelated to the subsequent performance of the interviewees during residency training; and the interviewer himself said that he did not think it was a very relevant variable. Nevertheless, an examination of his comments about the men he interviewed showed that he had noted "poor voice" for 75 percent of the men he expected to do badly and for only 21 percent of the men he predicted would do well.

There are only two ways to prevent first impressions from being influenced by stereotypes and extraneous characteristics such as physical appearance: by becoming fully aware of these effects and trying to allow for them or by avoiding direct contact with the person being appraised lest his personal attributes prejudice us. Since the latter course would cut us off from most of the valuable sources of information about personality, it is best to follow the former.

Moods and Need States

Our *moods* and *need states* can also bias perception and judgment when we encounter another person. All the world may seem to love a lover in part because his elation acts like a pair of rose-tinted glasses, and in part because his mood may be infectious and bring out the best in others. On the other hand, an anxious or depressed person is likely to perceive others with one of two distortions: He may see others as exaggeratedly frivolous or carefree in contrast to his own misery, or he may project his own mood and find it reflected all around him. In an ingenious experiment involving a house party of young girls, Murray (1933) showed that in the overwrought state following a scary game of Murder his daughter's guests rated men's faces as significantly more "mean" and threatening than they did in a calm and relaxed condition. More recently, Kleiner (1960) was able to bring about an increase in the rated attractiveness of a person who made a special contribution to the success of a small group in solving problems. In each of his experimental trios (whose members were previously unacquainted with one another), one person was always a confederate who knew the solution to puzzles in advance; the more threatened the group felt and the larger the improvement in the group's performance produced by the stooge, the more he was rated as someone the other members wanted to get to know better.

Depending on the situation and the nature of the need state, there can be other types of distorting effects on the formation of impressions. In general, the presence of an active, unsatisfied need tends to make a person especially attentive to the presence of a gratifier or goal object: Hunger will alert the eyes of the berry picker, sometimes even making him momentarily mistake a pebble for a berry. A young man who is longing for a girlfriend will often wishfully endow with great virtues any passably attractive girl who expresses an interest in him. A frightened, lone sentry more easily forms the impression that a stranger is hostile or dangerous than he would if he were to meet the same man on a city street under civilian circumstances.

Defenses and Blind Spots

Everyone has blind spots in appraising others, which are generally caused by the operation of his own defenses. A hysterical person who follows the model of the famous three monkeys may be able to see and hear no evil in others as part of his struggle to speak—and do—no evil himself. Put more technically and less moralistically, when a person defends himself against hostile impulses by denial, he may have difficulty perceiving hostility in other people. Conversely, self-knowledge can help to overcome the distorting effects of defenses in the formation of impressions.

Projection, Empathy, and the Self-Concept   One defense, *projection*, is of special interest as a source of error in impressions of personality. The term is understood here in the sense Freud used it to explain paranoia (not in the broader and looser sense he and a number of others have used it, to refer to any distorting or selective effect of a person's inner world on his perception or conception of the outer world). In its narrower meaning, projection is a distortion of reality that occurs when a person's desires conflict with his moral values and when his self-concept is too rigid to admit any frailties. Almost everyone uses this defense mechanism at times, but its use is especially pronounced in some seriously disturbed people.

Projection is a kind of opposite to empathy. In empathy, a person perceives the anger that is actually another's by allowing some of that emotion to develop within himself but attributes it to his percept of the other (see page 34). In projection, as a person's anger arises, he attributes it to his percept of another in order *not* to recognize that it originated in himself, since that would be intolerable to his righteous picture of himself. There are more complicated forms of projection, such as when a person begins to imagine that other people suspect or accuse him of having the evil thoughts he finds so intolerable. (Further discussion of projection and additional examples may be found in Mahl, 1971, Chapter 7.) Obviously, anyone who uses this defense very extensively will make many errors in his informal assessments of others, though it should be added that paranoid people are often shrewd enough to fasten their suspicions on people who do have somewhat more anger (or whatever quality is in question) than average, even though it may not be obvious on the surface.

Projection and empathy are two forms of one basic process in the perception and judgment of other people, but projection distorts the accuracy and depth of understanding, whereas empathy enhances it. The basic process might be called subjectivity, or egocentricity; whatever name we give it, it is the almost universal tendency to judge everyone else in relation to the self-concept. A person inevitably compares everyone else to himself. He himself is, after all, the person he knows best and longest and for whose welfare he makes the most continuous efforts.

In an experiment on the effects of subliminal stimuli on thought, Fiss (1966) showed how the self-concept of his subjects (college girls) affected even their perception of nonhuman figures. Before showing each subject abstract linear designs for .33 sec. in a mirror tachistoscope, he briefly flashed (for .01 sec.) either the word ANGRY or just a blank card; the subject then rated the "angriness" of each design. Under the conditions of the experiment only the longer-exposed image was visible. There was no significant difference in the average ratings given the drawings that were preceded by the word and those preceded by the blank, so at first the experiment appeared to have failed. But the subjects were also asked to rate themselves on a scale of interpersonal hostility, and this rating correlated significantly with the tendency to judge in accordance with the subliminal suggestion. In other words, only girls who were willing to describe themselves as having hostile thoughts and feelings rated the figures as if they were influenced by the subliminal stimuli.

From experiments like those described above we are only beginning to learn something about the extent to which perceptions and judgments of personal and emotional qualities are made with reference to the self-concept, and no doubt the process is a complicated and subtle one in many people. Yet the involvement of the self-concept in perception is a working hypothesis that brings together quite a number of observations, particularly those concerning errors in first impressions that are induced by the emotional and motivational states of the observers. The experimental findings also suggest that people are capable of unconsciously using subtle cues in making judgments of personality; indeed, such use of unnoticed evidence may have something to do with the "uncanny" skill of some diagnosticians.

Lack of Abilities   Errors in forming first impressions may arise from a lack of various clearly relevant abilities, including general intelligence, observational ability, and sensory acuity. The observer's interests and values obviously determine what he pays attention to and how he judges it; and anything that interferes with effective cognition, from brain damage to faulty education, can affect informal assessment.

Oversimplification and Tolerance for Ambiguity   First impressions are necessarily incomplete and fragmentary, for any personality is too complex to be completely grasped in a brief time. Naturally, the most common sort of error in such informal assessments is *oversimplification*. The danger of oversimplification is obvious, yet some people find it inordinately difficult to suspend judgment and to live with the realization that they cannot possibly know another person thoroughly on brief acquaintance. As a result, they jump to conclusions, prematurely crystallize their judgments, and are rigidly impervious to new information. An important dimension of people, therefore, is the degree to which they can hold back their need for a perfectly clear view of the world. Psychologists call it *tolerance for ambiguity*; it is one dimension of cognitive style, or one way of taking in and processing information about the world.

The concept of tolerance for ambiguity was first suggested by Else Frenkel-Brunswik (1949). In studying authoritarian personalities (see also Adorno, Frenkel-Brunswik, Levinson, & Sanford, 1950), she found that persons with an exaggerated deference to authority tended to have a highly simplified view of the world about them and the people in it; they described their parents, for example, in stereotyped and usually laudatory terms. Only students who had relatively democratic ideologies were able to describe personalities in balanced terms, seeing both good and bad.

In a well-controlled experiment, Scodel and Mussen (1953) demonstrated the relevance of authoritarianism to one kind of oversimplification—the direct attribution of aspects of the self-concept to others. They gave several hundred college students the F scale, the main instrument used in research on authoritarianism; this scale measures "protofascist" or radical-right attitudes. From this population the investigators chose 2 groups of 27 (each containing 12 women and 15 men), one having the highest and the other the lowest scores. The subjects were studied in pairs, each of which was made up of a high scorer (authoritarian) and a low scorer (nonauthoritarian). The members of each pair were introduced and were asked to discuss radio, television, and movies for 20 minutes. Each subject was then taken into a separate room and given a fresh copy of the F scale to fill out as he thought the other member of his pair had done. As was expected, the authoritarians saw the nonauthoritarians as being like themselves and predicted for them significantly higher F scores than they actually had. The low scorers correctly predicted that the high scorers had authoritarian attitudes, though less extreme ones than the high scorers had actually attained. Thus, the high-scoring group naively assumed that the low scorers were not significantly different from themselves, and the low-scoring group saw their authoritarian acquaintances as prejudiced but not as much as they actually were.

SOURCES OF ERROR IN THE PERSON JUDGED

Characteristics That Make a Person Hard to Know   Personalities differ in almost every way imaginable, including what might be called transparency versus inscrutability—how easy or difficult it is to form correct impressions of them. In addition there are several types of inscrutability. Some people are like turtles, so withdrawn into a shell of reserve and inhibition that it is hard to guess whether their inner experience is rich with sensitive perceptions and vivid fantasies or whether it is as drab as their shy exterior. Others are like porcupines, so bristling with suspicion and defensive hostility that it is hard to get close enough to them to learn more than this obvious fact. Then there are the lions, the nonintrospective men of action who are so much more complicated than they realize that they can give relatively little useful information about themselves. Chameleon personalities also lack insight and are hard to know because, not having a stable sense of identity, they adopt different

roles in every context. Brief observation may thus give an entirely misleading impression of them, as it may also of those sly foxes who deliberately
mislead others to throw them off their scent. And some people are so color-
less that they do not even bring to mind a zoological analogy to help us
caricature them; such a nondescript "average man" blends into the crowd,
standing out too little from his background to make it easy to find anything
distinctive to say about him.

Paradoxically, we also find it difficult to form correct first impressions
if a person is *too* different from ourselves. For example, it is proverbial that
all members of another ethnic group tend to look alike: we are often more
impressed by characteristics that a member of another nationality shares
with his compatriots than by the traits that set him apart from them.
Moreover, we may find that our usual inferential rules do not work, that we
lack appropriate concepts to make sense of his behavior and discern the patterns in it, and that our expectations are violated so often that we become
confused and disoriented.

The "Best Foot Forward" Error

Most people intuitively recognize that it is
possible to bias first impressions in their
favor by good grooming, smiling rather than scowling, and the like, and so
there is an almost universal tendency to try to take advantage of these effects. The result is what might be called the *best foot forward error* in first
impressions. This error is especially important if the observer's behavior or
the context is such as to arouse the subject's suspicion, hostility, or anxiety
and thus to make him defend himself by dissembling in this way. The observer may also contribute to the best foot forward error by giving cues about
the kinds of words or actions that will win his approval.

Deception

A certain amount of mild deception is involved when a person tries to be judged in
terms of his most attractive side, but most people—not just the "foxes"
spoken of above—go further. Voltaire was not the first cynic to note that
men use speech to conceal their thoughts; nor was Freud the first to see
that the person from whom a man wants most to hide his true feelings on
many topics is himself. Psychoanalysis has taught us, however, that these
processes are mostly involuntary self-defensive operations, not conscious dis-
simulations. We all engage in unconscious (as well as some conscious)
duplicity, at least occasionally deny our true motives, and lie about our
intentions or our reactions, hiding whatever would expose us to ridicule,
scorn, or other forms of social rejection. To be sure, we typically anticipate
more rejection than we would get if our dreadful secrets came to light,
because most people are not only tolerant but blessedly indifferent, having
many of the same secrets themselves and being more concerned with the

impression *they* are making on others than with sitting in judgment on them.

In any event, deceptive maneuvers greatly complicate the task of formal and informal assessment. Study and practice can, however, make it possible to penetrate some defensive smoke screens and to grasp part of the truth, even in initial contacts. Here is an area where the study of psychology can pay off in an increased ability to understand other people and deal with them effectively.

FURTHER IMPLICATIONS
OF ERRORS IN FIRST IMPRESSIONS

Because personalities are far more complex than first impressions of them, it is obviously easy for two people to disagree completely in their view of a third man and yet for both of them to be right. Cartwright and French (1939) demonstrated this point experimentally, showing that the validity (agreement with an assessment in depth) of two judges' impressions of a person exceeded their reliability (agreement with one another) because they were struck with quite different aspects of their man. In a way, this is the story of the blind men and the elephant all over again—each of the blind men had hold of part of the truth of what an elephant was like, though there was no overlap in their impressions because each came into contact with a different part of him.

What causes two people to form different impressions of the same personality? They may approach him with different sets or expectations based on hearsay, looking through the variously hued spectacles of different moods and needs, subject to the interferences of different defenses—in short, all the sources of error in first impressions also turn out to be determinants of variation in impressions from one observer to another. Not everyone is equally prone to such biasing influences as the halo effect or projection—seeing oneself in others. This last fact has a dual significance: It helps to explain observer-to-observer variation in first impressions, but it also suggests that the assessor of personality might do well to pay attention to the sources of error reviewed above as they operate in people who are themselves being assessed. Man is a social creature, and a subject's ability to size up others, as well as his susceptibility to various types of error in perceiving people are aspects of behavior worth noting.

This survey of the sources of error in first impressions has repeatedly brought out how intimately the process of impression formation involves emotion. So far, we have been concerned with the emotional reaction of the perceiver; let us turn now to the complementary point that a good deal of what we notice first about another person has to do with the latter's emotional state.

Perceiving Emotions
in Face and Voice

Much of the early research on the expressions of emotions and how well they are recognized proceeded on implicitly atomistic, rather than configurational (*Gestalt*), assumptions. It seemed not only a reasonable procedure, but the only proper one, to begin by asking subjects to match drawings or still photographs of people with the names of the emotions they were attempting to express. Although in these studies some subjects judged facial expressions with great accuracy and others did badly indeed, the overall results were positive—significantly better than chance. Consider, for example, the two poses in Figure 2-1; Feleky (1914) found that one of them was called *surprise, astonishment,* or *wonder* by 74 of her 100 judges and the other was called *disgust* or *repugnance* by 50 percent. Moreover, there was hardly any overlap in the lists of adjectives applied to the two pictures. Yet, as Davitz (1964) pointed out, textbook writers who have cited such work have often concluded that emotions *cannot* be judged from facial expressions. Perhaps they came to this conclusion because they were looking for uniform laws of behavior and considered individual differences an uninteresting nuisance. The differences among people are the main subject matter of personality assessment, however, so let us consider what seem to be the main sources of variability in the accurate judgment of emotions. Because the experimental evidence deals only with mien or voice (or both), it will be necessary to disregard posture, gait, gesture, and such physiological signs as pallor or flushing, trembling, and perspiring, though these cues obviously can tell an observer much about emotions.

THE PERSON JUDGING

Almost all the relevant research has indicated a great range of ability in judging the emotions expressed by face or voice. The ability to assess emotions from tape-recorded voices is significantly (but not highly) correlated with verbal I.Q. (Davitz, 1964). Usually there is no consistent

[handwritten margin note: emotions expressed by face or voice; learned ability]

Figure 2-1 Pictures from an experiment on judging emotions. (From Feleky, 1914)

superiority of one sex over the other, but when a difference is found it is in favor of the females.

Clearly, the ability to interpret facial and vocal cues correctly is learned, for it can be improved by specific training and practice and improves with age, at least from age 5 to age 10 (Dimitrovsky, 1964). Even so, the youngest children who have been tested have performed significantly better than chance. Gates (1923) found that children under 3 years of age can recognize laughing faces in still photographs; and that at 5 to 6 years they can recognize pain, although the subtler emotions like contempt are seldom accurately identified from pictures by preadolescents.

THE PERSON BEING JUDGED

Some people have impassive, "wooden" faces and monotonous voices; others are highly expressive. If an experiment requires the subjects to simulate emotion in facial expression or in voice, those who are trained in emotional communication—actors—are generally more effective than non-actors in getting a message across, although ordinary college students do remarkably well (Thompson & Meltzer, 1964; Levitt, 1964). In a Russian experiment (Kalina, 1960), where nonactors and actors posed for photographs of various emotions, the superiority of the professionals showed up only in the more complex emotions.

Not a great deal of research has been done on the characteristics of the "sender" of emotional communication, but it has been demonstrated that the facial expressions of 10-month-old babies are less recognizable than those of children and that emotions enacted by members of one's own culture are usually (though not in all studies) easier to recognize than emotions that are transmitted across cultural barriers. Much depends, however, on the emotion in question, and cross-cultural recognition of emotions has been found to be consistently better than chance in studies involving Americans and the supposedly inscrutable Chinese (May, 1938—photographs), and Americans, Israelis, and Japanese (Davitz, 1964—voices).

THE CONTEXT AND AMOUNT
OF EMOTIONAL COMMUNICATION BEING JUDGED

An emotion is not a static, detached state but a fluid and literally *moving* process that is part of a situation. Thus, in everyday life we rarely base our judgment of how someone feels on a momentary expression; we observe the total pattern of his behavior in the context of some situation. Several experimenters, realizing this point, demonstrated that accuracy and agreement among observers increased when they had information about the *situation* of the pictured person. Such findings were at first widely interpreted in a negative way: Emotion could not be judged from facial expression; it was all a matter of inference from knowledge of the situation. According to this theory, we learn that dangerous situations arouse fearful behavior; therefore, we perceive fear in the expression of a person who is in danger, no matter what his expression may be.

There is good evidence against this theory in the data of a well-known experiment (Munn, 1940) in which college students were shown candid pictures of people experiencing various emotions. First, they saw enlargements of the faces only; a week later they saw pictures of the entire person in the natural setting. When the feelings in question were joy, terror, pain, anxiety, surprise, or disappointment, correct judgments on the initial showing ranged from 65 percent to 99 percent, and performance was *not* improved when the context was added.

Other studies show that the overall accuracy with which emotions are recognized from facial expression alone increased when still photographs were replaced by short movies (Frijda, 1953) and that adding a sound track to silent movies of faces increased accuracy in judging fear and surprise (though not other emotions), even though the voices were merely reciting irrelevant, neutral material (Levitt, 1964).

THE NATURE OF THE EMOTION BEING JUDGED

In several of the investigations mentioned above, it was clear that the results varied greatly depending on the particular emotions involved. If the affective state is basic and elemental—that is, if a person is laughing heartily, weeping with sorrow, in agonizing pain, or ragingly angry—very little visual or auditory information is necessary to convey the message to the beholder. When it is a question of such extremes, particularly the unpleasant emotions like sadness and anger, communication is good despite cultural differences, lack of context, the age of either person involved, or the intelligence of the judge (Levy, Orr, & Rosenzweig, 1960). The more subtle, complex, and weakly expressed emotions—for example, nostalgic, quizzical, or ambivalent feelings—are correspondingly harder to identify because they are expressed in less dramatic and less uniform ways by different people; success in these cases depends more on the skill of the judge and on completeness of information about the behavioral situation.

INNATE FACTORS AND CULTURAL LEARNING
IN EMOTIONAL COMMUNICATION

It is difficult to obtain good evidence from human subjects about the degree to which emotional expression and recognition are inborn, biological endowments. Smiling and laughing are universal expressions of pleasure, and anguish of any sort tends to produce weeping in all cultures and at all ages. Obviously, however, it is difficult to determine just when in infancy we become able to recognize the emotions of others around us.

Some suggestive evidence comes from work with subhuman primates.

Miller, Murphy, and Mirsky (1959) found that monkeys clearly avoided color slides of other monkeys in a frightened state, discriminating them from pictures of calm monkeys. Another experimenter (Sackett, 1966) strikingly demonstrated that the ability to recognize emotion is innate, though not completely developed at birth. Eight rhesus monkeys were reared in individual, enclosed cages from birth to 9 months, during which time they saw no other living creatures. One wall of the cage was a translucent screen on which color slides were projected daily. Most of the pictures were of monkeys in various positions and emotional states, but some were control slides of human beings, landscapes, and miscellaneous scenes. The experimenter observed the monkeys' reactions to each picture through a one-way vision screen. All pictures of monkeys consistently stimulated more responses than did the control slides, indicating an innate "species identity," but two types drew most responses of all types: pictures of other monkey infants and of threatening adult monkeys. Typical responses to pictures of babies were attempts to play with them and exploratory behavior. The threatening expression of an adult monkey seemed to be innately meaningful, for the threat pictures caused more responses of almost all kinds at each age level, and had a specific effect that peaked at 3 months: The baby monkeys would squeal, rock, huddle, and shrink back in obvious fear on seeing the threat pictures. These negative responses were not called forth by any other slide.

It is possible that evidence may someday be found that human beings also have some inborn capacity to respond differentially to expressions of basic emotions in others. Surely the emotional expressions found in man and other animals have survival value as a means of direct, nonverbal communication among members of the species and, often, across species. The creature who is innately able to tell at a glance whether he is confronted by an angry or a contented specimen of his own or of some other kind is more likely to survive and pass along this ability to descendants than is his less sensitive brother.

It is equally evident that emotional expression is heavily influenced by culture. A young Chinese girl, for example, is taught not to show her teeth when she smiles; the gestural expansiveness of many Mediterranean peoples contrasts with the stolidity and impassiveness proverbially associated with American Indians and Orientals, who probably have as much depth of inner feeling as anyone else.

The cultural standards for emotional expression that constitute a vocabulary of nonverbal language are perhaps most clearly expressed in the theater. Actors develop a good deal more uniformity and clarity of facial expression than do nonactors, just as they tend to enunciate words more clearly. Most cultures teach the language of facial expression in their graphic arts, too. Since a painter must convey his message with a single momentary expression, it may not exactly match any one frame of a motion picture of a person who is realistically experiencing the same emotion, yet it may communicate feeling equally well. These pictorial standards of expression, epitomized and sharpened by the caricaturist and cartoonist, constitute a constant and pervasive indoctrination in ways to express our feelings. It is no wonder, therefore, that the first experimenters in this field assumed that still pictures were perfectly adequate material for studying the recognition of emotion.

Rival theorists in psychology once advanced extreme theories claiming that some aspect of behavior was innate *or* that it was determined by learning. We are now beginning to recognize that there are important genetic contributions to behavior up and down the line; at the same time there are hardly any aspects of behavior that do not show some shaping by the cultural environment of the individual. At this time more is understood about learning than about behavioral inheritance, although recent developments in the biochemistry and biology of heredity may reverse the situation. Psychologists stress environmental determinants because it seems that more can be accomplished currently by training, re-education, and therapy than by genetics, at least in human beings.

Empathy and Understanding

An important means of understanding the emotions of others goes by the somewhat abused term *empathy*. This concept was first introduced around the turn of the twentieth century by the German psychologist-philosopher Lipps, who based an esthetic theory on the observation that many people made small involuntary movements when observing certain works of art. He claimed that the sagging, drooping lines of a funereal sculpture (as shown in Figure 2-2) or of a weeping willow appear to us that way because they evoke similar dejected postures in us, while the linear qualities of a monumental building convey a sense of heroic strength by stimulating us to throw back our shoulders and stand more fully erect. We are not aware of our own movements and stance, said Lipps, because the evoked qualities are perceived as *in* the work of art or nature.

Such observations contain a clue to the way perception sometimes works: through a kind of identification or subjective merging of self and non-self. Although processes of this kind have been difficult to approach by means of systematic research, they play a major role in informal assessment and therefore deserve our attention. Despite their relative lack of control, the observations of psychoanalysts and other clinicians have a good deal to teach us about empathy (see, for example, Schafer, 1959).

There are five kinds of phenomena to which the concept of empathy is applicable. Besides the *esthetic empathy* mentioned above, there is the closely related process of what Murphy (1947) calls *autistic* (or magical) *participation*, more familiarly known as "body English." Golfers try to help push the ball into the hole by involuntarily leaning in that direction. If you have ever fed a baby or watched anyone else do it, you know how irresistible

Figure 2-2 *What are your empathic responses to this study by Rodin for his "The Burghers of Calais"?*

is the irrational impulse to get that little mouth to open by opening your own (see Figure 2-3). Behind all responses of the types mentioned is the automatic and unconscious identification of every normal human being with any other he encounters, which seems to be part of a phenomenon called *basic species identity*. In the infant, the first observable form of empathy is the direct transmission of emotional arousal by *emotional contagion*. Finally, the healthy human adult is capable of *mature empathy*. We will look most closely at the last three of these types.*

* Deliberately omitted is any discussion of the recent experimental literature that purports to deal with empathy but is actually concerned with predicting another person's test responses. What at first looked like a promising approach to measuring empathy turned out to be subject to many methodological complications and flaws.

Figure 2-3 "Open wide, please!" An example of autistic participation.

BASIC SPECIES IDENTITY

The ability to recognize a member of one's own species is widespread among the higher animals. It is rather remarkable, when you stop to think about it, that a cat acts toward her kind as if she *knows* that she and they are all cats. A story like Hans Christian Andersen's "The Ugly Duckling" seems to say that animals have an inborn knowledge of what they are: The forlorn hero of that tale ultimately responded appropriately when he encountered other swans and no longer felt like a substandard duck. Indeed, an experiment summarized above (Sackett, 1966) seems to show that monkeys do respond innately to their own in this way. Much recent research by students of animal behavior indicates, however, that whether a hatchling feels itself to be a duck or a swan depends on which species it happens to encounter in a precisely determinable, short period of time during the first days of life. By managing to be the only moving thing in sight during such a critical period, Lorenz (1952) imprinted a jackdaw chick with a permanent interest in human beings, to the exclusion of other members of the bird's own species. Even when the jackdaw became sexually mature, it heard no "call of the wild" that lured it off to an appropriate romance; instead, it gave every sign of having fallen in love with the German naturalist and courted him by tenderly stuffing his ears with tasty worms.

No direct evidence exists as yet of either an innate sense of humanness or a critical period of imprinting in the human infant. Nevertheless, the sense of species identity somehow gets inculcated. It is surely part of being human to recognize every other member of the species *Homo sapiens* as fundamentally like yourself. Furthermore, the greater cognitive complexity of man means that we are likely to attribute to other people a great deal of

Empathy and Understanding   35

what we know about or experience within ourselves. Inevitably, much of what we attribute to others will be true of them (many philosophers and psychologists have argued that we are all more alike than we are different), but much will be false, also. If I scratch you where you don't itch, it is likely to be because I *do* itch there. Even the paranoid's overalert sensing of hostility all around him is the pressing of an originally nonpathological capacity into the service of defense (see page 24).

EMOTIONAL CONTAGION

In Chapter 1, the concept of emotional contagion was introduced with an experimental demonstration that babies cry more when their mothers are anxious. In the first year, an infant has no way of resisting the emotions of others, no barriers to prevent their spread; his smile in response to his mother's is as helpless as his squeals when she tickles him.

There is good observational evidence that emotional responsiveness to others depends greatly on the child's experience of being loved, having his own feelings perceived and responded to appropriately, and developing close relationships to his parents. Institutionally raised babies are less responsive to people than are babies who have been cared for by their mothers, particularly if no one worker in the institution serves as foster mother. According to Harlow (1962), even infant monkeys show similar effects when they are taken from their mothers and raised without contact with their kind. After they grow up, such monkeys never develop fully normal social responsiveness, and have disturbed sex lives. If a socially deprived female monkey does succeed in becoming pregnant, she seems devoid of mother love and is unable to care for her own young (see Figure 2-4).

From a developmental point of view, the significant fact is not so much that the infant responds directly to his mother's fright or loving warmth but that the older child grows out of this emotional contagion stage and can learn to be relatively indifferent to the emotional states of others. For to do so he must have a clearly differentiated sense of self, a feeling of his own separate identity and where its boundaries are; this sense is acquired only gradually during the first couple of years. When he does learn that every one of us is, to some extent, an island, he does not have to make a separate discovery that these other creatures in the world also have feelings; he has only to separate out of the welter of his own emotional states the ones that originate with himself and those that are to be attributed to the other person.

preadoles - adoles. must know self before true empathy

Redl (1966) has used the term *contagion* to refer to the rapid spread of a mood or a form of expressive behavior in a group of preadolescents or adolescents. For example, sometimes a boy who has no particular prestige in a group will impulsively yell at a teacher or throw a plate in a mess hall, and at once the whole place gets in an uproar as the others unexpectedly follow suit. According to Redl's analysis of such instances, the group takes over the emotional state and the acts of one of its members when he ex-

Figure 2-4 Typical behavior of an unmothered mother monkey toward her infant. (From Harlow, 1962)

presses something that is latent (but usually not conscious) in all of them. The more mature the members of a group are, the more difficult it is for this kind of emotional contagion to take place and the more controlled its manifestations are. Emotional contagion seems, then, to be a developmental stage preceding the controlled awareness of the feelings of others that we call true empathy.

PREREQUISITES FOR MATURE EMPATHY

The difference between the passive emotional contagion of animals and children and adult forms of empathy can often be seen in cases of schizophrenia, the most common form of psychosis. A preschizophrenic or schizoid person may sometimes be sensitive to others in a mature way, in that he is able to detect the feelings of others in a socially useful manner and without losing distance or objectivity. But after a psychotic break, some schizophrenics display the vulnerability to contagion by their emotional surroundings that characterizes a baby. Such sensitivity is too passive and involuntary to constitute usable empathy, although at times it can make a severely psychotic and apparently withdrawn person astonishingly responsive to concealed feelings and impulses in the doctors and nurses who try to work with him. For example, Stanton and Schwartz (1954) found that when the staff of a mental hospital had internal disputes that they tried to suppress, the schizophrenic patients seemed to sense it and became more disturbed and upset than they were at any other time. This openness to emotional contagion accompanies other evidences of breakdown in the boundaries of the self, such as these patients' bizarre difficulties in drawing pictures of people (see Figure 2-5).

A long process of social learning must take place before empathy works smoothly and automatically. A typical nursery school tussle exemplifies the process in miniature: Bill won't let Barbara have the tricycle. He is in good contact with part of the emotional truth, for he can see very well that she wants it as much as he does. But the teacher tries to introduce a new set of considerations: "How would *you* feel, Bill, if she had it and wouldn't share it with you, even for a little while?" Here is a homely example of the ways children are taught to imagine as fully as possible the feelings of the other person—as sociologist G. H. Mead (1934) put it, to "take the role of the other."

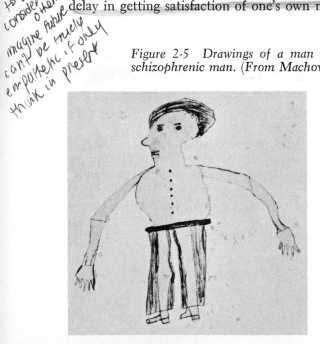

A Secure Sense of Identity

Paradoxically, mature empathy presupposes a clear separation of self and other and a secure sense of identity. To be willing to let go of his own immediate interests and to participate imaginatively in someone else's world, a person must have the security of knowing that he can slip comfortably back into his own skin. Mature empathy also requires the ability to tolerate enough delay in getting satisfaction of one's own needs to be able to consider those

Figure 2-5 Drawings of a man and a woman by a paranoid schizophrenic man. (From Machover, 1949)

of others, which in turn means being able to imagine the future. Anyone who lives only in the present is bound to the urgency of getting what he wants when he wants it; overcoming this impatience is an important part of growing up. Freud expressed this aspect of maturing as the change from the pleasure principle (acting only for immediate gratification) to the reality principle (deferring momentary pleasure so as to attain lasting and important goals).

② **Genuine Communication**   Mature empathy is not only an active but an interactive process; it is trained and refined by the interplay of communication. When young children first play together, they are more properly described as playing *alongside* one another. Piaget (1926) called their conversations "collective monologues." Some people never wholly outgrow this phase; although they may seem to be animated conversationalists, they do not listen, so that genuine interaction with them is not possible. The attempt to talk with such a person, even if it is merely to pass the time of day, can be extremely frustrating and annoying. Why should that be? Apparently, a normal person feels a need to establish some emotional contact with anyone he meets and to communicate, if only by exchanging conventional symbols of friendliness and of caring about one another's welfare. By failing to supply the expected feedback, an unempathic person thwarts this need.

An understanding person does not have to be an intuitive wizard who knows exactly what is going on inside you before you say a word; indeed, he may be preoccupied with his own concerns when the exchange begins and greet you cheerily when you are in pain. But he shows his empathy by noticing that you do not react in the way his gaiety presupposes, and by becoming appropriately serious and concerned.

③ **Practice**   The ordinary principles of learning are adequate to account for the development of empathy in a person who is not blocked in some way from being interested in others, from listening to them and to his own inner response, and from giving the other person a chance to talk about himself in the true sense of a dialogue. In the process of consistently attempting to respond appropriately to what the other person is trying to communicate, we become more and more alert to subtle cues to complex states of mind and feeling. Indeed, it takes practice to maintain the empathic skills. Marooned sailors and other involuntary hermits typically find it difficult on first reentering society to participate in ordinary social interchange, and they often make social blunders because their empathic capacities are rusty. By the same token, one of the early signs of the emotional withdrawal characteristic of schizophrenia is the appearance of inappropriate language and emotion and a resulting awkwardness and eccentricity in social behavior.

Caring
About Other People

Clearly, affection and empathic perception are closely connected. Whoever lacks the capacity to care about others will be sealed off from understanding them fully. An example of such a person is the psychopathic personality or sociopath, who has the kind of character disorder often found in criminals. These people are usually wholly self-centered and interested in others only for what they can get out of them. Psychopaths may be very shrewd in spotting a victim who can be easily deceived and in exploiting his weaknesses, yet it is an old saying among policemen that a really honest person seldom gets exploited in a confidence game. The apparent cleverness of the psychopath in assessing personality is limited to recognizing those qualities that he himself can experience (such as greed and willingness to cut moral corners) or that he can exploit (such as naive gullibility).

The Ability
to Experience Emotions

Since empathic understanding is based on a person's re-experiencing within himself what he sees the other person undergoing, empathic range is limited by the extensiveness of a person's experience. If you have never lost a person who was very dear to you, you may find it impossible to empathize fully with someone whose mother has just died. Yet this principle does not necessarily operate in a literal way: To have loved a pet that died may enable you to build in your imagination a sense of what the bereaved person feels so that you can respond in an appropriate and helpful manner.

Another clinical observation illustrates some conditions limiting mature empathy and some prerequisites for it. People whose defensive make-up is so rigid as to shut them off from fully experiencing their emotions lack the empathy that would enable them to get along with others easily. A common example is the dry, overly intellectual, compulsive person who isolates emotion and tries to live a life of dispassionate fact. He tends to treat people like objects and is unaware of their nonverbal signals of distress. Capability in informal assessment, therefore, requires that a person be aware of what goes on inside himself; in particular he must be in touch with his own feelings. Not that an empathic person spills over with emotion; he may be restrained in his outward expressions while still being very much in tune with his own affective life, and thus with that of other people.

Several psychoanalysts who have observed and pondered mature empathy agree that it is a process of temporary and controlled partial identification, similar to the process by which the self is formed (see Schafer, 1959). It must be partial, or the empathizer loses his distance, and instead of (or in addition to) perceiving the other person as anxious, he feels the anxiety as his own. People who are learning to become psychotherapists often go through a phase of just this type. They must open themselves to the emotional states of their patients; and until they learn to control the process of identification, they become overidentified with them and experience considerable personal turmoil. Indeed, research on the training of psychiatrists has shown that the men who eventually become the best therapists tend to go through such a phase, whereas those who from the beginning are unruffled by contact with disturbed people tend to be too closed off by their own defenses to develop much empathy (Holt & Luborsky, 1958).

How We Develop
an Understanding of a Person

METHODS OF INFORMAL ASSESSMENT

As we get beyond first impressions, we use three main methods in getting to understand a person: (1) observing his behavior in a variety of situations, (2) conversing with him, and (3) getting information about him from other sources.

Observation   In the process of learning to know a friend thoroughly, we scrutinize him carefully and repeatedly in his home, at work, at parties, and so on. By seeing for ourselves how he behaves in a variety of situations, we automatically winnow the aspects of his conduct that are situational and are left with the enduring dispositions that make up his personality. In addition, we can increase the range of our information about him by calling *more* of these personal dispositions to the surface. Thus we can overcome the unrepresentativeness of the sample of behavior from which we formed our first impressions.

Conversation   It is the exception rather than the rule when, in getting to know a person well, our observations occur in any way other than through interacting with him. Verbal interaction, or conversation, is especially valuable, since it enables us to find out rather directly our friend's feelings about things and people, his thoughts, his organization of his world, and especially his subjective sense of what he wants and is striving for. The primary means of comprehending behavior is through learning about a person's motivation—how behavior is organized by the attempt to attain goals of all kinds; therefore, to understand a person it is essential to know his ambitions, his aims in life, and the values he holds dear. There is hardly any substitute for personal discussion as a way of finding out about these matters; indeed, even though we can learn a great deal by watching what a person seems to be trying to accomplish and by piecing together the observations of others, our understanding is incomplete if we do not know how he thinks and feels about these matters himself. The very fact that he might not know or be willing to admit that he consistently tried to attain social status, for example, would be important for understanding his behavior and might illuminate aspects of his motivation that would otherwise remain obscure or puzzling.

To be sure, there are pitfalls in the conversational method; it has the drawbacks of subjectivity and personal involvement. Fortunately, however, the very attempt to keep up a series of conversations with a person tends to be somewhat self-correcting. As long as we remain open and do not intrude too much nor rigidly shut off the feedback from our successes and failures at communicating, we can continue to learn more and more about a friend, thereby deepening and enriching our understanding of him.

Information from Others No matter how long one person has been acquainted with another, it is always possible to learn new things about him from other persons, who see him in different contexts and relationships. A person reveals somewhat different faces depending on the situation, and whatever is known about the informants themselves adds to the meaning of the behavior and conversations they report. The dangers of hearsay are reduced when the opinions of one informant can be checked against those of others and against personal knowledge. The range of observations from others can be enormously increased to the point where they cover almost all the subject's life.

FORMING A SCHEMA FOR UNDERSTANDING

These three methods of getting data constitute only half the story of informal assessment; a conceptual and integrative step must follow as separate facts are woven together to form a schema for understanding. It is possible to collect a great deal of information about a person, and even to predict aspects of his behavior successfully, without any sense of understanding him. Common metaphors provide clues to just what is meant when we talk about understanding someone: We speak of wanting to know "how he is put together," or "what is his game," or "what makes him tick." These are causal and configural questions, which point to the existence of something like a theoretical model as the basis for understanding a particular person—a set of facts linked by causal propositions to yield expectations. This formulation unfortunately sounds excessively abstract, verbal, and intellectual, whereas it should give the idea of an implicit and affective understanding of someone we know well. In place of "theoretical model," let us borrow Piaget's term *schema* to refer to the basis for this affective understanding.

Ask a friend to tell you what sort of person his father is, and you may be surprised by his difficulty in finding things to say that convey more than one layer of feeling about a man he has known as long and as closely as anyone. To be sure, the very fact that such intense and conflicting emotions are centered on a parent makes it difficult to talk about him analytically. He is likely to be the focus of so many desires and such an important obstacle to, or means for the fulfillment of, others that his own son cannot be expected to come up with a disinterested, objective appraisal. Nevertheless, your friend knows a great deal more than he can put into words—an instance of Polanyi's *tacit knowing*. He knows "how to work the old man" for something he wants in the same way that he knows how to ride a bicycle, for an intimate familiarity is there that is readily available to guide behavior, though not in a verbal form. Psychologists assume that a complex schema is built up about every person we know well; this schema guides behavior in relation to the person and need not be verbal in order to be effective.

✳ *The Systematization of Informal Assessment*

It should be clear by now that the methods of informal assessment used in everyday life are subjective, empathic, and even intuitive; yet they *can* be subjected to rigorous, objective investigation. We can study the validity of these methods; for example, we can check the extent to which the statements one person makes about another's personality are true by comparing them to some independent standard (or *criterion*) or, more indirectly, by translating them into explicit predictions, which can then be checked against future behavior. We can select people who are good natural judges of men and investigate the ways in which they differ from others who are ineffective. And we can attempt to train people in order to improve their skill.

As soon as the methods of science are applied to an informal, everyday process, it begins to turn into a discipline, perhaps eventually into a technology, and even a science. The first attempts to systematize informal methods of understanding personalities produced clinical assessment, to which we shall turn in the next chapter.

Roger Chillingworth scrutinized his patient carefully, both as he saw him in his ordinary life, keeping an accustomed pathway in the range of thoughts familiar to him, and as he appeared when thrown amidst other moral scenery, the novelty of which might call out something new to the surface of his character. He deemed it essential, it would seem, to know the man, before attempting to do him good. . . . [So he] strove to go deep into his patient's bosom, delving among his principles, prying into his recollections, and probing everything with a cautious touch, like a treasure-seeker in a dark cavern. Few secrets can escape [such] an investigator. . . . If the latter possess native sagacity, and a nameless something more,—let us call it intuition; if he show no intrusive egotism, nor disagreeably prominent characteristics of his own: if he have the power, which must be born with him, to bring his mind into such affinity with his patient's, that this last shall unawares have spoken what he imagines himself only to have thought; if such revelations be received without tumult, and acknowledged not so often by an uttered sympathy as by silence, an inarticulate breath, and here and there a word, to indicate that all is understood; . . . then, at some inevitable moment, will the soul of the sufferer be dissolved, and flow forth in a dark, but transparent stream, bringing all its mysteries into the daylight.

NATHANIEL HAWTHORNE. The Scarlet Letter

CHAPTER 3
FORMAL ASSESSMENT: THE CLINICAL APPROACH

C linical assessment, the effort "to know the man before attempting to do him good," began as an application of the common-sense methods of informal assessment to the problems presented by psychiatric patients. Thus the early practitioners of clinical assessment focused on direct methods. For example, the nineteenth-century German psychiatrist Kraepelin interviewed each patient and his relatives, observed the patient's behavior in the mental hospital over a prolonged period of time, and followed up to learn what became of him. He made limited use of somewhat formalized medical diagnostic methods, but primarily he relied on his eyes and ears and information supplied by other staff members of his hospital to discern so-called pure cases of what he thought were "diseases" and to describe their essential characteristics. He succeeded so well that recent attempts to isolate types of mental patients by statistical methods (for example, factor analysis) have substantially confirmed his work (Wittenborn & Holzberg, 1951; Lorr, O'Connor, & Stafford, 1957).

Since the time of Kraepelin, clinicians have added special, indirect methods of their own. The pages that follow will focus first on the direct methods of gathering data used in clinical assessment and then on the indirect methods, a discussion of which will lead into an analysis of means of interpreting data and integrating everything into an explicit schema.

Direct Methods
of Clinical Assessment

THE INTERVIEW

An important characteristic of the psychiatric approach to assessment is that it has always (but especially since the work of Freud) been concerned with the most important crises of human lives, and the diagnostic interview has always focused on the problems that troubled patients the most. Therefore, the psychiatric tradition has the great merit of looking first at the main issues in a person's life, regardless of whether they lend themselves to accurate appraisal or not, but it also has the possible drawback of a medical orientation to symptoms and disease.

As the process of talking with another person to learn about his personality has moved from conversation toward something technical enough to be called interviewing, it has been formalized in two quite opposite ways. These formal techniques are the *structured interview* and *free association*.

**Structured
Interviews** An interviewer generally introduces some degree of structuring by means of questions. To be sure, it is possible to interview someone by informal, relaxed, and normally discursive conversation, without specific questioning. Sometimes the subject's anxiety, wariness, or the like makes unstructured interviewing necessary; but it requires much discipline and experience to be effective, and it takes much time. At one extreme, interviewing approaches testing when the interviewer uses a list of set questions in fixed sequence and even a set of "canned" answers from which the subject chooses (as in the case of certain public-opinion interviews that use multiple-choice questions). Most clinical assessors distrust the rigidity of such set methods and prefer to structure interviews according to *objectives*, or goals. Suppose, for example, the interviewer decides ahead of time that he wants to find out about the subject's home life; he will make himself a set of notes to cover the main facts about the family (what persons lived together at various times in his past, whether the family was broken, the ages of brothers and sisters, and so on), the nature of the emotional relationships that existed in the family, and the subject's informal assessment of his principal relatives.

The main problem for the interviewer is managing to steer the best course between oversubjectivity and overobjectivity. Too great subjectivity involves several kinds of dangers: The interviewer may get so emotionally involved that he forgets his goals or injects too much of his own personality into the interaction; he may reword questions so that they no longer get at what was intended or so that they suggest certain types of answers. He must take particular pains not to influence what the subject says, beyond pointing him in the appropriate direction and encouraging him to speak freely, for the whole point of an assessment interview is lost if the information elicited is seriously biased in any way.

The dangers of overobjectivity, on the other hand, are that the interviewer may become clinically insensitive and mistake rigidity for consistency. A uniform procedure is highly desirable, but the interviewer cannot assume that using the same words with all subjects will automatically bring about the same understanding of what he intends. It is being overobjective, also, to plod through a list of questions, disregarding the subject's signals that he is interested in a particular area and ready to talk about it even though it does not happen to be next on the schedule, or to ignore indications of anxiety, embarrassment, or guilt—signals that the interviewer should tactfully change the topic and approach the sensitive area later in a different way.

Whatever the technique of interviewing may be, it can sometimes yield a great wealth of information and, at other times, merely huge quantities of words with little in the way of useful fact. In any case, a major part of the interviewer's job is not just to elicit the subject's words but to record them in some way—in writing, on tape, or in his memory. The tradition in clinical interviewing has been to rely on memory, though in research settings electrical recordings are increasingly being used.

Free Association   The unique type of interview Freud developed has been used for diagnostic as well as therapeutic purposes. Freud became convinced that because most neurotics did not consciously know what was bothering them, direct questioning had limited value. At the same time, the conflicting motives underlying neurosis, as he understood it, were capable of steering the course of thought and talk when external formal structuring was removed. Therefore, he encouraged his patients to speak their thoughts freely, to talk about anything that came to mind whether it seemed relevant or not, while trying not to censor their words by any polite conventions or by the desire to please him through saying "the right thing." To minimize his own influence on the "free associations," he refrained from direct questioning and sat behind the patient (who lay on a couch), so as not to allow even his facial expression to give cues about what was wanted or expected.

The resulting method, free association, is unexcelled for providing data about the inner longings and fears that impel people, particularly data from which their unconscious motives may be inferred. Although the process of free association sounds easy, few people can immediately relax their conscious and unconscious defenses enough to do it, so learning the method usually takes many hours. Moreover, the analyst needs extensive training not only to interpret the subject's wanderings but to cope with the emotions that are often released: The subject may find himself unexpectedly faced by such painful thoughts and wishes that he needs not just acceptance and reassurance but skilled psychotherapeutic help.

Because Freud listened to his patients talk about anything they chose to over months and years of interviews, which were held four or five times each week, he grew to know and understand them better than any therapist had before him. Because of his conviction that all behavior was lawfully determined by conscious and unconscious motives, he listened when the neurotic men and women who came to him told him about their dreams and fantasies, instead of impatiently dismissing such stuff as irrelevant. In this way, the interview became to a great degree an *indirect* method of assessment. (Free association is not included among the indirect methods discussed later in the chapter, because it is little used in psychodiagnosis, except by psychoanalysts.)

TESTS

Some tests strongly resemble the highly structured interviews in which the questions are all written out. The Eysenck Personality Inventory, for example, consists of 57 questions, the first of which is: "Do you like plenty of excitement and bustle around you?" A place is provided for the subject to check his answer, Yes or No, by each question. Other such tests usually consist of many separate items, each of which is stated as a question that either might be asked in an interview or could easily be turned into one. (This and other direct, nonprojective tests will be discussed further in Chapters 4, 6, and 8.)

An intelligence test is the prototype of another sort of nonprojective, direct test that relies less on conversational means and more on setting the subject tasks to perform. Any test of abilities is generally presented in a straightforward manner. Thus it is a direct method of gathering data, even though it has to be administered and scored according to technical rules and even though it is not always obvious how an item should be solved. So-called group intelligence tests, of the self-administered type, exist in considerable variety, but clinical assessment usually relies on individual tests of intelligence administered by a skilled psychologist. The best known examples are the Stanford-Binet Scale, the Wechsler Intelligence Scale for Children (WISC), and the Wechsler Adult Intelligence Scale (WAIS). These are actually compound tests with many varieties of items testing relatively specific abilities; thus, they yield general intelligence quotients (I.Q.'s), but they also enable the experienced examiner to assess many qualitative aspects of the way a person thinks, reasons, solves problems, and copes with objective demands.

OBSERVATION

Any contact between assessor and subject is an opportunity for many interesting types of observable behavior to emerge, which are concrete instances of a variety of the behavioral dispositions or traits making up the subject's personality. Since observation yields the most direct type of evidence, it is a cardinal rule of formal assessment to take advantage of every opportunity to observe a subject's behavior during testing and interviewing or at any other time. The assessor must observe as sharply (though inconspicuously) as possible and record the observed behavior, with its context, as soon as he can.

An assessor's notes might include, for example, the observation that the subject became red in the face and perspired freely when asked to disrobe for a physical examination. Or they might contain a report of a subject's conversation with one member of a clinic's staff while the subject waited for an appointment with another, including observations of his attempts to ingratiate himself and get some information about how he was doing. Valuable as such incidental observations are, they must be interpreted with some caution and with the realization that they are based on a small sample of behavior, often in an atypical situation.

PERSONAL DOCUMENTS

Autobiographies   When the subject is cooperative and intelligent enough to carry out the assignment, an excellent method is to have him write an autobiography. If no specific instructions are given, a good deal can be learned by his choice of topics and by the kinds of things he omits, such as any mention of a much disliked brother. The usual procedure, however, is to suggest general areas for the subject to cover, so that the assessor may have direct information on the topics that concern him most. The structured extreme of this procedure is the *biographical inventory*, an instrument that contains a series of specific questions and, sometimes, sets of alternative answers, one of which is to be checked.

For example, Siegel (1956) developed a biographical inventory containing 372 items of the following kinds, which fall into ten clusters. Here are 5 items exemplifying five different clusters; the subject checks True or False for each:

> *Father has taught me to fish or enjoy some other individual sport.* (Action)
> *I have taken a trip of more than 100 miles with friends.* (Social Activities)

I never have dates. (Heterosexual Activities)
Mother is active in a political group. (Political Activities)
Father is active in a church group. (Religious Activities)

Such inventories have proved useful in large-scale research on selection of personnel.

Diaries   Diaries are personal documents of the greatest interest to the clinical assessor if they are something more than bare records of external events. Yet even a set of appointment books can yield objective, direct evidence about the breadth of a person's acquaintance, his pattern of work, his orderliness, his involvement in community activities, and so forth. Sometimes researchers will ask subjects to keep special types of diaries recording a form of behavior under study, such as dreams (Schonbar, 1959) or fantasies (Singer, 1966).

Personal Letters   Although personal letters can be extremely revealing, they are difficult to obtain and are not usually asked for in routine clinical assessment. If a collection of letters does become available, it may be an invaluable source of information about a personality that is otherwise inaccessible for assessment. For example, Sigmund Freud wrote a series of letters to a close friend and colleague, Wilhelm Fliess, during the years when he was forming his basic psychoanalytic ideas; most of the letters, discovered about 50 years later, have been published (Freud, 1887–1902). They give a sense of direct acquaintance with a genius during an important phase of his life, and they have been of great value to his biographers.

Without the evidence of these letters, even so close a disciple as Ernest Jones might not have known that Freud suffered from a moderately severe neurosis during the 1890's, and he surely would have been ignorant of the subjective nature of Freud's symptoms. Jones quotes a letter of December 6, 1897, in which Freud described "spells where consciousness would be greatly narrowed . . . with a veil that produced almost a twilight condition of mind [Jones, 1953, p. 306]." And it is only because Freud's letters to his fiancée some years earlier were preserved that we have a glimpse of the intense, romantic love he was capable of feeling; without them, we

> could easily have formed the impression that his marriage had been a simple affair of two people suited to each other being drawn together and deciding to marry. . . . How different was the truth, as revealed in the love letters! There we are confronted with a tremendous and complicated passion, one in which the whole gamut of emotion was evoked in turn, from the heights of bliss to the depths of despair with every grade of happiness and misery being felt with unsparing intensity [Jones, 1953, p. 99].

Letters from Jenny, edited by G. W. Allport (1965), shows how a collection of letters may be subjected to several kinds of systematic psychological analysis.

The direct methods that yield the most valuable results in some cases tell little in others; but this is characteristic of clinical assessment as a whole. For every great diarist or letter writer, there are hundreds of people whose personal documents are scanty, impersonal, and even misleading in the impression they give of a prosaic or shallow person. The same is true of any method in which subjects have any degree of freedom to respond, including tests and interviews. It is not difficult to learn through conversation, observation, or personal documents if a person is in fact taciturn, constricted in his thinking, or secretive, but it is often hard to learn more about his inner life of feelings and desires. As we saw in Chapter 2, people differ greatly in their openness, or transparency. The more defensive or otherwise inscrutable a person is, the less can be learned by direct methods. The *indirect* approach therefore plays a leading role in the clinical tradition of assessment.

Indirect Methods
of Clinical Assessment

The special methods involved in the indirect approach are the *projective techniques* of studying personality; but the indirect approach is also an orientation and a way of using data that can be applied to virtually any sort of information about a person—even to the results of objective tests.

It was Freud, again, who originated indirect assessment. He soon discovered that the dark stream of free associations is not always transparent, and because of the technique's permissiveness, a good deal more than the painful mysteries of the patient's suffering emerges. His dreams, daydreams, and the trivial mistakes of everyday living often have no obvious bearing on the problems that brought the neurotic into treatment, but Freud found that they constitute valuable indirect data when examined for their latent, rather than their manifest, content.

Freud learned to interpret dreams through studying his own. As he unravelled the tangle of determinants that brought a dream into being, he found that the same principles unlocked many of the mysteries of neurotic symptoms. After turning his attention to the psychological causes of slips of the tongue, momentary lapses of memory, and other types of seemingly unimportant errors, he was able, with the aid of the subject's free associations about such a slip, to reveal the impulses and defenses that brought it into being. In doing so, he laid the foundation for projective techniques and for all indirect methods of studying personality, and he provided the main interpretive rules.

HOW PROJECTIVE TECHNIQUES
AND OTHER INDIRECT METHODS WORK

The assumption underlying both the specific techniques and the whole indirect approach to interpreting assessment data is that when a person can respond relatively freely, his total behavior betrays many of the determinants that brought it about. Let us take a closer look at this highly condensed formulation.

**Freedom
to Respond**   Freedom to respond does not imply freedom of the will in the metaphysical sense of an absence of determinism. Rather, it simply acknowledges the fact that behavior is sometimes highly constrained by the requirements of a situation, and at other times a person has many more behavioral options open to him. The more freedom to act a person has, obviously, the less are the particulars of what he does and says dictated by forces external to him and thus the more is his behavior determined by the tendencies within him that make up his personality. Thus, the question, "What type of job are you looking for?" offers far less scope for personal dispositions to affect the answer than does "What are your main goals in life?"

"Total Behavior"   The phrase "total behavior" in the formulation calls our attention to the fact that at any one time a person is actually doing many things. Consider someone who is taking an intelligence test and simply responding correctly to the question, "How much are $5 and $4?" He may say "$9" in a straightforward, bored, haughty, tentative, or supercilious manner, indicating that he finds the question gratifyingly easy, or insultingly so, or that he suspects a trick, and so on. Or his answer, while technically correct, may be so peculiarly stated that it suggests a serious disturbance. The following example came from a nearly psychotic doctor: "That's 500 pennies and 400 pennies. Shall I add them?—A total of 900 pennies.—Oh, I guess you want me to say $9."

The subject's reaction time will often be significant: He may be so eager to show his skill or his contempt for the test that he blurts out his reply before the examiner stops speaking, or he may be so fixed in a pattern of caution that he ponders the question and checks his answer before responding. At the same time, he may display a characteristic posture: He may sit bolt upright, his stiff spine never touching the back of the chair, or slumped down in an attitude of overcasualness; or he may fidget in unconcealed anxiety. He may also spring up and pace the floor while replying, or he may crane his neck to see what the examiner is writing down. Meanwhile, his facial expression may be appropriately relaxed and calm, tense, depressed, frozen, smirking, or angry.

Although this by no means exhausts the range of behaviors that may occur while a subject is giving a routine, correct answer to a question that seemingly allows him very little leeway, it should be enough to suggest the wealth of diagnostically significant behavior that may be going on simultaneously. Some questions do in fact tend to constrict response, and the very situation of taking an intelligence test exerts subtle restraints on behavior to which most people unconsciously respond. Nevertheless, a human organism has many channels of response, and what seems to be a one-dimensional measurement provided by an arithmetic test is actually the result of ignoring most of the behavior that goes on. If you put a schizophrenic patient into a bare little room where there is a lever he can press, as some operant conditioners have done, he may bang his head on the walls, shout incoherent delusional speeches, or have murderous fantasies; but by concentrating your attention on just the number of times per hour he presses the lever, you can act as if the single aspect of behavior you are measuring is all that is really going on. The tradition of clinical assessment, by contrast, emphasizes sharp observation and accurate recording of all the subject's important behavior patterns.

The point about accurate recording deserves some emphasis. If the tester does not write down every word the subject says as nearly verbatim as possible and if he does not make notes on any behavior that deviates from the normal, most of the richness of his observation will soon vanish in the welter of impressions left by a session of testing. If he just records a plus for the arithmetic question, he will have only that single bit of information to work with later on when he is surveying and interpreting all his data; the residue of unverbalized understanding may then continue to resist translation into words.

The Multiple Determinants of Behavior

A major implication in the statement of assumption we are discussing is that any given act, mannerism, or personal characteristic has many determinants. Freud was struck by the superficiality of the answers people would give to such questions as "Why did you do that?" and in particular by their blindness to the unconscious motives their actions often expressed in addition to the conscious intention by which they sincerely tried to explain them. The fact that an act or thought had more than one motive Freud termed "overdetermination."

The principle of overdetermination may be generalized far beyond the realm of motivation, however. At a minimum, the following classes of determinants operate in bringing about any single answer given by a person who is being assessed: (1) the general situational context; (2) the immediate perceptual impact of the stimuli to which the person is responding, including the personality of anyone he is speaking to; (3) the directing sets that steer his attention and thought according to preconceptions about what is going on, what is wanted, what it is appropriate to do under the circumstances, and so on; (4) the processes of identification, which greatly affect the way the subject responds to other persons actually present or pictured in test materials; (5) the whole hierarchy of motives that are more or less active in the person at the time; (6) the defenses that control these motives; (7) the cognitive elaboration of response, as it draws on various kinds of information stored in his memory (his own life history, his self-concept and identity, his attitudes and values, and his store of general information); (8) the enabling and limiting effects of abilities, including not only general intelligence but also specific capacities that are relevant to the immediate task or situation; (9) the internal climate of moods and affects that give emotional flavor to the cognitive process; (10) the personal style of the subject's cognitive organization and of the words and gestures he uses to express his thoughts and feelings.

Several of these ten headings could be further broken down, and the whole list could be supplemented by looking at the behavior in question not psychologically but from the point of view of the other behavioral sciences and disciplines relevant to understanding man. A subject's behavior in answering questions put by a tester or interviewer can be viewed from the vantage point of the ethnologist, who would point out the extent to which the behavior is culturally determined; from that of the sociologist, who would stress the role relationships of the two persons and their relative places in a social structure; from that of the economist, who would remind us that part of the subject's motivation is the money he is being paid or is paying for services rendered in the context of a capitalist, free-enterprise system; from that of the biochemist, who would inquire into the chemical composition of the subject's blood and perhaps relate his fast reaction time to a momentarily high secretion of adrenalin because of stress; from that of the physical anthropologist, who can expertly analyze the subject's physique and relate it to his behavior; and so on. Much of the information that would be developed by the work of these and other specialists might be integrated into a broad conception of personality, but much would simply be too peripheral. For the most part, therefore, we assess personality with a psychological orientation. Nevertheless, we should not lose sight of the fact that many other sciences are concerned with behavior and that it is determined on many levels other than the one that may interest us at the time.

The "Betrayal" of the Determinants

The final assertion made by the italicized formulation a few pages back is that an action or verbal statement *betrays* many of its determinants. The metaphor is intended to suggest that a full understanding of behavior presupposes a process like the penetration of a disguise. Few of the many factors responsible for the detailed structure of behavior are visible to the untrained eye, yet the content and style of what a person says and does contain many subtle indicators of what motivates him. To change the figure of speech, the instruments of thought often leave their toolmarks on the final product, enabling the trained observer to discern and infer what the important determinants were. This last process is *clinical interpretation* (or clinical inference), which plays a central role in projective techniques and in the indirect analysis of most other kinds of data. The process is described later in this chapter and is illustrated in later chapters with an actual case. Likewise, the nature of projective techniques will become much clearer in Chapter 6, as we examine one man's responses to two standard projective tests (the Rorschach and the Thematic Apperception Test).

Projective techniques differ from direct methods in that they do not depend on the subject's willingness to give information about himself. They are designed to encourage freedom of response so that the material the subject produces will have the most opportunity to reveal its own determinants; they yield information about the person only by enabling him to furnish a thought product that we can interpret by reconstructing the determinants that brought it about. For some years clinical assessors assumed that the essential feature of projective techniques was the ambiguity or unstructuredness of the test materials, the immediate stimuli to which the subject responded. It has become clear from theoretical analysis and from research data that the pictures about which the subject tells stories in the Thematic Apperception Test, for example, may be quite clear and specific with no loss in the test's effectiveness; the task itself, making up an imaginative story, permits so much freedom in responding that the answers are not unduly constrained by the specificity of the pictures.

A BRIEF SURVEY OF PROJECTIVE TECHNIQUES

All of a man's behavior expresses his personality to some extent, and almost any observations can be useful. Nevertheless, the great advantage of working with relatively fixed and standardized methods is that they provide a constant backdrop against which the individuality of each subject may stand out in bold contrast. A projective test presents the subject with a standard set of inkblots (the Rorschach Test or the Holtzman Inkblot Test), a standard set of pictures about which to tell imaginative stories (Thematic Apperception Test, or TAT), a standard set of incomplete sentences to be finished (Sentence Completion Test) or of words to which the subject is to respond with the first word that enters his head (Word Association Test), a standard group of toys the child is invited to play with (World Test), a standard set of pictures of people out of which the subject must select those he likes and those he dislikes (Szondi Test), or a standard set of geometric figures to be copied (Bender Gestalt Test). The procedure is the same for everyone, the instructions are relatively fixed, and the examiner tries to maintain the same attitude of unbiased readiness to hear and record whatever the subject wants to say. The test's materials are usually varied enough so that they present a variety of challenges, or bring to mind a full range of generally important topics or situations, or otherwise elicit as rich a sample of reactions as possible.

Without the degree of constancy provided by standardized methods, it would be much more difficult to compare the subject's behavior with that of others. But by holding the stimulus situation constant, the examiner hopes to be able to account for the variation of responses in terms of differences in the internal organization of his subjects. Even graphic techniques that lack structured stimuli, like figure drawing (the Draw-a-Man Test or House-Tree-Person Test), easel painting, or finger painting, follow the same rationale.

Clearly, there is no limit to the types of standardized materials a person might be confronted with and asked to talk about, manipulate, construct something with, or the like. During the first decade after World War II, the heyday of projective techniques, clinical psychologists turned their ingenuity to the development of many more instruments of this type than can be listed here, a number of which have their staunch advocates. Those who have retained their enthusiasm for projective tests tend to place more emphasis now on building up better norms and a stronger base of clinical experience with a small range of instruments with established usefulness rather than on trying out new ones.

The subject's freedom to respond, which enables him unwittingly to reveal so much about himself, is also a weakness of this type of test. A Rorschach or TAT protocol (the record of a subject's responses and behavior) may allow a skilled clinician to make inferences about almost any facet of personality—abilities, motives, defenses, past history, pathological trends, values and attitudes, and much more—but there is no guarantee that he will be able to make *valid* statements about any one of these areas for any particular subject. One man's figure drawings will tell worlds about his inner experience of his own body; another's drawings will tell little beyond the fact that he is a conventional and guarded person.

An Introduction to Interpretation
in Clinical Assessment

Projective techniques, and the methods of clinical assessment generally, are no better than the man who interprets them. They have little, if any, intrinsic validity, since they are not direct measures of any one aspect of personality. Instead, they are devices to scoop up samples of thought and behavior, which must be interpreted before they can be of value; and interpretation of this kind of material is an expert performance requiring a blend of art, experience, native shrewdness and intuition, and science, or at least technology. Science is included because interpretation demands a thorough knowledge of personality theory and a disciplined way of handling evidence—by forming and verifying hypotheses—which closely resembles the scientific method.

To interpret clinical data properly, one must be able to form hypotheses or to make inferences freely, drawing on experience, empirical rules about what means what (statistical inference), and hunches, but ideally deriving hypotheses (possible interpretations) from a theoretical understanding of how the test responses come about. This is the creative or inspirational phase of the job. It must be followed by a hard-headed and dispassionate scrutiny of each hypothesis, when one tests it against as many kinds of data (other than the fact it was based on) as possible. No single test, not even the most elaborate projective technique, can be a sufficient basis for statements about an entire personality. The best clinical assessment, therefore, is *multiform*; that is, it draws on as many different sources of information as can be practically obtained. The best tradition of clinical assessment emphasizes the use of a balanced set, or *battery*, of tests, including both objective and projective types.

By the same token, the clinical assessor generally uses both direct methods, such as the interview, and indirect methods, in which the subject is baffled about how his responses can be of any value. He observes behavior directly, gets reports of what his subject has done in the past, and makes inferences from the content of test responses and from formal features of these responses. To illustrate this last process, one can infer conscientiousness (1) from TAT stories about people who are scrupulous in living up to their obligations (that is, from content) and (2) from a subject's serious, orderly approach to the job of telling stories of just the kind specified by the examiner (a formal aspect of the TAT).

Much of the task of interpretation, therefore, consists of putting together a theory about a particular person, which accounts for as much as possible of what is known about him. The examiner forms a schema, just as in informal assessment; but in formal clinical assessment he has the additional task of making explicit what is usually in large part implicit and of setting his formulation down in well-chosen words so that it makes sense to someone else. Sometimes (chiefly in research contexts) part or even all the output will be ratings on a set of personality variables; usually there will be a prose report of manageable length.

Like much of the rest of the material in this chapter, the general remarks on interpretation above will become more meaningful when applied to the concrete data of one subject, treated in Chapters 6 through 9. First, however, we must take a close look at a very different way of gathering and working with data in the formal assessment of personality—the "objective" method.

Better to measure cloth ten times and cut it once than the other way around.

Yiddish proverb

CHAPTER 4
FORMAL ASSESSMENT: THE OBJECTIVE APPROACH

The attempt to make the measurement of abilities and other personality traits a rigorous, objective discipline led to the development of a new specialty, *psychometrics*. This science of psychological measurement relies heavily on statistics and has its own technical vocabulary. Only an introduction to this subject can be given in this chapter, for it would be virtually impossible to present in a few pages a treatment of the objective, psychometric approach that would be simultaneously clear to the uninitiated and comprehensive in its coverage of the major issues. Because clinical assessment is closer to the informal ways of getting to know people, it is easier to present and to understand than objective assessment. It would be a mistake, which the reader should resist, to conclude from this irrelevant fact that the objective approach is less intrinsically interesting or less worth studying.

However it is done, assessing personality is in large part a matter of measuring various kinds of traits—dispositions to behave in specifiable ways. Precise, objective, quantitative measurement is certainly preferable to vague, sloppy, ambiguous description, as long as it does not get in the way of more important considerations. Good measures of personality traits facilitate both the research that tests psychological theory and the applied, more immediately usable kind (like research to establish methods of selecting students or employees). Some psychologists, unfortunately, make such a fetish of numbers and objectivity that they care more about getting quantitative measures than about what the numbers mean or whether they contribute to understanding. The difficult task for a science of personality is to find a path between the swamps of oversubjectivity and the deserts of overobjectivity. Nevertheless, those who have zealously pursued the ideal of objective measurement have learned a great deal that can and must be adopted by those who are more clinically oriented, if the latter are to translate their insights about individuals into transmittable scientific knowledge.

This chapter briefly surveys the contributions of the "objective" approach to assessing personality. The quotation marks (which will hereafter be dropped) are a reminder that the ideal of entirely eliminating clinical judgment and interpretation is unattainable. Even when a testing device manages to do without a subjective rating or report by anyone, its relevance to personality has to be established ultimately by reference to someone's judgment, whether that of an expert, the subject, or his friends. And, as we shall see, most objective techniques involve subjective estimates even more directly.

The pursuit of objectivity has led to the gradual crystallization of two very useful ideals of measurement, along with ways of finding out how close any particular technique of assessment approaches those ideals. A perfect measuring instrument would be completely *reliable* and completely *valid.*

Reliability and Validity

The term "reliable" primarily means "consistent"; but since there are several kinds of consistency, reliability is an ambiguous word unless the type of consistency is specified. The two most important types are internal consistency and consistency in time (repeat reliability). In the first of these senses, a test is reliable if its components all measure the same trait; in the second, a test is reliable if it continues to give constant results when it is repeated after a lapse of time.

Common usage can be a confusing guide here. We generally say that something is reliable if we can rely on it to do what it is supposed to do; but this rather vague merit encompasses both reliability and validity, as they are understood in the technical terminology of psychometrics. A test, rating, or other measure is "valid" to the extent that it demonstrably measures what it claims to measure. Since there are various ways of demonstrating a claim, validity too can have several different meanings, as we shall see later.

In addition, the two concepts of reliability and validity are interdependent. If a test happened to give a valid measure of a trait at one time but at another time its score fluctuated for unknown reasons, this lack of repeat reliability would lower the validity. Also, if a test proves internally consistent and stable over time, it must measure something (even if not necessarily what it purports to assess); on investigation it may turn out to be a useful measure of some aspect of behavior.

Let us pause for a moment to consider how a test measures a trait of personality, using the example of an ability—say, immediate memory for symbolic units, such as numbers. An examiner reads strings of digits aloud (for example, 4, 7, 2, 9, 1, 5) and then the subjects write them down. One subject may have been able to retain and reproduce 9 digits in correct order, another only 5. We assume that, in some way, the brains of these two people differ, so that one is generally better at taking in and recalling units like letters or numbers. If the test is repeated a week later, a few of those who did badly the first time will do much better, some of the original top performers will stumble, but most subjects will get approximately the same scores. The more the scores differ from one week to the next, of course, the poorer the reliability. But why should scores change? Does the ability— the assumed although unknown property of the brain—itself fluctuate? The standard psychometric assumption has been that it does not; all abilities tend to improve up to about age twenty, after which a very gradual decline begins, becoming noticeable only a few decades later. The mathematical theory of probability, on which statistics is based, encourages the assumption that there is a "true score" for everyone, which does not change in the short run, but that there is also a certain amount of random error in measuring it. An "error of measurement" should be carefully distinguished from indeterminancy; it does not imply at all that the test scores fluctuate for no reason, only that we do not usually know what the causes are and that in the long run they tend to be distributed in a certain fashion (according to the normal curve of errors).

In the case of the digit-span test just described, it is not difficult to imagine some extraneous determinants of the score. The sound of distant music drifting through a window may be ignored by all the subjects except one girl to whom the song has special meaning; a fly may light on another subject at a critical moment, distracting him from the numbers; a third may be in unusually good spirits for personal reasons and may be functioning better than usual. None of these particular small influences on performance is at all likely to operate in the same way a week later: The last subject may have lost sleep the night before and perform below par, and the formerly dreamy girl may now be on her toes. Hence, scores change more easily than brains do. Among the distractions that have been found to interfere with digit-span performance, one of the most common, anxiety, is of interest in itself. Rapaport, Gill, and Schafer (1945) divided a group of unselected highway patrolmen into an anxious and a nonanxious group on the basis of a psychiatric interview and then found that though the anxious policemen were not generally less intelligent, they got significantly poorer digit-span scores than the nonanxious ones.

If we could know *all* the determinants of all aspects of performance

[margin note: other determinants that affect results]

on a test, we would be able to say how much of the variance (the man-to-man variation in score) was attributable to a specific form of immediate memory, how much to anxiety, how much to a variety of trivial external influences, and so on. There would then be no need to distinguish between reliability and validity, and in fact we should have solved the problems of interpretation as well. At this time, however, we must make do with coefficients of reliability and validity.

Reliability is never perfect. We can never get rid of every unwanted influence and concentrate only on the degree to which a test score is determined by—and therefore measures—the enduring aspects of personality in which we are interested. Nevertheless, anything short of total confusion or psychotic delusion is unlikely to cause a person to change his answers to some questions (for example, "Are you male or female?"). The aim of those who construct self-report tests is to write items that have this degree of stability.

There is less agreement about the ideal of internal consistency, or homogeneity. Probably the disagreement arises because some tests attempt to measure simple, unitary concepts, in which case a high degree of homogeneity is desirable, but others aim at broad, general aspects of personality and can be validated only by predicting some form of behavior (see Cronbach, 1960, and Cattell, 1964). Tests of general intelligence, which are usually validated against performance in school, are a good example of the latter type; as we shall shortly see, Binet long ago found that very homogeneous tests of conceptually simple functions were inferior to more complex tests as predictors of grades.

Any test that is not scored in a completely objective, mechanical way is subject to another kind of unreliability—disagreements between scorers. The more clinical judgment is involved, the more difficult it is to get scorers or judges to agree, which is one of the good arguments for objective tests. All too often, however, the kinds of simplifications that are necessary to achieve objectivity undermine validity. We shall return to some of these issues in Chapter 10, where the relative strengths and weaknesses of the various techniques of assessment are considered further.

Intelligence Testing
and the Psychometric Tradition

The concept of a "mental test" was developed by Galton in the last quarter of the nineteenth century, and J. M. Cattell was using 50 tests (measures of sensory sensitivity and the like) by 1890. The first practically useful test, however, was constructed shortly after the turn of this century by Alfred Binet, a Frenchman of wide interests and catholic curiosity. He is known as the man who figured out how to do what all the other testers had wanted to accomplish—to measure an aspect of human capacity that had practical and social significance.

Given the task of separating the bright students from the dull for the Paris school system, Binet had the insight to start with miniatures of real-life problems, not with "elementary functions of the mind." Thus, instead of measuring how quickly a child could press a telegraph key when a signal light went on, as Cattell was doing, he asked his subjects to follow a set of orders or to state the ways objects were similar. He saw also, with practical eclecticism, that tests of various types would be needed (tests of memory, attention, comprehension, and seven other functions) and that they would have to be appropriate to the levels of attainment characterizing children of different ages. His scale grouped items according to the ages at which a majority of normal children could pass them, so that a child who could perform at a given level was said to have that mental age. These practical considerations, and the administrative need for a single score, over-ruled Binet's convictions about the manifold nature of intelligence, which might otherwise have led him to provide several scores (Guilford, 1967).

William Stern, a German pioneer in the study of individual differences, contributed the insight that if mental age (as Binet measured it) were divided by chronological age, the resulting quotient might remain relatively stable as the child grew up. When, in 1916, a group at Stanford led by Terman issued the American translation and revision of Binet's test, which was to become the American standard for the next 20 years, they called this ratio by the name that has stuck ever since: the intelligence quotient, or I.Q.

USES OF INTELLIGENCE TESTS

Testing caught on in the United States because tests like Binet's were useful in predicting how well a child would perform at school. It also quickly became apparent that intelligence tests could be used in vocational guidance and selection, because different occupations required different levels of measured intelligence.

The First World War caused a great spurt of growth in the testing movement. A man had to have certain basic abilities even to be a foot soldier, and the mentally defective had to be eliminated as quickly as possible from huge numbers of recruits. Therefore, a group of Army psychologists who were familiar with individual intelligence tests invented the first group test of intelligence, the Army Alpha. This test and its successors have been useful not only in screening out the unfit but in identifying those capable of complex and responsible jobs.

The years following the war saw a rapid increase in the variety and popularity of tests. Many kinds of performance tests were used in vocational selection; some attempted to measure generalized motor abilities, and others were frankly miniature standardized samples of the kind of work a man would have to perform on a job (for example, putting together a disassembled lock). As the number of tests grew, their content differing for different purposes, it became apparent that a number of more or less independent abilities must exist. But just how many were there, and just how independent were they?

FACTOR ANALYSIS

Such questions as those above could not be answered by theoretical analysis alone; special statistical techniques were required, especially *factor analysis*, which came to its first great flowering in the 1930's. The first step in a factor analysis of several tests is to give them all to a group of subjects and find out to what extent the scores achieved on any one test can be predicted from a knowledge of scores on any other. Through the statistical method of *correlation*, invented by Galton and Pearson, his student, it is possible to calculate precisely the degree to which doing well or poorly on a given test is related to performance on another test. This relation is expressed as a number between 1.00 (perfect positive correlation) and −1.00 (perfect negative correlation), the midpoint being .00 (total absence of any relation). If the people who obtain high scores on one test uniformly get low scores on a second one, and the low scorers become high scorers, there is a high negative coefficient of correlation. As a rule, however, tests of abilities tend to be positively correlated, and negative coefficients are exceptional.

Let us assume that we have persuaded several hundred high school students to take 12 tests of intellectual abilities, which we wish to factor analyze. We would compute the 66 coefficients of correlation, arranging them in a matrix, which makes it easy to see how each test is correlated with the others. If the numbers were all close to zero, each test would then measure a separate and independent ability. By the same token, if all the coefficients were very highly (and positively) intercorrelated, it would be reasonable to conclude that the tests were alternative measures of one ability. The more usual case, however, is that subgroups of tests form clusters that are more highly intercorrelated than any of their components are with the other tests—yet the clusters usually overlap somewhat. In such a state of affairs, common sense is no longer much help. We need a method by which we can comb through the tangled skein of interrelationships and find the smallest number of independent abilities that could account for the results. Factor analysis is a mathematical method that does just this. It extracts from a correlation matrix a set of independent (or orthogonal) dimensions, called factors, which account for the clustering of the tests (or other variables). It seems reasonable to identify the factors in aptitude tests as abilities.

There is more than one method of factor analysis, however, and the various methods give somewhat different results. The first factor analyst,

Spearman, developed a method that always yielded one major general factor; working with intellectual tests, he called this factor *g* (for general intelligence). For several years, many psychologists did not understand the fact that Spearman's "discovery" of *g* was a necessary consequence of his mathematical method, and so accepted the conception that intelligence was basically one unitary ability, of which vocabulary was an excellent test. The controversy is by no means over, but a rival conception vigorously advanced by Guilford (1967) seems to be gaining favor. According to this point of view, many independent intellectual abilities exist, a fact that could not have been foreseen from the early factor analyses of small groups of tests.

This discussion so far has focused on intelligence tests because the first great advances in psychometric method occurred in the testing of abilities and intellectual achievements. But factor analysis was only one of many technical advances in psychometrics. Other refinements of method have been developed that make it possible to produce ever more precise, reliable instruments to measure psychological variables. The goal of psychometrics is not to understand the complex patterns of behavior that constitute personality, but to find a way of measuring one thing at a time with maximal precision and objectivity. To this end, psychometricians have invented techniques of item analysis (ways of finding out which items in a test are best) and scale construction (ways of putting together groups of items that apparently measure the same construct or aspect of personality).

Objective Tests of Personality

We shall next consider a few representative examples of objective tests of personality developed in the psychometric tradition. They are called objective because the subject responds by bits of nonverbal behavior, like checkmarking pre-set answers, which can be scored according to mechanical rules. The scores may then be subjected to various statistical manipulations, which do not require any human judgment, subjective estimate, or the like. Since subjectivity always opens the door to bias and since it is not as constant in its operations as a machine, there are undeniable advantages to objective tests, at least in principle.

THE DIRECT APPROACH

**Personality
Inventories**   The first objective tests to be developed were adjustment inventories. As part of the effort to save time in processing recruits for World War I, Woodworth invented the first personality inventory, which he called the Personal Data Sheet. Essentially a self-administered psychiatric interview, it presented the

subject with 116 questions about common physical and mental symptoms to be answered with checkmarks by the appropriate answers (Yes or No). The total number of Yes's was taken as a measure of general maladjustment. The approach is perfectly straightforward, obvious, and *direct*.

In the surge of testing that followed the war, the authors of many other adjustment inventories followed in Woodworth's footsteps, usually revising and extending his items. Sometimes the revisions amounted to little more than changing an item from one format (Do you daydream a great deal? *Yes No ?*) to another (I daydream—*Almost always Frequently Occasionally Rarely Almost never*). In the attempt to measure the trait of adjustment, all such inventories list personal problems, worries, or symptoms. If a person attains a *critical score*, this is considered an indication of a need for counseling. A critical score is one chosen in such a way that most members of a group of psychiatric patients (such as neurotics) score that high or higher, but most members of a normal group obtain lower scores.

The number of similar self-report tests of various traits mushroomed in the 1920's and 1930's. Some, like the Bernreuter Personality Inventory, included a measure of adjustment, among other traits, which were scored on a logical or theoretical basis: The author thought about a trait like introversion, drawing on what the concept's originator wrote about it (Jung, 1921), and made up a set of items describing various aspects of introverted behavior. When Flanagan (1935) subjected Bernreuter's test to factor analysis, however, he found that all the information it provided could be accounted for by two independent factors, which he called measures of sociability and confidence. This example shows one of the shortcomings of the logical (theory-based) method of constructing scales, as well as the apparent superiority of the factor-analytic technique.

Guilford, Thurstone, and R. Cattell are among the best known of the psychologists who followed with other personality inventories constructed by the aid of factor analysis. A recent example, "How Well Do You Know Yourself?" (Jenkins, 1959), provides factorial measures of 17 variables; it is a shortened version of an unpublished, longer form (described in Jenkins, 1962) measuring more than 100 interrelated traits, as well as two independent, general "superfactors" (superordinate factors derived from the intercorrelations of the trait scales). Because it covers many aspects of personality in a relatively short time, such an instrument can be useful in personality research with subjects who are motivated to describe themselves as well as they can.

The validity of direct and undisguised self-report tests depends greatly on the subject's honesty and self-knowledge, since these tests are generally quite transparent and thus susceptible to the strategy of "faking good" and "faking bad"—that is, of presenting yourself as either less or more troubled than you really are. Even when a person is trying to be completely honest, his particular problem may not be covered. Despite these disadvantages an inventory can be useful in such situations as military selection, because it takes very little time of a psychiatrist or a psychologist; the inventory can be given and scored by a clerk, and the few men who do admit to many symptoms can subsequently be interviewed.

As an example of what can be achieved by a relatively simple self-report questionnaire, consider the ~~Neuropsychiatric Screening Adjunct~~ (NSA) developed by the Army in 1944 for use in induction centers during World War II (Star, 1950). The ~~objective of this questionnaire was to identify men who might later break down and thereby to reduce the ne-cessity for psychiatrists to interview~~ every draftee. The 23-item questionnaire contained 15 questions dealing with psychosomatic symptoms to detect neurotics (for example, "Have you ever had spells of dizziness?") and 8 additional "stop items" to pick up nonneurotic conditions such as psychosis ("Did you ever have a nervous breakdown?"), addiction ("Do you ever take dope?"), and psychopathy ("Were you ever sent to reform school?").

In a preliminary study, the test was given to a group of hospitalized neurotics and a group of ordinary working soldiers; a *critical score* was found, which correctly identified 90 percent of the neurotics. True, 30 percent of the "normal" soldiers scored this high or higher on the test and thus looked like potential psychiatric casualties (a kind of error called "false positives"). It was judged important, however, to keep the number of "false negatives" (actual neurotics undetected by the test) as low as 10 percent even at the cost of having to interview many men who would make satisfactory adjustments. This is the nature of a screening instrument: If it is to be useful, it must identify for more intensive study almost all the potential breakdowns ("true positives"); and if it can cut down the amount of interviewing significantly, there is a net saving in scarce psychiatric man-hours, even with many false positives.

A test of the NSA's effectiveness was made in induction centers all over the country in July 1945, when more than 100,000 men were given the questionnaire and were also interviewed by psychiatrists. (The latter could see the scores on the test if they wanted to, and it is not known just how much they used or were influenced by them.) The results of applying the critical score from the preliminary study as a cutting score are shown in Table 4-1. Even under the hurried, stressful conditions of induction, the test agreed well with psychiatric judgment. For example, the psychiatrists judged 57.7 percent of the total sample to be acceptable for service (left column of the table); of this group, 21.8 percent got a critical score on the test as potential psychiatric casualties, which means that test and doctor agreed on 78.2 percent of them. Likewise, the great majority (80.8 percent) of the small number rejected by psychiatrists as neurotic were also picked out by the test's critical score. Furthermore, the rates of rejections (and specific diagnoses) by psychiatrists varied far more widely from station to station than did the test scores. A longer test with less obvious questions might conceivably have worked even better, but this performance was good enough to justify the routine, official use of the NSA.

Table 4-1 Effectiveness of U.S. Army Neuropsychiatric Screening Adjunct (NSA) in Agreeing with Psychiatric Judgments

Categorization of draftees by psychiatrists (with proportion of total)	Percentage of each category picked out by test as potential psychiatric casualties
Men judged acceptable for service (57.7%)	21.8%
Men rejected for medical reasons (27.1%)	30.3
Men rejected for all psychiatric reasons (14%)	69.5
Men rejected as neurotics (5.6%)	80.8
Men rejected as psychopaths (3.9%)	68.2
Total (100%)	31.9

Based on data from Star, 1950.

Tests of Vocational Interests In 1927 the first of a new type of test appeared—the Strong Vocational Interest Blank, followed 7 years later by the Kuder Preference Record. These remain the best known and most widely used tests of vocationally relevant interests. Both are self-administered, pencil-and-paper questionnaires composed of many small items that present specific topics or foci of interest; the subject indicates how he feels about each item by making a mark next to his choice from a set of possible answers.

More than 50 scoring keys for Strong's test are available; each is the result of administering the test to hundreds of people in a given vocation. Strong compared the average answers of any one occupational group, such as lawyers, with those of a large miscellaneous group of subjects and retained for a key only the items that discriminated lawyers, say, from men in general (see Table 4-2). This procedure is known as *empirical keying.* The scoring method gives a quantitative expression of the similarity of a subject's pattern of answers to those of people in each of the keyed occupations.

Kuder's test was built quite differently, by the method of *homogeneous keying.* He made up many forced-choice items; each requests the subject to indicate the one possibility in three that he likes most and the one that appeals to him least. The following is an example from the Kuder Preference Record—Vocational (1948):

a. Collect autographs
b. Collect coins
c. Collect butterflies

Table 4-2 Example Using the Item "To Be an Actor" *
Showing How Scoring Weights Are Derived for
Occupational Scales in the Strong Vocational Interest Blank

Occupational groups tested	Responses of occupational groups			Responses of men in general			Differences			Scoring weights		
	L	I	D	L	I	D	L	I	D	L	I	D
Artists	40%	30%	30%	21%	32%	47%	19	—2	—17	2	0	—1
Chemists	16	34	50	21	32	47	—5	2	3	0	0	0
Carpenters	11	32	57	21	32	47	—10	0	10	—1	0	1
Ministers	42	33	25	21	32	47	21	1	—22	2	0	—2
Musicians	34	48	18	21	32	47	13	16	—29	1	1	—3

* To which the subjects responded Like (L), Indifferent (I), or Dislike (D). Adapted from E. K. Strong, Jr., 1943.

Kuder intercorrelated items and by means of factor analysis identified groups of them that represent the same type of interest. In this way he put together 10 general dimensional scales (Scientific, Artistic, Mechanical, and so on), giving an easily surveyed profile of interests, which is useful to a counselor in guiding a person into occupations to which his profile is known to be relevant.

Neither of these tests is particularly successful as a means of *selecting* suitable people for a job, because a person can easily fake his answers in order to be hired. The items are on the whole too transparent; the responses that can make one "look good" are too obvious. The tests are, however, of proved usefulness in vocational guidance and counseling.

THE INDIRECT APPROACH

In this approach, any kind of item on an objective test is worth using as long as it can be reliably measured and it is statistically associated with one type of person only. The item does not have to make much sense or be intuitively meaningful to the tester. This conclusion follows clearly enough from the logic of indirect measurement in the realm of personality: If a psychologist cannot measure a trait directly in a way that is convenient enough to constitute a practical test, he can try to find some other form of readily measured behavior that happens to be highly correlated with what he is really interested in and that will serve as an indicator of it. The correlation coefficient takes the place of understanding, so an item can be anything that works.

Notice two points about such objective indirect assessment. First, a measure of this type can never be any better than its correlation with something different in kind, and it is unlikely therefore to have very good validity. Second, its rationale is similar in several ways to the logic of projective techniques (or of any other indirect assessment), for they too rely on a correlation between easily accessible test behavior and relatively inaccessible behavior of greater intrinsic interest. The difference is, first, that each bit of information a projective test provides is not treated mechanically but is interpreted clinically by means of a theoretically illuminated understanding of the inner relation between test response and the aspects of personality that determine it. Second, projective techniques have the disadvantage that they typically do not yield precise, objective measures, or at least do not do so as easily as objective tests.

Personality Inventories

After the example of the Strong Vocational Interest Blank, an indirect type of objective inventory has been introduced, which relies less than early inventories did on the face validity of the items and on the subject's ability to report his own feelings and behavior accurately. It uses, instead, the method of empirical keying. The best-known example is the Minnesota Multiphasic Personality Inventory (MMPI), published by Hathaway and McKinley in 1943 after considerable preliminary research. It comes in a group form with printed answer sheets and in an individual form in which the 550 items are printed on separate cards, which the subject sorts into three slots in a box (marked True, False, and Can't Say).

A typical item is a statement that might have been taken from a psychiatric interview; indeed, many of them were. Some are frank statements of rather extreme, psychotic symptoms ("My soul sometimes leaves my body"; "I see things or animals or people around me that others do not see"); some represent milder psychological and physical symptoms ("I have a great deal of stomach trouble"; "I brood a great deal"; "I feel weak all over much of the time"). Some items describe past history ("In school I found it very hard to talk before the class"); and some are statements of belief or attitude ("I like science"; "I am entirely self-confident"; "Horses that don't pull should be beaten or kicked"). Many are quite innocuous, whichever way one answers them ("I used to keep a diary"; "I enjoy detective or mystery stories").

The original aim of the authors of the MMPI was to create an aid to psychiatric diagnosis. Accordingly, they administered their items to groups of patients with known psychiatric diagnoses and compared the answers of each group of patients item by item with those of a large group of non-hospitalized persons (relatives and other visitors at a hospital); only those items that distinguished the schizophrenic patients, for example, from the nonpatients were retained for the schizophrenia (Sc) scale. Eight of the basic nine clinical scales are named after types of psychopathology (see Figure 8-1, page 169).

In practice, the examiner rarely looks to see whether a subject answers any one item True, False, or Can't Say. Instead, he scores the answers on the empirical scales and then draws inferences from the resulting profile. Even at that point, he does not rely on his understanding of the nature of the diagnostic categories that give the scales their names, for the test happens not to have been notably successful when used in the way it was originally intended. That is, if a person's highest score is on scale 2, depression (D), it does not necessarily mean he is clinically depressed, even if the score is above 70 (which is presumed to be in the pathological range for each scale); and if he is depressed, that scale alone will not indicate whether the condition is of neurotic or of psychotic degree. Instead, the test's authors recommend taking into account the rest of the profile and interpreting the meaning of each scale in terms of accumulated clinical experience with the kinds of people who tend to get high or low scores on it.

Hathaway and his collaborators made a determined effort to enhance the usefulness of the MMPI by providing several correction keys to alert the user that a subject's answers may not be taken at face value. Anyone who does not want to commit himself on an item, does not understand it, or feels that neither True nor False is the right answer for him can omit the item in the group form or sort it Can't Say in the individual form (scored "?"). Because some subjects will overuse this escape hatch, the simplest control score is just a count of these ?'s; if as many as one-fifth of the items are answered this way, the test is considered invalid.

Another possible cause for invalidity of the test is that the subject may deny all difficulties so as to look as normal as possible. It should be possible, Meehl and Hathaway (1946) reasoned, to distinguish such a subject from a genuinely untroubled normal person by measuring his tendency to deny some "symptoms" that most normal people will actually admit to (for example, "I get angry sometimes"). About a dozen such items were included, constituting the L (lie) scale. The F (false) scale is somewhat similar; it consists of 16 items very rarely answered in the scored direction, which for the most part is pathological. Thus, both a person who is trying to look as "sick" as possible and a careless or inattentive subject may get a high F score.

The K control scale was derived from the common answers of a special group of people—psychiatric patients whose scores on the scale most appropriate to them were not high enough to fall in the pathological range. These items are taken to measure a kind of defensiveness or denial that anything much is wrong. Fixed proportions of the subject's K score are therefore added to his raw total on five of the clinical scales to correct directly for the tendency toward defensive understatement.

Although the idea behind such special keys is excellent, they have often proved disappointing in practice. Some recent work on another test suggests the reason. Norman (1963b) hoped to develop a test of five personality factors (see page 87) that would be valid even when a subject was trying to put his best foot forward. He administered the test twice to a large group of college men, first with the usual instructions to answer as frankly and accurately as possible and then again with instructions to answer so as to make the best impression for getting into Officer Candidate School. From the differences in responses under these two conditions, he was able to develop a special key, or scoring method, to detect faking. When he repeated the dual procedure with a similar group the key correctly identified 94 percent of the faked tests while erroneously tagging only 6 percent of the "frank and accurate" ones as phony. Later, a third group of students took his test twice, the second time in the way each thought would maximize his chances of being accepted by the Peace Corps. The faking key, which had worked so well before, now did a very poor job of distinguishing the new set of faked answers from the subjects' honest answers, because the subjects' conception of the ideal Peace Corps trainee was quite different from the conception of a promising Officer Candidate. It is therefore dangerous to assume that subjects will respond in only one way in an effort to look as good as possible, for their definition of "good" will vary according to the nature of the situation. (Further data on the reliability and validity of the MMPI are given in Chapter 8.)

The problem of response sets. In discussing the problem of how to assess motives, long before the first work on the MMPI was begun, Murray raised the possibility that

> we might solve our problem by getting the subject to state his desire. We might ask: what are you trying to do? Here, however, we are confronted by more problems; for the S [subject] is often unconscious of his motives or, if conscious, is unwilling to reveal them. The S may have a host of secondary conflicting motives. He may want to show himself in the best light, to be consistent, to exhibit independence, to be different, to give the normal response, to mislead or please the E [examiner], to amuse himself, and so forth [Murray, 1938, p. 245].

About twenty years later, psychologists interested in objective assessment began to take these problems seriously. Today, under the name *response sets*, rather than "conflicting motives," they are widely recognized as limiting the questionnaire approach (which is, in effect, simply asking the subject, "What are your desires, and how do you usually behave?").

A response set is an enduring disposition that helps determine a subject's answers to a questionnaire but one that is different from and usually irrelevant to the kinds of traits the questionnaire is intended to measure. The sets generally assumed to be most important and troublesome are *acquiescence* and *social desirability*. The majority of items in tests like the MMPI make their points straightforwardly; hence, if a person was susceptible to the traditional medical student's disease of imagining that he has a symptom as soon as he reads about it, or if he had a habit of being obliging, or a trait of suggestibility, he might answer Yes indiscriminately, and through this acquiescent behavior end up with a set of pathological scores. On the other hand, if a person was concerned (consciously or unconsciously) about how he was "coming across" to the examiner, if he wanted "to show himself in the best light" and "to give the normal response," his answers to questions might be heavily determined by his idea of what most people would consider the good, right, or socially desirable response. Few of us are wholly immune to the effects of such secondary conflicting motives; yet obviously some people are much more prone to behave in one or both of these ways than others are. Therefore, the effects of response sets are widespread but not uniform, which makes it more difficult to cope with them: Any correction has to be differential, not uniform.

When the importance of response sets became apparent a few years ago, they were overemphasized at first. With the alleged discovery that most of the variance in the MMPI scales could be traced to acquiescence (Couch & Keniston, 1960; Messick & Jackson, 1961) and social desirability (Edwards & Heathers, 1962), many workers with the MMPI jumped to the conclusion that this test was best interpreted in terms of response sets rather than in terms of the content, or meaning, of its items. One step in the disillusionment of the psychometricians who had been the MMPI's main supporters was the repeated demonstration that in the bewildering variety of scales that had been developed, only two factors of any size were to be found (for example, see Messick & Jackson, 1961; Block, 1965). In a series of ingenious analyses, however, Block (1965) has shown that the meaning of the items remains the most important determinant of people's responses to the MMPI and that acquiescence and social desirability play insignificant roles. By balancing the number of responses keyed True and False, he constructed acquiescence-free scales; he then showed that these scales contained the same two factors, one of which had been widely interpreted as a measure of acquiescence. Likewise, he eliminated items with strongly positive or negative social desirability and again showed that the resulting scales had these two factors. Finally, he explored the meaning of the two factors in five different samples of subjects who had been intensively and independently assessed. He found that the first and largest factor seems to measure psychological health, or adjustment versus maladjustment—a conclusion also reached by several other investigators (for example, Tyler, 1951; Kassebaum, Couch, & Slater, 1959), though Block prefers to term this factor Ego-Resiliency. The second factor, which Welsh (1956) had called repression and Kassebaum and his colleagues (1959) had identified with introversion-extroversion, Block labels Ego-Control. At one extreme, this factor measures overcontrol—an excessive delaying of impulse and gratification; at the other extreme, undercontrol—"insufficient modulation of impulse and an inability to delay gratification [Block, 1965, p. 115]."

The final chapter of the MMPI story has yet to be written, and it may turn out to contain more interpretable variance than Block's impressive researches would seem to allow. Meanwhile, the developers of new inventories will do well to eliminate the unwanted and unnecessary effects of the principal response sets.

The ethics of personality testing. It should be clear from experiments cited above that self-report inventories can easily be faked. Yet the whole point of such tests is lost if they are given in a context in which the subject cannot feel confident that he is acting in his own best interests by telling the truth. It may be that the development of empirical keying and other indirect methods got some test constructors off on the wrong foot, so that they conceived of their job as outwitting the subject and getting from him information he did not want to give. However it started, the fact is that in recent years inventories like the MMPI, which contain many highly personal questions and which try to get information indirectly, have been used in contexts where the subject's answers may expose him to some danger, like that of not getting a job for which he is applying.

The question has therefore been raised whether such use of personality tests is ethical. Members of the American Psychological Association subscribe to a Code of Ethics, which is designed to give guidance in all aspects of their work. One principle from the code states:

> The psychologist's ultimate allegiance is to society, and his professional behavior should demonstrate an awareness of his social responsibilities. The welfare of the profession and of the individual psychologist are clearly subordinate to the welfare of the public. . . . in service, the responsibility of most weight is the welfare of the client with whom the psychologist is working.

In the judgment of many members of the profession (Lovell, 1967), the client whose welfare must be protected is the person being tested, even when the psychologist is hired by a company to select employees. It is therefore an ethically questionable practice to ask people to take tests and answer questions that they might consider an invasion of their privacy in situations where they have little effective freedom to refuse.

Not surprisingly, such abuses led to a rash of books attacking the MMPI and similar personality tests (for example, Whyte, 1956; Gross, 1962; Packard, 1964) and finally to senatorial and congressional investigations in June 1965. Our society offers all too many examples of the unwarranted invasion of privacy by government and business, by politicians and market-research firms; and recent years have seen the rise of "thought reform" (misleadingly called brainwashing; see Holt, 1964) and other authoritarian attempts to use psychology to invade and control the innermost thoughts of citizens.

Is personality testing an invasion of privacy? The main issue of invasion of privacy grew out of the application of the MMPI to the selection of people for government employment, but the use of such tests in research has been attacked as well. Because the issue can easily be overgeneralized, we need to see clearly that in the matter of privacy, context makes all the difference. Thus, when a lawyer asks his client personal questions in order to prepare a defense, the accused person is likely to react quite differently to the probing than he does when the same questions are put to him by the prosecuting attorney in open court. What is necessary and helpful in one context is an intolerable breach of privacy in another.

Let us consider what is meant by "privacy." If someone comes into your home, inspects the premises, looks at the titles of the books on the shelves, and asks you questions about various possessions you have scattered around, is that an invasion of your privacy? If he is a friend, surely not; you may even have "conversation pieces" just to stimulate such inquiries. Or if he is an expert you have asked to appraise your furniture, by coming into your home he is doing you a service for which you will pay. If, however, you go to the door to answer an unexpected ring, and a stranger demands to come in, inspects your belongings, and asks you questions about them, the whole situation changes, and you are likely to feel that your privacy is being invaded.

The psychologist's role is like that of the expert appraiser—he appraises personality when he assesses it by means of tests. If he does so in a clinical setting where a client has gone to seek help with personal problems, it is appropriate for him to ask personal questions; in this situation the confidences of the client are protected by the ethics of the psychologist's profession. If a girl applies for a job as a typist, she will expect to be asked about her familiarity with office procedures or to have her typing speed tested; but she may understandably resent being asked her views about religion and sex.

For these reasons, official representatives of the American Psychological Association made it clear in their testimony at the 1965 hearings that tests like the MMPI were not intended for this kind of selection and that such use violated the Code of Ethics. They also pointed out that when personality tests are given to a subject in a research project, his answers remain anonymous and are used only in the attempt to increase scientific knowledge about personality. A subject in such a study always has the option of refusing to answer a question that upsets him; on the other hand, if he records his response honestly he can be certain that his confidence will not be abused and that his cooperation in research will be appreciated. Ironically, the MMPI is often scored by machines or by other impersonal means so that the psychologist does not see any particular person's answer to any specific question; he is generally concerned only with the summed answers to many questions in scoring keys.

Nonverbal Tests There is no intrinsic reason why the method of empirical keying should be confined to verbal items (see page 68); it can be applied to many other kinds of behavior, and has been. The results have not been impressive, however, and few such tests have achieved much currency. Most of the existing nonverbal indirect tests of the objective type have been constructed by an alternative strategy, that of factor analysis: The investigator finds clusters of covarying scores from nonverbal tests and interprets them by examining their correlation with verbal tests of known significance.

The leading exponent of indirect, nonverbal testing of personality is R. B. Cattell (1957), who has declared that the ultimate goal of assessment should be to do away with self-report inventories and rely entirely on objective tests made up of motor, perceptual, or even physiological items. He has published batteries of Objective Analytic tests, as he calls them, based on factor analyses of more than 200 scores derived from such tests. To establish the significance of his performance-test factors, he does not use empirical keying but depends rather on correlations of his test factors with behavioral ratings and with factors from tests of the self-reporting type.

Eysenck (1960) has pursued a program of research along somewhat similar lines, using objective tests of conditionability and the effects of various drugs as well as sensory, perceptual, and motor tests similar to Cattell's.

These indirect nonverbal tests have been criticized on the grounds that (1) the results bearing on validity are not impressive; (2) the approach is clumsy and time consuming; and (3) though the tests are not subject to faking, they are not satisfactorily reliable (Vernon, 1964). The underlying difficulty seems to be that if a test is to measure an important aspect of personality, the performance that produces a score must itself be rather directly determined by the personality trait in question. And since, as we saw in Chapter 1, a trait is a disposition that is inferred, ultimately, from a person's behavior in real-life situations and is not itself an entity with an independent physical existence, it is not surprising that the approach has had little success.

Cattell is under no illusion that self-report inventories are about to be made obsolete, therefore; indeed, he works actively with them. The sort of variable his factor analyses of inventories and judges' ratings has led to is typified by his factor E: dominance versus submissiveness; or C: Ego-Strength versus neuroticism. These are complex patterns of behavior, which are ultimately dependent on some kind of stable anatomical-physiological patterns in the body and nervous system. In apes and monkeys, for example, dominance versus submission is an obvious behavioral pattern, which is much affected by the animal's hormonal status (Clark & Birch, 1945) and which can be drastically changed by electrical impulses to certain regions in the midbrain (Delgado, 1966). At present, however, it is impossible to assess a personality by studying the brain in any direct manner; even if experimenters could practically and ethically undertake such a study, they would not know what to measure. For the time being, therefore, investigators must rely on behavioral indexes of traits, and the sorts of measures Cattell has provided (for example, his 16 P-F Test) have been found useful by many workers in assessment.

Objective Measures
from Physical Anthropology and Biology

Some psychologists are convinced that an excellent angle from which to approach personality assessment is that of the body, long studied by physical anthropology. Almost as long as there has been interest in personality, people have been struck by the association of certain temperamental traits with aspects of physique: The fat man is traditionally supposed to be easygoing, the muscular man vigorous, the thin man contemplative. The German psychiatrist Kretschmer (1921) gave such observations an apparently scientific basis, though his methods were too casual and slipshod to be convincing. He described three main types of physique and claimed to have found a predominance of *pyknics* (stout builds) among manic-depressive patients and a dearth of them among schizophrenics, whom he classified as either muscular (*athletic*), thin and weak (*asthenic*), or disharmonious mixtures of the principal types (*dyplastic*).

SOMATOTYPING

Sheldon (1940), the best-known recent worker in the field of physique and personality, attempted to follow up Kretschmer's work. First he replaced Kretschmer's typology with three variables or components of physique, which he called endomorphy (fat), mesomorphy (bone and muscle), and ectomorphy (leanness). Using a standardized photographic technique and a method of inspection backed up by various objective measurements, he rated each of the three components on a 7-point scale and found 76 combinations, or somatotypes (types of body build). Figure 35-1, for example, presents a standard picture of a 4 5 1—that is, this young man's

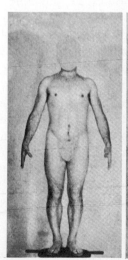
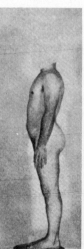
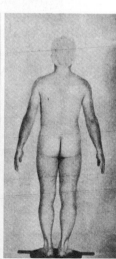

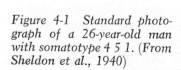

Figure 4-1   Standard photograph of a 26-year-old man with somatotype 4 5 1. (From Sheldon et al., 1940)

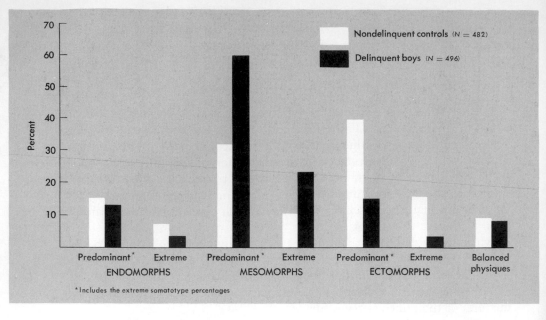

Figure 4-2 Distributions of somatotypes in delinquent and nondelinquent adolescents. (Based on data from Glueck & Glueck, 1950)

body is rated at the midpoint (4) on endomorphy, just above the middle of the scale on mesomorphy, and at the minimum on ectomorphy. He would thus be classed as a mesomorph, since the second component is predominant, though he is by no means an extreme mesomorph.

Sheldon then published a study (Sheldon & Stevens, 1942) in which he claimed to have isolated three components of temperament, each of which was correlated very highly with one component of physique. But critics (such as Adcock, 1948) have pointed out that he made no effort to get objective, independent measures of physique and temperament; he rated everything subjectively, a procedure that makes bias inevitable when the rater has an expectation about how the variables ought to be related. In a study of state-hospital patients, Sheldon (1949) claimed to find equally strong relations between somatotypes and three components of psychosis: Roughly, the bulkier the patient, the more he was inclined toward affective exaggeration; the more lean but muscular, the more paranoid hostility he showed; and the frailer, the more hebephrenic characteristics he had. Another study by Sheldon in the same book found a disproportionate number of overdeveloped muscular and fleshy physiques among delinquent adolescent boys. Again, however, he presented no satisfactory control data, and his conclusions cannot be taken at face value.

A number of Sheldon's claims have been checked by others, with mixed results. The better-controlled study of delinquents by Glueck and Glueck (1950) did tend to confirm Sheldon's last finding, for they found twice as many mesomorphs among their 500 delinquents as they found among 500 controls (see Figure 4-2). Bellak and Holt (1948) found that the somatotypes of a sample of schizophrenics differed significantly from Sheldon's published norms based on college students—though not, as he had reported, by containing an overrepresentation of frail ectomorphs. Rather, they contained a disproportionate number of wiry (slender but secondarily bony and muscular) somatotypes and a dearth of pronounced mesomorphs (the brawny "Mr. America" types). Moreover, the schizophrenic patients were *not* significantly different from a matched control group of patients with paresis, an organic psychosis resulting from syphilitic infection (see Table 4-3). To some extent, the findings could be accounted for, if

Table 4-3   Distribution of Somatotypes
Among Schizophrenics, Paretics, and College Students

Groups of somatotypes	Proportions having these somatotypes		
	Schizo-phrenics	Paretics	Sheldon's college students
The stout (all endomorphs, endomorphic mesomorphs, and endomorph-meso-morphs)	16%	21%	27%
The brawny (predominant mesomorphs and ectomorphic mesomorphs)	8	3	22
The wiry (mesomorphic ectomorphs and mesomorph-ectomorphs)	50	58	13
The frail (predominant ectomorphs, endo-morphic ectomorphs, and ectomorph-endomorphs)	16	15	19
Balanced physiques (no component pre-dominant)	10	3	19
Totals	100%	100%	100%
Number of cases	50	33	4000

Adapted from Bellak & Holt, 1948.

it could be proved that psychosis caused a wasting away of muscles through inactivity and a loss of interest in food.

Despite Sheldon's claims, some investigators have found that somato-type measures change with age and with nutritional status. On the other hand, well-controlled studies, in which physique has been measured by objective physical measurements or else by somatotyping and personality by means of self-report tests and inventories, have often found small but positive correlations in the direction of Sheldon's hypotheses. Psychologists tend to discount Sheldon's claims because of their dogmatic and undemocratic tone and because of his faulty experimental designs. Nevertheless, his conclusions seem to contain some valid insights, which need to be verified by more truly objective methods (see Chapter 6).

BIOCHEMICAL MEASURES

It has often been suggested that measures of physique are persistently, though never very strongly, related to personality because of some third factor that is more directly related to both, such as the operation of the endocrine glands. This hypothesis gains plausibility from repeated clinical observation of the marked changes in personality that accompany known endocrine disorders. For example, in Addison's disease the cortex of the adrenal gland is progressively destroyed, so that the production of its hormones is cut down; as this occurs, apathy, negativism, and paranoid attitudes often appear. Similarly, when the blood contains more than the normal amount of cortisone (a hormone produced by the adrenal cortex) as a result of treatment for such conditions as arthritis, other marked changes in behavior and mood often occur, most notably euphoria. Despite such observations, there is little evidence that normal variations in mood are related to changes in amounts of hormones. Moreover, both a deficiency and an excess of some biochemical substances can produce similar effects, and the same hormonal abnormality can be associated with very different personality changes in different people.

The situation is similar in other biological branches of psychology. Exciting discoveries are occurring—the effects on behavior, thought, and emotion of direct electrical stimulation of the brain or of introducing small amounts of various chemical substances—and the relations usually turn out to be more complicated than they look at first. Although more is being learned about, for example, the significance of certain parts of the brain for emotions and motives, more detailed findings are needed to throw light on stable individual differences. The important advances made in recent years in endocrinology and biochemistry may eventually help to illuminate the biological basis of some aspects of the human personality, but most psychologists who are experts in assessing personality and who follow these developments feel in no immediate danger of being thrown out of work by endocrinologists or biochemists.

PSYCHOPHYSIOLOGICAL MEASURES

In the past, great hopes have been pinned on such psychophysiological measures as the galvanic skin response (GSR), which indexes the activity of part of the autonomic nervous system by measuring sweating. Since many chronically anxious people tend to perspire freely, which changes

the electrical properties of their skin in a way that is
psychologists have assumed that the GSR and othe
autonomic function, such as the rate of the heartl
might make good objective tests of emotionality, anxi

Ultimately, some measures of this type may prov
of personality assessment. At present, however, the a
related to aspects of personality in ways that are 1
useful. As one of the leading workers in the field o
put it:

> The relationship of the autonomic nervous system to behavior in general,
> and to the problems of neurosis and psychosis, is a vast and controversial
> field. . . . the autonomic response is a part of the total behavior of the
> subject . . . the "meaning" of the somatic response must be *interpreted*
> in terms of the transactions of the individual with his environment, and in
> terms which involve judgments, or at least statements, of "molar" psycho-
> logical states and behavior [Lacey, 1959, pp. 160, 174, 178].

He reached this conclusion after a thorough review of many attempts
(mostly unsuccessful) to find objective, external, physiological measures of
some of the intangible changes in personality accompanying psychotherapy.
Nevertheless, Lacey is quick to add that psychophysiological investigations
can contribute greatly to research on psychotherapy when they are used
interpretatively and not in an attempt to avoid dealing with psychological
phenomena by direct psychological means.

Objective Measures
of Cognitive Style

A rationale often offered for projective techniques is that everyone has his own personal world—his peculiar way of looking at reality,
conceptualizing things and people, and organizing experience. Psychologists
of personality such as Klein (1951) and Witkin (1954, 1962), whose earlier
research was in the experimental psychology of perception, saw that their
standard methods of analyzing visual and kinesthetic phenomena could tell
something about the subject's personal world if they were used in a new
way. Formerly, experimental psychologists were interested only in group
averages, because they wanted to learn the laws of perception in general. If,
however, you ask how far any individual subject deviates from the average,
you can measure rather directly an aspect of his unique way of viewing
things, his cognitive style. By the logic of indirect measurement, this might
also give clues to related and less strictly cognitive aspects of personality, as

. Thus, the recent emergence of tests of cognitive controls or titutes a promising development in assessment.

Leveling versus sharpening. Consider, for example, a dimension of gnitive style that Holzman and Klein (1954) call leveling versus sharpening. Working with certain classical psychophysical methods, in which subjects estimated the sizes of squares or the heaviness of small weights, they found first that people tended to be consistent in their perceptual judgments, some (sharpeners) making sharp discriminations and following closely any changes in the nature of the stimuli, others (levelers) tending to miss changes in the level of stimulation because their memories of what they had just experienced became confused. An interpretation in terms of memory—that is, how well a person can keep records of successive similar experiences separate rather than letting them blend into one another—was suggested to Holzman, Klein, and their co-workers by the results of a larger study in which they gave many cognitive tests to a group of subjects and then did factor analyses of the results (Gardner, Holzman, Klein, Linton, & Spence, 1959). Leveling-sharpening emerged as a factor made up of scores not only from the perceptual tests just mentioned but also from such tasks as giving free associations to the word "dry"; levelers used a good many words in talking about each topic that came to mind but stayed quite close to the starting word, while sharpeners flitted about quickly from one idea to another, ranging far afield.

The general cognitive sluggishness of levelers was shown also in their slowness to recognize the effect of distorting spectacles and to name the colors of ink in which rows of asterisks were printed. More clinical data suggested that the levelers tended to have repressive, hysterical defenses (see Chapter 8). A number of experimenters have taken up the dimensions of cognitive style that Klein and his co-workers developed and have suggested that these may have many other ramifications in emotional as well as cognitive behavior.

Field independence, or psychological differentiation. Like Klein, Witkin has headed a team of investigators who have spent more than fifteen years developing measures of cognitive style and relating them to many aspects of their subjects' lives. Witkin's group has concentrated on a dimension of cognitive style that he called first *field independence* and then *psychological differentiation.* The impetus to this work came from the armed services' concern about the fact that some pilots, after flying into a cloud and losing sight of the ground, would fly out the other side with one wing up, or even upside down. They literally did not know which way was up. Through experimental studies of how people told "up" from "down," Witkin found that two kinds of information played a role in this orientation—the visual field and the inner experience of the pull of gravity on the body.

Let us suppose you have suddenly found yourself in a chair inside a small room. You were blindfolded when you took your seat; with the blindfold off, you can see that your chair is tilted, at least in relation to the room. But the room is devised so that it too can be tipped one way or another from the true vertical; and the chair can be tilted quite independently of the room (see Figure 4-3). If you were asked to operate a control that changed the position of your chair, would you be able to "fly by the seat of your pants" until you were *actually upright,* even though the appearance of the room would make it seem that you were out of line? People differ greatly in the extent to which they can perform such tasks, depending on how much of the two kinds of information (external and internal) they use.

One reason Witkin changed the name of the dimension was that when he gave various other cognitive tasks to his subjects, the "field-dependent" ones showed a general difficulty in articulating, or differentiating, complex stimuli, such as the puzzle pictures of the Gottschaldt Test. (An example from a similar test is shown on page 188 in Figure 8-4.) Subjects who had been able to select the bodily sensations of gravity out of a total mass of stimulation also proved best able to select the simple design out of the complex figure in which it was embedded. Moreover, they seemed to have more differentiated body images; Witkin found large and significant correlations between field independence and such aspects of figure drawings as the amount of realistic detail (see Figure 4-4). When the subjects were clinically assessed, largely by means of projective techniques, the less differentiated proved to be significantly more passive in coping with their life situations, less insightful, and more afraid of their own impulses (Witkin et al., 1954). Linton (1955) found less differentiated subjects to be more easily influenced by suggestion than more differentiated, or field-independent, subjects. Though these relationships are interesting, cognitive styles are important to assessment for their intrinsic interest rather than as indirect measures of other traits.

Figure 4-3 Tilting-Room–Tilting-Chair Test.

Figure 4-4   Left, figure drawings by a field-dependent man. Right, figure drawings by a field-independent woman. (From Witkin et al., 1954)

Criticisms of cognitive-style research. Critics (for example, Postman, 1955; Gruen, 1957) point out that much of the work of Witkin, Klein, and other exponents of cognitive style concentrates on extreme groups, when in fact most people fall somewhere nearer the middle. They also object that the links of perceptual and other cognitive phenomena to what is usually thought of as personality are vague, analogical, or just empirical correlations —for instance, it is known that field-dependent people are often passive in social situations, but it is not understood *why,* or where the causal connection is. Researchers on cognitive style have been accused of claiming findings of general validity more quickly than the small and selected samples of subjects in their experiments would allow. Undoubtedly it will take years before enough research has been done to answer these objections. The issues that have been raised by both sides are important ones, and the effort to answer the questions of the critics is advancing the psychology of personality.

Judgments of Personality
as Objective Measures

Some psychologists take the position that personality is purely a matter of social perception—that it is meaningless to speak of anyone's personality apart from the particular people who interact with him, get impressions about him, and use trait terms in describing him. The weakness of this position, as Allport (1937, 1961) pointed out for thirty years, is that it neglects the problem of how a person's friends could get a consistent conception of him as, let us say, warm, if there were no actual consistency in his behavior. As we have seen, first impressions can be biased by hearsay and prejudice, but in the long run a specious judgment is unlikely to be held by more than a few rigid people who have need to maintain a fictional view about someone for some personal reason.

The purely social conception of personality may partly account for the profusion of research studies using inexpert judges to provide measurements of personality. Regardless of one's definition of personality, there is value in such judgments, and they do have the great advantage of being far easier to obtain than expert (clinical) judgments. Most of the published research on ratings of personality deals with inexpert judges, because there are so many more of them than of highly trained and skilled assessors of personality. Understandable though this imbalance is, it has the regrettable effect of concentrating research on the most superficial aspects of personality, which *can* be fairly adequately rated by amateurs.

HOW TO OBTAIN JUDGMENTS OF PERSONALITY

Who could give the most accurate picture of your personality? You may perhaps think of close relatives, those people you have lived with and who have been able to observe you under the greatest variety of conditions for the longest time; perhaps close friends, in whom you confide inner thoughts and feelings, some of which you might be reluctant to tell even a parent, brother, or sister; or perhaps someone with whom you have had a long-term loving relationship, who undoubtedly knows you better in many ways than anyone else.

Obviously, these people are well qualified in many ways to assess your personality; yet one fact immediately casts doubt on their usefulness as informants—they are biased. Anyone who loves you is going to have a hard time being objective, particularly when the assessment touches on socially valued aspects of behavior—and there are extraordinarily few aspects of personality that are not to some degree considered admirable or base, good or bad, attractive or unattractive. To ask a man's mother or wife to rate his personality is doubly dangerous; not only would the judgments, if you could get them, probably be biased but the very attempt to do so would violate the privacy of both the subject and the informant. For such reasons, personalities are rarely assessed by obtaining judgments from the people who know a person best, although they are used as informants whenever possible.

But if a person has only casual contacts and is not emotionally involved with the subject, does he know him well enough to judge his personality? It all depends on the *aspects* of personality in question. Students who live together in a dormitory for months or years may not know one another's deepest longings and ultimate goals in life, but they may know more than anyone else about one another's patterns of everyday social behavior.

The judgments of a person's acquaintances are classified under objective methods of measuring personality as *peer ratings*. Objectivity in this context properly refers to intersubjectivity; in other words, if a consensus of apparently normal adults agrees that something is true, it can be accepted as true unless there is good reason to believe that they are all laboring under a common handicap. One such handicap is the lack of any opportunity to form independent judgments by direct contact with the facts, in which case prejudice or some form of reliance on the judgments of other people may operate or the judge may try to infer the truth through use of some theory. The crucial point, then, is to *have an acquaintance rate or judge only those facets of a subject's behavior that he has had the best opportunity to observe directly and not those he has not observed.*

One of the best ways to get useful quantitative measures, which are substantially equivalent to judgments or ratings, is to ask members of a group of acquaintances to choose or nominate "one of the four best leaders" or "the five kindest members" of the group, or the like. This technique, called *sociometry*, was developed by Moreno (1953), who has based a branch of social psychology on it.

PERSONALITY VARIABLES BEST RATED BY PEERS

What aspects of personality are best assessed by the ratings of acquaintances? Clearly they must be overt patterns of behavior. A leading figure in the objective approach to assessing personality, R. B. Cattell, decided that the psychology of personality would be much aided by having available a comprehensive, clearly intelligible vocabulary for describing observable behavior, the outermost layer of personality. Allport and Odbert (1936) had started the job by pulling out of the largest unabridged dictionary all words that could be used to describe personality—18,000 of them, of which just over 4500 clearly denote traits, or consistent and stable modes of behaving. Cattell (1957) sifted through this latter list, grouping words that were essentially synonyms; he found 171 clusters, from each of which he selected one term that seemed to express its core meaning.

At this point, Cattell called on the services of a large group of people to rate their acquaintances on each of the 171 traits. Cattell thought it likely that the judges would be able to make a much smaller number of real discriminations. He intercorrelated the ratings, therefore, and found 36 clusters of traits that were so highly correlated they seemed to be expressing the same judgments. As expected, for example, the terms *talkative* and *silent* proved to be highly, but negatively, correlated; the other clusters also contained such logical opposites. Cattell thus obtained a set of paired (or *bipolar*) trait names, which he subsequently expanded slightly to a total of 46 pairs by drawing on the special terminologies of personality theorists.

Many personologists (psychologists who specialize in research on personality and its theory) have used this comprehensive list in a variety of re-

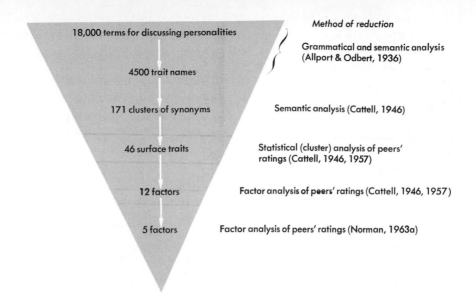

The following rows appear inside the figure:

	Method of reduction
18,000 terms for discussing personalities	Grammatical and semantic analysis (Allport & Odbert, 1936)
4500 trait names	
171 clusters of synonyms	Semantic analysis (Cattell, 1946)
46 surface traits	Statistical (cluster) analysis of peers' ratings (Cattell, 1946, 1957)
12 factors	Factor analysis of peers' ratings (Cattell, 1946, 1957)
5 factors	Factor analysis of peers' ratings (Norman, 1963a)

Figure 4-5   The attempt to achieve a manageable vocabulary of traits.

searches. A number of them, including Cattell, decided to examine the set of paired traits further by factor-analyzing sets of ratings using the list. At this point, the story becomes quite technical, for as was pointed out earlier (page 64) there are quite a number of different techniques of factor analysis, which make different assumptions and give different results. Cattell himself claims that in his 46 overt traits he finds "twelve very stable and two or three less definite primary personality factors [1957, p. 73]." Other workers (such as Norman, 1963a) have analyzed some of Cattell's data as well as their own and just as repeatedly find only 5 factors (see Figure 4-5). Meanwhile, yet another team (Glueck, Meehl, Schofield, & Clyde, 1964) have started all over again with Allport and Odbert's 4500 traits, which they have supplemented from 72 other sources to make a total of 6682 items. After going through rather similar procedures of clustering the terms, they came up with a list of 329 phenotypic items, or overt traits, defining 176 factors, and 101 genotypic items (similar to what Cattell calls source traits).

Let us take a look at the smallest list, that of 5 dimensions. These factors seem to be suitable for acquaintances to judge, for they have emerged from studies in which the ratings were made by small groups of casual friends —fraternity brothers, college-dormitory friends, graduate students of clinical psychology who spent a week together while being assessed, and U.S. Air Force officer candidates. Each factor name in Table 4-4 is followed by the 4 specific bipolar ratings that best express it (that is, have the highest loadings on that factor).

Table 4-4   Five Major Factors
in Ratings of Personality

1. **Extroversion**

talkative	vs.	silent
frank, open		secretive
adventurous		cautious
sociable		reclusive

2. **Agreeableness**

goodnatured	vs.	irritable
not jealous		jealous
mild, gentle		headstrong
cooperative		negativistic

3. **Conscientiousness**

fussy, tidy	vs.	careless
responsible		undependable
scrupulous		unscrupulous
persevering		quitting, fickle

4. **Emotional stability**

poised	vs.	nervous, tense
calm		anxious
composed		excitable
not hypochondriacal		hypochondriacal

5. **Culture**

artistically sensitive	vs.	artistically insensitive
intellectual		unreflective, narrow
polished, refined		crude, boorish
imaginative		simple, direct

Adapted from Norman, 1963a.

WHO ARE THE BEST JUDGES?

Whenever a group of friends rate one another's personalities, some are bound to come consistently closer to the consensus than others. Therefore, if we single out those whose judgments are closest to the mean (comparing them with the most deviant ones) and examine the ratings they have *received*, we have a quick formula for a study on the characteristics of the good judge of personality. There has been a good deal of research along these lines, from which much can be learned if the inherent limitations of this kind of data are kept in mind. In the better studies, the qualities of good judges are determined by other means as well, usually by tests. The fact that the various studies converge on the findings outlined below increases the likelihood that these generalizations are meaningful.

Not surprisingly, the better judges are generally more intelligent and more mature than the poorer ones. Their tendency to excel in social skills and to be warm and socially adjusted may indicate that their ability at judging is attributable simply to the fact that they see people the way most of their friends do, for the socially successful should be most in touch with the group's ways of perceiving and judging. It is just as plausible, however, to argue that possessing such abilities as accurate judging is a distinct social asset.

In forming judgments, it helps to be similar to the people being rated: The best judges resemble their subjects in sex, age, and ethnic and cultural background, a finding that again may be partly valid (for we can understand best those whose experiences have been like our own) and partly an artifact (Bruner & Tagiuri, 1954; Taft, 1955). The latter may be true because a person who was actually like most others in the group he had to rate and who proceeded almost entirely on the basis of naive projection, assuming that everybody was like himself, would show up as an apparently shrewd judge of men.

A hint that some very general kind of sensitivity may be involved in rating personalities comes from the repeated finding that judging ability is related to literary and artistic interests and skills. The good judge has a relatively complex and differentiated set of concepts for thinking about people rather than a set of simple stereotypes. Such a statement comes very close to saying that the good judge should be psychologically minded (in Murray's term, *intraceptive*)—concerned with the subjective and interpersonal dimensions of experience. This quality has been found to be lacking in the authoritarian personality, as measured by tests of prejudice against minority groups, notably by the California F-Test of fascist-like attitudes. A couple of studies have found that authoritarianism does in fact show up more strongly in people who are poor judges of others. So does reliance on the defense of projection, which is part of the authoritarian syndrome.

There are some data available on the characteristics of the best *expert* judge of personality. In the original explorations of personality at the Harvard Psychological Clinic (Murray, 1938), groups of 12 to 24 subjects at a time were studied intensively by teams (or diagnostic councils) of 6 expert judges, who rated them on the needs and other variables developed and defined by Murray. In one experiment, the diagnostic council had been working together long enough to rate one another on the same variables of personality that they had been using to express their understanding of the subjects. When the ratings an expert had given were compared with the ratings given him, a general tendency to judge subjects in terms of contrast became apparent; that is, an expert who was rated as highly orderly tended to give ratings of the need for order that were low on the average, while the judges who were considered somewhat disorderly by their colleagues rated the same subjects as higher on this need. Even a highly trained judge will tend to take himself as the standard. In addition, the results showed that the experts tended to do the best job of rating subjects who were most like themselves and who had similar cultural backgrounds, and to mark inaccurately those who least resembled them. The best judges were generally more experienced in assessing personalities. On the whole, these findings have been upheld by subsequent research and are congruent with the findings from the research on inexpert judges.

Judgments of personality have brought us full circle, back to clinical assessment. The clinical and the objective traditions do overlap, for both approaches can be used together, and often are—as they were in the study of Morris Brown, with whom we shall now proceed to become acquainted.

All that a man does is physiognomical of him. You may see how a man would fight by the way in which he sings; his courage, or want of courage, is visible in the word he utters, in the opinion he has formed, no less than in the stroke he strikes. He is one; and preaches the same self abroad in all these ways.

THOMAS CARLYLE. Heroes and Hero-Worship

CHAPTER 5
MR. MORRIS BROWN: AN ILLUSTRATIVE CASE STUDY

So far, we have been considering assessment in the abstract, the general case. The issues will become much more meaningful as we look at a case study of a real person and examine how he was actually assessed. As we saw in Chapter 1, personalities can be assessed in a number of different settings. Though the aim of assessment in almost any context is to understand a person, the extent and focus of understanding does differ a good deal from one setting to another. Therefore, to be most useful, the example chosen cannot be taken from routine practice of diagnostic testing or of any other kind; it should come as close as possible to satisfying the ideal requirement of *complete* understanding. Before considering the actual case of Morris Brown, which is by no means ideal, it may help to take a close look at what is meant by "complete understanding" of a person.

Specifications
for an Ideal Assessment

VARIABLES TO BE ASSESSED

First we will want to know, What is he like? An ideal understanding of a person requires a comprehensive description of his personality at some point. It will include:

1. Physical, biological personality—appearance, physique, and physiological characteristics.

2. Temperament—characteristic level of energy and emotional states (moods, affects, strength of drive), especially the frequency and intensity of anxiety, guilt, shame, helplessness and hopelessness versus enjoyment of life, zest, hope, and buoyancy.

3. Stylistic, expressive aspects of personality, including gesture and voice.

4. Manifest traits of other types by which people who know him classify and recognize his characteristic behavior. (See Table 4-4, page 88.)

Such a description does not so much provide understanding in itself as help us frame more penetrating questions. We begin to approach understanding when we can ask, Why does he act this way? This question reflects the desire to ask our subject what he is trying to do, what he is aiming for, and what his intentions are. Yet we should recognize that just asking him alone will not suffice, because he cannot be expected to know all the answers. We must include in our description some consideration of personality dynamics:

5. Conscious and unconscious motives, their sources, and the sources of the affects listed above (2), such as anxiety.

6. Values, ideals, interests, and attitudes.

The organizational (configural) approach to understanding is another way to go beyond description. This approach has two distinct though related objectives: On the one hand, we are interested in the enduring inner conditions that make behavior possible and set limits to what a person can or will do; and on the other, we want to know how the pieces fit together, how a person is organized. Implied, then, are:

7. Defenses and controls, in relation to impulses.

8. Thought organization, cognitive style.

9. Abilities and achievements.

10. Identity—self-attitudes; sense of competence; self-concept; insight; sense of integration with his occupational role, social group, and culture.

To understand a person, we must not limit ourselves to studying the processes and organizations inside him, even though (as in 10) they have outward reference; we must also know about the actual relations between *him and his environment*. Involved here are the enormous issues of the person's relations to society and culture and the large question of his adaptation. The following variables are particularly important:

11. Situational origins and setting—cultural tradition, family background (ethnic, religious, ideological) and the degree of the subject's rootedness in it; significant persons who have helped shape his personality; present ecological context; major "press" (opportunities for gratification, frustrations and demands upon him, types of stress).

12. Adequacy of his adaptation to situational origins and setting—pathological trends and potentialities, conflicts, symptoms.

13. Nature of his principal relationships to people and feelings about them.

In the process of attaining understanding, we sooner or later want to ask, *How did he get that way?* The *genetic* approach to personality thus requires that we learn:

14. Major facts of his past history and the chronological development of main trends.

Finally, we come back to organizational considerations, for everything has to be put together into

15. An *integrative synthesis*, linking the separate pieces into a coherent whole that, in Carlyle's words, "preaches the same self abroad in all these ways."

METHODS OF ASSESSMENT

An ideal case study would provide all the kinds of understanding described above; obviously, in order to do so, it would demand the use of many methods (multiform assessment), since no single technique can provide all the necessary information. An ideal study, then, ought to make use of the following types of methods for gathering data:

1. Application forms, face sheets, objective public records.

2. Interviews, ranging from highly structured to free-associative.

3. Autobiographies and other personal documents (letters, diaries, biographical inventories).

4. Self-descriptive inventories and questionnaires, direct and indirect; self-ratings.

5. Projective techniques.

6. Physical and physiological measurements, as well as other biological approaches.

7. Judgments by others (behavioral observations and ratings, sociometric ratings by peers).

8. Objective and situational tests, such as tests of cognitive style.

9. Tests of intelligence and other abilities.

10. Sociological and anthropological techniques of studying the person's societal and cultural origins and setting.

All this makes up a rather tall order, especially when we add to it the stipulation that the data should be gathered and interpreted by experts who have optimal talent and training for the job.

The case study chosen for presentation below is far from ideal in a number of ways. The data were initially gathered by two graduate students without prior experience in assessing personality (one was studying sociology, the other psychology).* In addition, there are gaps in the coverage of variables assessed; therefore, no claim is made for anything like a complete understanding of the subject. But the case of William Morris Brown has two unusual qualifications to exemplify multiform assessment: First, a wide variety of methods was used, which represented each of the 10 categories listed above and resulted in a great mass of data. Second, the relatively rare opportunity of a long follow-up was presented when the subject allowed himself to be reassessed after a lapse of 26 years.

An Informal Assessment

The two assessors began their report with the following description, which conveys the general impression Morris Brown made in casual social and business contacts around 1940.

If you were to meet William Morris Brown, you would probably find him likable and eager to please, although not very unusual. He talks with apparent relish, racing along from one thing to another with a naive sort of eagerness at once disarming and refreshing. His face is alert and mobile, and in spite of a smile that seems a little too ready, you would probably put him down as a happy extrovert who would fit into the local service club with ease and satisfaction. At 26, Morris looks like any other energetic young businessman, well satisfied with himself, the world, and all the good "business prospects" in it.

Morris is large and compact, without much excess fat, although he is beginning to have trouble keeping his weight down to 194 pounds. The fat is starting to cover a strong and uniformly well-muscled body, creating the impression of a sort of surface softness. He carries his 6-foot frame well and easily, however, with a trace of the athlete in his walk. The same softness shows in his face and at times gives a juvenile look to what is otherwise a quite mature appearance. Not handsome, he is not hard to look at either, with features that are smooth and regular, although slightly heavy. Morris is overly aware of a hardly noticeable Jewish cast to his full lips and long broad nose and sometimes worries about being mistaken for a Jew (he is not Jewish).

His well-fed look of stability and maturity is probably a help to Brown in his business. He is a securities salesman and is quite successful for his age. He carries around with him a mimeographed office periodical sheet showing that he led his agency in business volume one month. Since graduation Morris has been

* The student of sociology was Robert F. Bales, now Professor of Sociology at Harvard and a distinguished contributor to his field. The psychology student, Robert R. Holt, is the author of this book.

living in the eastern city where the large and well-known university he attended is located. At present he lives alone in an inexpensive rooming house near the college; he makes a considerable proportion of his sales to members of the university community, including undergraduates. Within the last few months he bought a new Studebaker from the fellow who was his roommate before leaving the city, but, on the whole, Morris does not spend much money. He appears prosperous; recently a credit report on him rated his income and his total worth at, he says, about double their real value.

His present life goes along pretty smoothly, to outward appearances. He works hard and takes an afternoon off every few days to play golf, at which he excels. Almost every weekend he gets away for a while to work on a cabin he is building in the country. On these trips he almost always takes along at least one companion, usually of college age, to help with the work. He has a rather large number of friends whom he sees with about equal frequency, but no intimate ones. Morris rarely goes to a movie because he says movies hurt his eyes, but he likes to read, mostly biographies. He seldom has a date and knows few girls.

HOW THE ASSESSMENT WAS MADE

This assessment relied in part on observation during numerous informal contacts. For example, the investigators gave a large party and invited the subject; he came by other evenings for casual chats and parlor games; the psychology student spent a day with Morris in the country helping him build his cabin; and there were occasional meals, rides in Morris' car, and visits to his apartment. These were, then, more than first impressions. Let us try to reconstruct how these contacts resulted in the characterization above.

Interest in the Subject

The assessors would not have learned much about Morris if they had been unable to get interested in him. The very first assertion in their description—that he was likable—attests to the fact that they did not try to remain "scientifically detached," wholly unmoved by their subject. Although their original motivation was to carry out an assignment for academic credit, before long both students were much more deeply engaged by the intrinsic interest of the task—learning about another human being in as much depth as possible— and by a growing friendly interest in Morris himself.

One component of this interest may have arisen from the subject's tendency to define the situation implicitly as one in which the graduate students were experts who could see into mysteries that were closed to him. His relationship with them was characterized by friendliness, deference, and extraordinary cooperation; he went out of his way to satisfy all their requests for information and personal documents and made an honest effort to be as frank and open as possible in answering their probing questions. The investigators explained in the beginning that they would want to inquire into all aspects of his life, including matters that were most secret and private; after agreeing, Morris never complicated the investigators' task by conscious withholding or distortion.

It would have been difficult not to like someone who clearly wanted so much to be liked and who did all he could to satisfy the investigators' demands. Nevertheless, it might be added that Morris was in a number of respects quite different from other members of the graduate students' circle of friends, in whom intellectuality and a kind of sophistication were prime values, which Morris lacked.

Empathic Perception The investigators learned a fair amount about their subject *empathically*, without doing so deliberately or being focally aware of it. His eagerness to please, for example, was a characteristic they directly perceived; it was not inferred, nor did he state it about himself in so many words. In fact, the first three sentences of the assessment above (up to the "happy extrovert" characterization) are primarily based on direct, empathic perception. To be sure, the description required no particular depth or subtlety of interpersonal perception. The levels of species recognition and emotional contagion (see Chapter 2) were sufficient to tell the assessors that this was a smiling, non-hostile fellow man. Only the observation that his smile was over-ready suggests anything like mature empathy. To make such a point, the assessors needed an implicit set of standards by which to judge the appropriateness of common affective expressions, and a modest capacity for simultaneous detachment and responsiveness.

On the whole, however, neither of the graduate students had great natural empathic ability or any training in its use. Both were bookish and studious rationalists, committed more to attaining knowledge by the exercise of reason than to enriching their affective lives by cultivating an emotional sensitivity. Close examination of their work shows how many times they missed empathic communications or suppressed awareness of what was going on in the interpersonal relationship instead of recognizing and using it. For example, when we examine Morris' TAT stories, we shall see evidences that beneath his overt effort to cooperate seriously there was a level of teasing, almost mocking, resistance. Being wholly unskilled in handling resistance, the examiners not only did not deal with it but remained unaware of it.

Direct Observation The third channel through which the informal assessment operated was *direct observation*, both of behavior and of the subject's physical personality. The latter aspect might have been less emphasized had the psychology student not been enrolled in a seminar on constitutional psychology with W. H.

Sheldon (whose work on somatotypes and temperament was reviewed in Chapter 4, pages 77–80); the study was also serving to satisfy one of that seminar's assignments. The kind of observation encouraged in Sheldon's seminar is exemplified by the remarks on Morris' carriage and athletic walk and indeed by all of the second paragraph of the description except for its final sentence. In general, the majority of the assertions made in the description are factual and are derived either from direct observation or from essentially public and objective information readily provided by the subject.

CRITICISM OF THE ASSESSMENT

If we turn from analysis of this informal assessment to criticism, perhaps we can agree that it is hardly remarkable in any way. It does mention a few traits, some interests and activities, and some (though not all) vital statistics. It may at least help you to form an image of the man, a concrete nucleus for the schema you will build up as you read on. Although this assessment shows no obvious signs of being seriously inept, it is perhaps disappointing because it says so little. It drops only a hint or so that there may be more to the subject than appears on the surface, but this is hardly surprising, since the authors' intent was precisely to present Morris' social front before penetrating to a psychologically more interesting level.

They made no attempt to exhaust the possibilities of informal assessment or even to raise questions for more systematic exploration. To be sure, in their informal contacts with the subject the investigators did form a host of impressions that are neither recorded here nor explicitly set down in any other part of the original case study—the written product of the first assessment. These impressions may be sensed throughout the document, however, for they are an integral part of the schema formed by the complex interaction of formal and informal processes of assessment. Such a schema operates like a frame of reference or a group of orienting sets, anticipations, and guiding assumptions; it helps in choosing material to present, judgments and evaluations, and causal and organizational hypotheses. In this sense, informal assessment operates behind the scenes in every situation where it is given a chance.

Notice how much the attempt to depict the surface of Morris Brown's personality emphasizes his conformity and conventionality. It is as if the authors consciously intended to say to the reader, "This man can be counted on in many respects to behave predictably." They are, in effect, establishing a level of expectation against which deviations will stand out sharply. The amount of conformity is also an important initial fact about any personality (see Chapter 1, page 9); it is regrettable that the level is so vaguely indicated, without any quantitative indication of the extent to which Morris' behavior was conventional.

Let us see how the sources of error in informal assessment described in Chapter 2 operate here. The examiner's emotional reaction to the assessed subject is usually feared and minimized because of the dangers of the halo effect, the leniency error, and need-fulfilling distortions of perception and judgment. The assessors in this case had been alerted to these dangers, and they made conscious efforts not to fall into any obvious traps. They also safeguarded themselves against these types of error by using many methods, including objective ones, and by prolonged study, which tested prejudgments against a constantly accumulating body of evidence.

In spite of their precautions their own somewhat antiphilistine value system can perhaps be sensed in the slightly snide tone of the second half of the first paragraph: If Morris had proved to be nothing but a happy, extroverted young businessman, they would have been disappointed. A slightly prejudicial stereotype of the typical member of the Junior Chamber of Commerce was operating here. (At this point we cannot evaluate how far it may have biased the assessment, but let us keep it in mind, along with the other sources of error just mentioned, as we go further into the case study.)

A Clinical Assessment

The assessors led into their attempt to provide a deeper understanding of Morris Brown by discussing next in their assessment the inconsistencies in Morris, the ways he was nonconforming and violated expectations:

> Morris doesn't like to think of himself as "having problems with a capital P," but suggested himself that the case study be undertaken when he learned that the writers were looking for a subject. He was most eager about the study from the start, frankly admitting that the idea of finding out about himself fascinated him. He has a friend who is a vocational tester and has taken all the tests he could get his hands on. Morris declared that he can't figure himself out and ventured that he would make an interesting, though normal, case. He has "turned inside out" psychologically "in the last five years or so," he said, and there are aspects of his personality now that are "just silly—don't make sense." It was the hope of clearing up some of these puzzles, then, as well as a characteristic desire for a new experience, that impelled Morris to submit himself for study, promising not to hold anything back intentionally.
>
> Morris feels independent, yet he has a strong need to have others around. "Apparently I'm the most independent bastard ever made," he writes in his autobiography; "you're supposed to tell me why. I have made many friends in the last five years but have never felt too close to or too dependent on any one of them." A fear of being alone, a desire for sympathy and response, is matched by

a fear of becoming too closely involved. Morris has a feeling that he is engaging in too many "extracurricular activities," referring to community enterprises like the Red Cross Drive. A fundamental conflict that has not reached a satisfactory solution may be seen here.

There is another basic clash of tendencies in Brown, with even more implications. He has a deep aversion to being hampered or tied down in any way. "You get in a rut, but not in the right things. Besides, I don't *want* to get in a rut." "I never have followed any pattern in my life . . . I don't want a settled married life—it would drive me crazy." "I would go crazy working for someone else: my work has to be something I can do on my own." Related to this theme is a certain lack of moral sensitivity, which Morris recognizes when he admits: "I don't think I have very much moral sense." Deception of his mother (she thinks his car was borrowed from a friend), keeping some of the money he has collected in fund drives, unconventional sexual practices—these are commonplaces of Brown's life; and though he wonders why he doesn't feel guilty, he says, "I just think about the nice angle on it."

Despite his impatience with restraint, Morris declares that his deepest desire is complete control of himself: "My greatest victory would be to go for a month for 24 hours a day doing what I decide to do. Keeping on schedule—even if it called for getting drunk every night. Doing what I *planned* to do." To this end, he involves himself in as many external constraints as possible, such as appointments. "What I need is a job where somebody will control me—help my self-control—the army would do me good for a year." Even when controls of this sort are self-imposed, he has the feeling that it "would be swell to have a whole day of appointments and then just say 'to hell with it,' and yet I don't." As recently as a year ago, he used to decide "that I wanted to take a trip and start off somewhere, not caring where." This idea of flight persists in constant plans and fantasies of travel.

Though he declares he does not really worry about it, Brown is concerned about his sex life. "Another thing I'm interested in is sex: Why isn't it more important to me? . . . I don't think I'm normal in this respect." "Maybe I worry about masturbating too much, but nothing particular about that. I don't want you to get the idea that I think I'm going insane or anything like that. I'm brutally callous. But I wonder why I've never been in love—but once." He has had at least as much homosexual as heterosexual experience and shows no signs of changing his ways.

The conflicts and inconsistencies described above, together with his puzzled lack of insight into them, form the outstanding problems in Brown's life.

We are now clearly beyond the realm of informal assessment and into the considerations with which a clinical assessment often starts—a person's problems. It is not so much the fact that conflict and inconsistency have entered the picture that takes us into formal assessment as it is (1) the explicit use of special techniques (in this instance, the autobiography) and (2) the nature of some of the problems, which involve socially taboo areas about which even a close friend might not know. (In fact, even his roommate was not aware that Morris engaged in any homosexual activity or that he lacked "moral sense" about money entrusted to him.)

As we saw in Chapter 3, the term "clinical assessment" covers a variety of processes, using several sorts of methods. Following Meehl's breakdown of clinical prediction (1954), we can usefully simplify this variety by distinguishing two major phases, or levels, of clinical assessment (see Table 5-1).

Table 5-1 Two Main Phases of Clinical Assessment

	First Phase	Second Phase
General character	factual	interpretive
Systematic emphasis	conscious content—events and meanings	latent structure—organization and causal relationships
Methods used	interview, autobiography, other personal documents	projective techniques, free association

Though the student-investigators made a stab at the second phase, they devoted most of their time and efforts to a first-phase clinical assessment, supplemented by a number of objective approaches. The remainder of this chapter will therefore concentrate on the methods and results of their first-level clinical assessment; Chapter 6 will focus on the objective assessment and the second phase of clinical assessment; and Chapter 7 will present an attempt to integrate these and all the remaining data.

FIRST-PHASE METHODS

The case study written about Morris Brown in 1940 was primarily his life story, based for the most part on more than two dozen interviews. The examiners took turns conducting these sessions, during which they wrote down in longhand as much of Morris' responses as possible. Before deciding what questions to ask they consulted several systematic guides, such as those contained in Young's *Personality and Problems of Adjustment* (1940) and Murray's *Explorations in Personality* (1938). These are outlines of major topics to be covered in a psychological life history; Morris' first assignment was to look them over briefly before writing his six-page autobiography. The inexperienced investigators at first felt the need to have written lists of questions at hand, but the interviewing quickly developed into a somewhat more natural process of following up topics the subject himself introduced.

The methods used here approach those of more sophisticated clinical assessment, which generally relies heavily on the interview as the fundamental method; and in research contexts, an autobiography of the kind obtained from Morris is often standard procedure. The assessment of Brown was unusual in two respects: A good deal more time than usual was spent in interviewing, and the subject provided much more information than is generally available by way of *personal documents*. On a visit to his home town, he collected the "baby books" and infant diaries his mother had kept, her genealogical tables and records, a sample of letters he had written to her during the summers of his adolescent years, his own diaries covering the years 1929 to 1939, themes and a few short stories he had written in high school and college, photograph albums giving a complete record of his growth and appearance up to maturity, a scrapbook filled with newspaper clippings about himself, expense accounts, maps of his home town, and records of results on vocational and similar tests he had already taken. The examiners gave him a list of questions concerning his birth and early development; he put them to his mother and wrote down her answers. The account of his first years is based on this indirect interview and on Mrs. Brown's records; hence, it tells something about her as well as about Morris.

Clinical assessment, even of an ambitiously multiform variety, does not require anything like this profusion of personal records. The assessors did go through all the material, however, using it largely to check facts and dates. During two brief periods of his life, Morris' diaries became full and introspective and thus psychologically useful; they are quoted in the life story that follows.

This story is the assessors' synthesis of the data gathered by the methods just listed; it is presented substantially as it was originally written. Quotations from the autobiography, when not specifically identified, may be recognized by Morris' characteristic preference for dashes as his principal punctuation.

FIRST-PHASE RESULTS:
THE STORY OF MORRIS BROWN TO 1940

Infancy   Morris was born in the spring of 1914, 11 days before he had been expected. He weighed 7 pounds and appeared hardy from the first.

During his infancy, his mother reports, Morris was never sick, aside from a case of baby jaundice shortly after birth and a little constipation in his first year, which apparently was not painful. He was breast-fed until he was 10 months old; his appetite was so great that he developed the habit of waking up in the night and crying until fed to his capacity. The doctor advised Mrs. Brown to continue with the night feeding when Morris could not be broken of the habit. Weaning took place gradually, and the transition to more solid foods was made by easy stages. Toilet training was a simple and objective matter, without punishment, and Morris was out of diapers in a year. Other sources of conflict in many infancies, such as enuresis and autoeroticism, were not present, if Mrs. Brown's reports are accurate. From all indications, Morris was a happy baby and thrived. His physical development was normal, except that he was always tall and heavy for his age.

In one respect, however, the course of his development differed significantly from the norm. At age 2, he would say only "bow-wow," "no," and "mama," although the average size of a child's vocabulary at this age is nearly 300 words. His mother wrote in January 1916, "he shakes hands, waves and grunts his way thro' conversations, but will not speak a word." Later, "at 2¾ years, he learned all his letters, then slowly began talking—'aw pick up' being his first real attempt to express an idea,"—referring to his blocks, with which he played actively and constructively.

His father had an explanation: Morris, he said, was long learning to speak intelligibly (note that he did vocalize indistinctly, "grunting") because he did not need to. His mother had some ability as a teacher and was devoted to her child; she was able to understand what he meant and wanted without his having to learn the strict conventions of language.

The first few years present a picture, on the one hand, of normal development of locomotion and dentition, and, on the other, of the formation of certain definite personality traits and problems. At 22 months, Morris' mother wrote in the diary she kept sporadically for him: "He is usually good, but very positive and determined, but will do as I wish in the end . . . loves to play with his sisters,—takes an old doll to bed with him, builds blocks, and plays with everything he can get hold of." Again, at age 2, "he is a real boy, cunning, sweet, spunky, determined, lovable." Looking back on the early years now, she remembers him as lively, very talkative (he was speaking distinctly by the time he was 3 years old), sociable; he liked attention and interrupted a lot. Little Morris was very headstrong, she says, and her greatest problem with him was his tantrums.

Mrs. Brown had a deep pride in her family and was determined not to let it down. Both paternal and maternal branches of her family had been in this country for a century and a half and settled in her home town as leading citizens. It was a shock, then, when her father, a well-to-do clothing manufacturer, was financially ruined through no fault of his own and died soon after, when she was 14. A short time later she became a teacher and a governess. In 1912, Nathan Brown, a widower who had married her best friend, asked her to marry him. She was 33 and may have thought this her last chance; in addition, her brother was about to marry Nathan Brown's sister. At any rate, she accepted him. They settled down in a large house in a nice residential area of a small city in the northeastern part of the United States, and she undertook to bring up her stepdaughters, Nancy and Marcia, 6 and 4 years old respectively. Morris was born the following year.

As Morris says, "Father and Mother were made so differently it was impossible for them to get along." She was practical, "nervous," concerned with the observance of the amenities; he was enthusiastic, impatient, independent, and irresponsible. There was, in addition, the difference in age—Morris' mother was 34 at the time of his birth, his father 50. Mr. Brown's speculative bent asserted itself in a characteristic way just before Morris' birth. He borrowed $50 of the money his wife had been saving to pay the doctor and went west to see some oil wells. He had previously made a considerable fortune from speculation in real estate and oil but had gone bankrupt just a month before Morris was born.

Mr. Brown "was no long-time worrier or planner," and as "he would dodge unpleasant things rather than get ruffled," he left the small city where they had settled and got a job selling insurance in a big city. He came home only on week-ends; he refused a $50-a-week job in a bookstore there when it was offered to him, to the great disappointment of his wife. The job wasn't "his kind of life—steady hours, etc.," Morris explained. Mrs. Brown simply "couldn't *understand*" his refusal to take a steady job when his wife and three children at home were in such desperate need of money. She viewed it as a "cardinal sin." Her only means of support was the income she got from renting the top two floors of their house.

This state of affairs—conflict over economic arrangements and Mr. Brown's never holding a job long, never staying at home for any length of time—continued until 1923 (when Morris was 8), at which time Mr. Brown left permanently for another state. Mr. Brown never contributed to the support of the family after 1924 and made overtures about a divorce some years later. The idea of being a divorced woman, however, was too much for Mrs. Brown to bear; Morris thinks also that she always hoped he would come back and be a real father to his children.

In addition, during Morris' early years, his mother had several physical difficulties: poor eyesight, internal disturbances from Morris' birth and from an earlier injury, and a major operation in 1923. Nevertheless, she worked hard, too hard—she not only had to make ends meet but had to keep up appearances. As the business section of the city grew up around her and her friends moved farther away, she apparently grew more determined that her children were not going to go down in the social scale.

Childhood   This overworked, unhappy woman did not have the time that she would have liked to devote to bringing up her son, whatever her theories of child guidance were. She grew less and less able to handle him. From "spunky" Morris grew to "very headstrong." When thwarted, he would go into a screaming tantrum, and all Mrs. Brown could do was remove him to some place where he would not be heard too loudly; she did try throwing water on him, too, but with slight success. Morris claims that his frequent spankings worked. Nevertheless, he continued to cry to get his own way when angry or disappointed. His mother tried repeatedly to get his father to punish him; Morris thinks that his father applied a reluctant hairbrush no more than two or three times and then only after her demands grew insistent. Morris' early memories of his father are mostly pleasant; in one recollection they are walking together through a cemetery while the father explains to the son about the different kinds of trees.

During his early years, Morris got along fairly well with people, at least when he was having his own way. He started to read at an early age and liked to read to the roomers who rented the upper floors. He had a few friendly contacts with them but made no particular friends there. He often quarreled with the few other children that there were to play with. A succession of most of the childhood diseases, severe pneumonia, removal of his tonsils and adenoids (twice), and a serious ear infection may have contributed to a rather marked social isolation during Morris' childhood.

Morris says that the two things he will always remember about his early life were "its extreme poverty and complete loneliness." What was an upper-class neighborhood on the edge of the thriving business section when Mr. Brown and his wife moved into their house became a disorganized rooming-house area during Morris' early childhood. The business section spread until the busiest corner was only a few blocks away, and the well-to-do families moved farther out. The large houses were converted into rooming houses, as Mrs. Brown had converted hers.

The people who lived in the area no longer knew one another. The neighborhood organization disappeared, and with it went most of the children, most of the intimacy, and most of the control that people in a neighborhood group exercise over one another's behavior.

These statements can be made with some confidence, because the sociologist member of the assessment team made a sociological study of the community in which Morris Brown grew up. Morris provided a good map of the city, and a library book on its recreational facilities and city plans yielded information about the location of industrial areas, new homes, business and other areas, all of which were marked on the map. From information Morris provided, it was possible to locate his parents' home, his schools, his church, the residences of his friends and his mother's friends, and various pertinent institutions. From this composite map, and from Morris' verbal characterization of various sections, the several *ecological zones* of the city could be located—the business area, the area of slums and rooming houses, the middle-class workingmen's homes, and the upper-class homes. Nationality groupings were also located. The graphic summary of all this information, partly subjective and partly a matter of objective record, made it possible to check some of Morris' statements about socioeconomic status relationships and to gauge more accurately the social status of his own neighborhood and play areas.

Morris' dominance and resistance to control continued, especially as his sister Nancy and his mother tried to enforce obedience. His sister Marcia was tactful, however, he says, and handled him by explaining why he should do what was required.

At the age of 4, Morris was sent to a Catholic kindergarten next door, which he attended for two years. He remembers that they had chapel once in a while, but apparently any religious teaching that he might have received there did not leave a noticeable residue of piety. When he was about 5, he and another neighborhood boy worked out a system of stealing the money from milk bottles. They bought soda pop with the money, but he was not otherwise close either to this boy or to the one other he knew. There was no neighborhood gang or play group; and this one episode, for which he was punished by his mother, is the only record of any behavior approaching delinquency.

When he was 6, Morris was enrolled in a grade school several blocks beyond the main business avenue, on the edge of the city's Polish section. Most of his classmates were the children of Polish mill workers. Morris regarded them as "very dumb." He made friends with one big Jewish boy by helping him with his lessons. Apparently he received admiration from this one boy, but he was constantly annoyed by two Polish boys who would tease him, wash his face with snow, and lie in wait for him as he went to and from school. Morris used to go several blocks out of his way to avoid these tormenters.

However hesitant Mrs. Brown may have felt about sending her boy to this school, she could not afford to send him to a private school as her family and friends did their children. It was all she could do to put the girls through private school. She tried to make up for this and to give Morris contact with "friends who were good enough for him," as she put it, by giving him piano lessons and sending him to the dancing classes attended exclusively by the children of her upper-class friends. Morris felt that he had nothing in common with them, hated dancing school, and on occasion merely pretended to go.

These efforts to do her best for him only widened the gap between Morris and his mother. "I never was one to hang around her," he reported. "She always visited school and so on—that drove me crazy." She wanted him to go to Sunday school and say his prayers, but after the age of 7 or 8 Morris gradually left off the prayers. A little later, he told the investigators, "I was going to build a houseboat, and asked the woman next door to go with me. I wasn't going to ask mother because she would make me do things I didn't want to."

Nancy, who was in high school at the time Morris was about 8 years old, was extremely embarrassed by her lack of suitable clothes and by other signs of poverty. She was nervous and cried a good deal. One day after she had visited her aunt, Mrs. Brown's brother came to the house for a talk. He told Mrs. Brown that she "wasn't fit to keep the girls," and he took Nancy to live with them. "Stabbed in the back," Mrs. Brown felt that nobody appreciated her efforts. For two years she was likely to cry at unexpected times. Morris himself does not recall being particularly sorry to see Nancy go.

Mrs. Brown's relatives were also vociferous in their condemnation of Mr. Brown for leaving his family in hardship while he lived elsewhere in comparative luxury. Mrs. Brown was in a dilemma—she wanted him to come back and play the part of the proper father, and yet she could not help condemning him. Morris did not defend his father, but "didn't exactly blame him," as his uncle and the rest of the family did. Morris does not believe that he imitated his father or identified with him, but in another interview said spontaneously, in contrasting his mother's "practicalness" about money with his father's attitude, that he has "taken more after" his father.

During his childhood Morris had little contact with girls other than his sisters. In his eighth year, he and the two little girls who lived next door were caught behind a woodpile, engaged in mutual display. He was put to bed without food for the rest of the day, which he considered "an awful punishment." On one or two occasions, Morris played "doctor" with his sisters. Once, when he was about 8, he looked through the keyhole of a locked door and saw his parents in the act of intercourse. He didn't realize the significance of it until years later, he says.

Morris did very well in school and was repeatedly moved ahead of others. Always much younger than his classmates, he had a sense of his own brilliance, which was appreciated neither by his teachers nor by the other boys in the school. He was also overweight, a poor athlete, and regarded as a "sissy" by most of the boys. To show that he was not a sissy he took a dare the March of his tenth year: He plunged into an icy pond and swam around.

Conditions did not improve much when Morris started going to another school in a middle-class area at the beginning of the seventh grade. He did well in his studies but still did not gain a single close friend. He sat under a tree with the teacher when the boys played baseball at the annual school picnic. He developed an interest in big-league baseball. He learned to play tennis and began to dream about being a really "big-time" player. He spent a great deal of time reading; biography and travel were his favorite topics. He asked his teacher to go to a movie with him and was very disappointed when she refused.

At the age of 10, just about the time he finished grade school, Morris decided to gratify his desire to travel. He took the money out of his savings account and bought a train ticket to a nearby city. Arriving there, he walked around a couple of hours and came back. In spite of his mother's objections, Morris learned to hitchhike the next year and made many trips to neighboring cities; one trip to play in a tennis tournament involved a considerable distance. His father, who was living in this city, gave him a couple of $5 tennis lessons and let him hitchhike back. Morris greatly enjoyed this form of being independent but not alone; his companions were often other boys he knew at the YMCA.

Adolescence   In high school Morris began to get fair but inconsistent grades. He cut class often and did not care especially how he did his assignments. His philosophy when grades turned out lower than he liked was, "What's the sense of *worrying* about grades— if you do, you do, if you don't, you don't. Let somebody else piddle around with the details—hell, there are always plenty of $18-a-week clerks." The "Y," only two blocks from his house, became a growing interest for Morris; it gave him the contact with other boys that he so much desired. He swam, played basketball and ping-pong, and continued with tennis, his best game. He made the high school team and played in a number of boys' tournaments, but his social techniques were still not satisfactory. He says he was "a lousy competitor—always folded at the wrong time." Outside of sports, he rarely participated in high school activities.

By the age of 11 there was a quickening of sexual desire, which manifested itself in several ways. After hearing some boys talking about masturbation, Morris "gave it a try. It was fun, so I kept it up, and have ever since." About two months later, in the gym after tennis and showers, he says, he and another boy masturbated together with no idea that they should not. In the next few years a number of incidents occurred similar to the following. One afternoon when Morris was about 13, his mother came home early from a club meeting and knocked on the bedroom door, behind which he and a boy friend were engaged in mutual sex play. She had to wait until they dressed before they unlocked the door; suspecting what had been going on, she reproached Morris in spite of his attempt to "brazen it out." He was ashamed of himself, but not overly, and he was not further punished.

At about age 12, Morris began to think of girls sexually. There was a pretty blond girl in some of his classes whom he admired from afar and thought of regularly when masturbating, but he never approached her. He was always un- aggressive with girls, and the very few formal dates he had were duties imposed by his mother in return for invitations to parties that he didn't like anyway.

Another major manifestation of sexual development in adolescence was the appearance of a "terrific case of hero worship," directed at a boy of 17 or 18 at a "Y" camp. Morris engineered his hero into taking his Sunday school classes and "used to think he was pretty near God. It almost broke my heart once when I heard him tell a dirty joke."

Beginning at about age 14, Morris made "one after another, a series of very close friendships, almost passionate, altho never any desire for sex relations of any kind. I couldn't stand the thought of that."

Morris grew very rapidly at puberty; at 13 he was a big, mature-looking boy, 5 feet 6 inches tall, weighing 147 pounds. When he was a sophomore in high school, his mother wrote that he "plays tennis, swims, and eats, all heartily . . . is a fine-looking boy, broad and straight, and usually very good." From what he says now of his disobedience and aggressive attitude toward her, that last thought must be considered in the light of an apparently wishful one: "He and I are alone now, so are everything to each other."

Morris' own view toward his mother was much the same as it had been earlier: "I've always done what I wanted; what she said didn't have any effect. I used to have battles with her until she saw it was useless." By the time he was 12, Morris came and went pretty much as he pleased: "What could she do? I had control of my own money."

At the age of 15½, Morris graduated from high school, with little idea of what he wanted to do next. He got a job as usher in a nearby movie theater that he had often attended, where he worked for the rest of the year (1929). In non-working hours he did postgraduate work at high school. His spare time was taken up with athletics, reading, and playing around with the "crush" of the moment. He began to be a very good athlete; a scrapbook contains newspaper notices from the winter of 1927–28 on, in both swimming and tennis. In August, he won second place in the YMCA tournament and was one of the city's outstanding tennis players. Public notice and approval were just what Morris wanted; he was considerably happier in these years than he had been in childhood.

Morris kept a very full and introspective diary at the time, almost entirely concerned with his ups and downs with George, another usher and a "crush" for months. He speculates for half a typed page about George's motive in insulting him—which was evidently not difficult to do, for he wrote: "I can't stand any kind of razzing." Resolutions to punish George by being cool to him are followed the next day by descriptions of the great time they had together, for example, hitchhiking. Morris indignantly rejects the idea that there was anything sexual in this friendship, or in any of his relationships of this sort. There was, instead, continuous aggression between the two boys, with occasional tussling. The mutual masturbation affairs continued all through this period, but, Brown stresses in the autobiography, "never with anybody I liked." Even so, several instances of overt sex play with a real friend have come up, each of which Morris characterizes as the only thing of that kind he ever did with anyone he liked.

Brown knew few girls; in his marginal social position the daughters of his mother's friends were superior to him and the Polish girls inferior to him. Although Mrs. Brown got him, much against his will, to go to some dances, "the effort on her part to get me social wore her out—we had some awful battles." At the time he did begin to find himself socially, he attracted friends by his athletic prowess and by slavish devotion, qualities that apparently got him friends among boys rather than girls. There was one girl whom he went to see frequently the summer he was 15, just "hanging around her house." He had dates with her off and on for two years. But his initial sexual experiences were all with boys; he had had no instruction from his mother in the facts of life, which he picked up around the "Y." It was a few years before he learned of the stigma that is attached to homosexuality, but even then he did not cease homosexual activities. Instead, he isolated them in his mind into a sort of neutral category, along with masturbation; he put disgusted rejection of "fairies" in another, and emotionally fraught friendships in still another compartment.

In the spring of 1930, Morris and his mother bought a used car, of which he was quite proud. After he got a job as clerk in a rayon mill in the summer, he took out a few of the mill girls who were reputedly easy marks but to his surprise was unable to get anywhere with them sexually. Morris complained: "Women can be so illogical!"

When the mill moved, shortly before he turned 17, Morris decided to go back to high school for four months to prepare for admission to college. He took on a heavy schedule; in June he got honor grades in college-entrance examinations. This time his social life in school was happier:

> for the first time I was in a gang—about 8 of us—and I loved it—two of those fellows are now the only friends I have in the home town, and I see them every trip home—I didn't get into any messes during that time for a change—(all through high school I had a series of fights with teachers, was always in trouble for doing one thing or another,—although my marks were always good).

This year was the height of Morris' tennis career, and he was kept busy winning the city championship and finishing among the first four in the state tournament. He was now at last captain of the school team and attracted wide notice.

Ever since he became old enough to start finding odd jobs, Morris was resourceful in earning his own money. With what money he saved, he began at age 15 to speculate in stocks. This was the year of the stock-market peak, when everyone was dabbling in the market. Despite the crash, Morris was shrewd or lucky enough to make some money; he kept it up for several years. It is interesting to note that in 1931 he wrote a school theme in which he made an impassioned defense of the stock market, with the most exaggerated claims for the moral nature of stock manipulators' motives.

At this time Morris was doing an increasing amount of small-time gambling, too. It became one of his most time-consuming interests and continued throughout college. The summer he was 15 years old he went to a famous nearby resort where he spent four seasons, first as a golf caddy, then as an assistant professional. He rapidly took to the game of golf and soon learned to like it as much as tennis. "I gambled incessantly the first two years, then had a well-rounded life the last two."

Morris still has many of his neat and careful expense accounts from these years, which give evidence of moderate expenditures that were well within his means. His gasoline record for his cars has the cost per mile to six decimal places. The problem of controlling himself was worrying him then as now, and this meticulous record-keeping appears to have been a means he took to discipline and get a grip on himself. A similar motive underlies the sporadic, usually brief, and almost always objective diaries that he has kept from 1928 to the present [1940]; they are filled with factual accounts of when he went to bed and when he got up, what he saw, makes of cars in which he hitched rides and the distance he traveled in each. His letters to his mother from the resort are of the same type. After the first few he wrote: ". . . please keep all the letters I send you, so that when I'm thru, they will be sort of a diary." Another quite typical letter ends:

> Write as often as you can—I always like to hear anything you like to say. Send me something like a big sticky gingerbread or some kind of cake. I'm eating everybody else's, so I've got to hit back some way. I would like my typewriter & topcoat; please *don't* send any more *old* sweaters; my old Hi-Y *red* and that old green sweater are no good—I need good clothes.
>
> Write,
> Morris.

College Years   In July of the summer he passed his entrance exams, Morris suddenly decided to go to college in the fall without waiting another year, as he had planned. He and his mother decided on a school of notably high and venerable reputation. He was given a small scholarship and got a job waiting on tables. This assistance, the money he had saved from working, and the philosophy that "things would work out" were enough to get him through the first year.

Though he was entering college at 17, Morris had attained his full 6 feet and weighed about 175 pounds; he looked hardly less mature than he did nine years later.

"I must make the right kind of friends, and use them to advantage," Morris wrote in his diary soon after arriving. "A freshman . . . is given every chance to go in for any form of athletics; and I'm going to take advantage of every opportunity . . . I might just as well start trying to leave a mark now." (Though he made no freshman teams, he often took advantage of the opportunity to play golf inexpensively on the university's course.) "I'll be taking the regular freshman course in every respect, which at least gives me an even chance, to get some good marks and high standing." "I like . . . the fellows. Some, it is true, are awful snobs, but the greater part will turn out to be nice fellows once we get acquainted."

Up to this time, there had been only one new development in Morris' sex life. Largely on a home-town girl's initiative, he had an evening of sex play. He enjoyed it enough to take the girl out several times afterward, hoping for more intimacies, but she did not permit them. After this experience, he began to seek lower-class "pick-ups" occasionally with some friend. He continued to find other boys who enjoyed mutual masturbation, and he made more intense, crush-like friendships, with the usual aggression and tussling, but apparently no overt sexuality. One difference at this point was that Morris was becoming aware of his overdependence on particular friends and began trying to prevent such extreme emotional involvement.

He had one date all freshman year. A month or so later he wrote in his diary:

> It's very peculiar the difference between me and say, Dick, or any of the other fellows. I get no real pleasure from a casual date or from the company of a woman: it seems a very ineffectual way to waste time, and one that costs a lot of money, or if you don't spend money on a girl, it should make you feel cheap.

Morris summarized his undergraduate days in his autobiography: Freshman year was "the most fruitful I have ever spent in my life—I ended up with 2 A's and 2 B's, and felt that I had done a good job. . . . The next three years show what college can do for a guy with no self-control—marks down each year, more and more time playing cards, going out chasing women, etc., etc.— . . . 3rd year—lost my scholarship and my job." He was then supported by money from his mother and by some contributions from his uncle.

> My roommates made other arrangements for my last year, and I moved into a single. There I managed to get studying again, wrote a good thesis and got a *cum laude*—was not present at graduation—had no desire to be—because I was with 3 other fellows sailing a boat—Played golf religiously, made the varsity my senior year.

Not excelling in stiffer tennis competition, Brown dropped it for golf, at which he has continued to improve, until he has now [1940] been state champion in his class. He had said, "My real goal is to make Phi Beta Kappa some time," at the beginning of sophomore year, but this goal apparently fell by the wayside.

The growing caution of becoming too involved with friends was sharply reinforced during his junior year by what Morris regards as a "traumatic" experience. That year he got in with a gambling gang, one of whom was a sophomore named Henry. The two soon became fast friends, playing ping-pong together, picking up girls for casual necking and petting, and "wasting a lot of time." Then one night everything went wrong. Walking home from an evening on the town, Henry proposed that they break the whole thing up. Morris was stunned. "That whole business was the greatest shock I ever had in my life." He broke down and cried when he was alone. Henry had been criticizing him a lot and calling him "Hoiman," because he knew Morris disliked being thought Jewish, but Morris was still very fond of Henry and had no intimation that their friendship was going to end that way.

The upshot of this crisis was to make Morris take a new attitude toward friendship. In its extreme form this attitude is a professed preference for doing things with people he doesn't know, getting to know strangers, but not too well. His friendships have become more and more extensive, rather than intensive, and there have been no more crushes. Looking back on those early affairs, Morris is confused and incoherently uncomfortable. He remembers many of the boys as "awful dopes," a fact that he even occasionally recognized at the time but with no effect on his attachment. "It was all so silly . . . usual at that age, but I really did overdo it."

Early Adult Years   College widened Morris' interests considerably. He began to be aware of the world of ideas, a process of growth that is still continuing; he is attaining some degree of intellectual sophistication but still lacks subtlety of response and is ill at ease with persons he considers intellectuals; such people have a good deal of prestige with him. An interest in concert music, which he traces back to his early adolescence, was stimulated and grew. Surgery began to fascinate him, and he began both to witness and read about it.

During his first postcollege summer, when Morris was 21 and was working as a lifeguard, a homosexual of the most obvious kind propositioned him. Morris was willing, four or five times in fact, though he declares himself disgusted by the man's entirely feminine reactions, affectations, and the like. Then why did he do it? His answers are all inconclusive and more or less evasive:—well, it was something new, he'd never known a guy like that, there weren't many people to talk to there anyway. But he also remarked, "I didn't care—just as soon; there wasn't any moral degradation about it."

In spite of at least half a dozen homosexual affairs, Brown has never admitted to himself their implications, nor has he seriously faced the question of what their nature was. It was a satisfaction; he accepted it and had no regrets. In his view it did not amount to anything. "If there's anything that disgusts me—a fairy, I just don't understand it—not getting any pleasure out of a woman . . . I can't imagine it—it just doesn't make sense, silly," he protested in an interview. "I'm absolutely sure I'm not a fairy, no matter what you decide."

The fall after graduation Morris returned to the city where his university was located, after only a few days at home. He soon became interested in the idea of selling securities, took a training course, and got a job. At the same time he was approached about working with the Boy Scouts, and he agreed to become a scout-master. Almost at once he experienced success, for he had always been able to get along well with boys younger than himself. After a few years of active interest and work both in camp and in the troop, he became one of the city's outstanding young scouters. Then one day the mother of one of his scouts accused him of making sexual proposals to her son. Morris denied the charge and had a scout executive investigate it. Nothing could be proved one way or another; Morris believes that the boy probably misunderstood one of his "filthy jokes." He could only make an issue of it or resign; realizing how he could be ruined if the accusation were made public, he chose the latter alternative and got out of scouting completely four years after he had begun.

This episode was a severe shock to Brown, but it did not have the effect of forcing on him a realistic view of his sex life. As recently as this fall [1940] he had an evening of extensive homosexual activities with a young man who was a good friend. Brown was embarrassed in telling about this (it was the only time he manifested such a reaction) because of the obvious connection of friendship and sex, which he strives to keep separate.

The same separation of "the sacred and the profane" is to be seen in his attitudes toward women. On the one hand, he mentions a desire for a wife, a distant romantic feeling that he has seldom felt with any vividness, and he has had a couple of instances of companionship with women, one with a woman older than himself. During the summer of 1940 he met Alison, his closest friend's girl; when the friend left the city Morris began seeing her occasionally. As his recent roommate said, "he never really saw much of her; it was just an idea he got . . . He never stood too much of a chance with her." However, Morris speaks of Alison as the one girl with whom he has been in love or has thought of as a possible wife. His fantasies about her have never gone further than thinking about her "in a bathing suit—I've never touched her, kissed her only twice." This idealized and rather tenuous affair was broken up by a misunderstanding about a date, which depressed and worried Morris for a month or so, but not seriously.

On the other hand, when he goes out with a girl Morris usually has hopes of some sexual fun, preferably with only a minimal prelude or aftermath. None of these dates has ended in intercourse; he says that the girl has always thwarted him at the last moment. Indications are, however, that he has no very active desire for heterosexual genital relations: "I'd rather stop at second base than at third, where it's no fun, when I know I can't have a home run. I do develop a feeling of shame after I've been messing around third base—wash my hands, etc." He has had intercourse twice, both times in his junior year at college, and with prostitutes. He went to a brothel with his pal Henry the first time, with neither much success nor enjoyment. After going back again within a week and definitely "proving his man-hood," he was quite disgusted and resolved never to have anything more to do with prostitutes.

A dream he had during the period of the interviews expresses several of Morris' attitudes about girls. He was walking up to an altar with Ethel Merman, who turned into a girl whom he has taken to a couple of dances but does not like much. They kneeled and a priest, "trying to calm me down," went through a marriage ceremony. After it was over, he thought: "What am I going to do with a wife?—I didn't expect this; how am I going to adjust all the little details of my life?" Ethel Merman, a "singer of hot songs in Broadway shows," who usually appears as a frankly and pleasantly bawdy wench, seems to represent Morris' sexual ideal in this dream; instead of attaining this, however, he gets involved in the constraints of marriage and with a less desirable but more probable sort of girl.

Morris has reached no consistent or satisfactory sexual adjustment. In the post-college years there have been occasional "streaks of taking four different girls out in five days," some seeking of pick-ups, and sporadic homosexual adventures; masturbation has continued unabated. Even in his autoeroticism, no emotion is connected with sex; the act is casually performed and usually with no fantasy that Brown can recall. At the most, he will think of voluptuous female forms or "a few male genitals," but in neither case are they personalized.

Of the years between the ages of 21 and 26, Morris said little except that he did a great deal of growing up. He has the theory, which he got from a friend, that a person has a certain amount of growing up to do, and he considers himself to have done it almost all in the last year and a half. It is interesting to note that in trying to define growing up, Morris, after a little incoherence, identified it with "whether or not you acted, governed your emotions with your reason."

About five years ago he heard a talk by a psychiatrist, which made a considerable impression on him. The man held that (1) it was most important to do what you planned to do and (2) you should "think *there*, not *here*." The latter advice Morris interpreted as meaning "think about what you are doing, don't introspect or analyze yourself." It was the first idea, however, that was most important to him. In the last five years Morris has been trying to plan his days and control his activities in this way. "I don't like responsibility, but I go after it now because I think it's good for me."

The first year away from the regulating power of either school or home, with a business that made few rigid demands by way of schedule, "I gambled hard, lived crazily . . . proved myself in everything I undertook very unreliable—as I always had. The next four years I have been gradually growing up—have tried the system of always doing anything I was asked to." To the end of "transforming his personality" he fills his day with appointments, makes himself speak at meetings, goes to parties where he doesn't know anyone. He keeps three marbles in his left coat pocket, and each time he makes a serious effort to sell a man some securities, he transfers one marble to the right coat pocket. His firm calculates that to be successful a man should make at least three such efforts per day.

In the autobiography, Morris wrote:

I have a yen for community activities—apparently I want to be a big man in town before I have proved my right to it—I have a good reputation as a guy who gets things done—if they only knew! . . . I have made many friends in the last five years, but have never felt too close to or too dependent on any one of them. And I feel a disdain for anyone who is not pretty self-sufficient—I keep myself busy all the time, often on very trivial things.

Scout work put him in touch with philanthropic and civic organizations, and he soon began taking part in them. It was hard at first; having always avoided parties and social affairs of a genteel sort, Morris was afraid of these social situations. It occasionally came out in interviews that he still fears meeting people, that he feels greatly relieved to get away to the country where he is not under the tension of selling to strangers. Experience has proved to Morris, however, that he can sell, he can make a speech, and he can get people to do things; and so most of the reluctance and fear has gone.

At present, Morris has worked his way to the top of such organizations as the Red Cross Roll Call, Junior Chamber of Commerce, and Community Chest, holding important executive positions in each. He is also the president of a businessman's athletic association that he organized and president of a business association in his office. A couple of other clubs claim him as a member. All these activities were undertaken gradually while he was learning to sell stocks and bonds, and though Brown has devoted a great deal of time to these nonbusiness activities, they have proved to be financially rewarding by getting him much publicity and favorable notice. Two years ago he resolved to get his name in the paper at least once every two weeks for six months—and he did. Usually he appears not to have been greatly affected by his public recognition, but when he gets drunk he has a tendency to recount his achievements and ask what it is about him that makes people want to honor him so signally.

Morris Brown is jolly, tells jokes fairly well and often, and has a ready laugh. But his approach is without the appeal of an original style; he once said, "I never made up an original joke in my life." He also says that he "seems to rub people the wrong way sometimes" and wonders why. Yet he says, without apparently seeing any connection, "If there's anything I'm not, it's tactful. Oh, I've learned a certain amount of superficial tactfulness, but dealing with people is still a new thing for me; I say things that are all wrong." For example, his attempts to use flattery at times fail from lack of subtlety.

In the past year or so, Morris has become quite interested in the Catholic church. He thinks he has read more than a score of books on it—"everything from the Catholic Question Box up" to Newman's *Apologia*. "If I get myself all screwed up mentally, I'll go sit in a Catholic church somewhere—just sit, not pray." Yet he will not join and could not imagine taking the step of accepting everything the church says. His most frequent condemnation of things is not a moral judgment, but a rational objection: "it's silly . . . . just doesn't make sense."

He has many liberal views, but hates to hear an idea or an institution challenged. "Martin Luther was one of the greatest criminals who ever lived, because he shook the faith of thousands of people." "In college you see a lot of Goddamn free souls wandering about with their own ideas—it's so crazy." "I don't like to be around skeptical people, it makes me doubt."

Morris' attitude to immortality is perhaps indicative of the function that his established beliefs have and that he would like the church to have, in his mental economy. "It's no use discussing it with someone who doesn't think we're immortal. . . . If you don't have such a belief, it takes the brakes off what you may do here—encourages the idea of living hard, fast, and loose."

Brown's gambling, referred to above, continued after college for a few years; and he went from speculating in stocks to taking fliers in the commodities market. In 1937 he bought a lot of wheat for a rise; but the price fell, and all of a sudden he had lost $1000. For a couple of days he was almost dazed by it, but he quickly determined never to gamble seriously again and has in the main lived up to his resolve. Occasionally—once a month or so—he will take a hand in a poker game, but not for high stakes.

Morris prefers to live in the present or plan, at most, for only a short time ahead. When asked what his goals are, he beat around the bush a little, then said that they were

> not very well thought out—always sort of immediate. I have a desire to be a big man around town. Most men have ideas about getting married, having a nice home, doing things for Mother with a capital 'M.' I know I owe her a lot, but never thought about setting her up. I hadn't thought of this—I'm changing my goals. . . . I want to be a really good golfer. I think it's silly of me to think of what I'll be 20 years from now. People who have their life all planned out bother me.

Morris feels that he has about reached the ceiling of prestige and status in his community activities; it is now a question of whether he seems to other people to be a success. Money, beyond enough for a modest level of comfort, means nothing to him. He is a little unsure about what he wants in the way of friends. The idea of knowing many different kinds of people, particularly important people, appeals to him: "I love it—you can *learn* something from them." He expressed no desire for intimate friends. The fact is that he has three or four reasonably close friends, but he is judging these relationships in the frame of reference of his former intense involvements.

Though he has a conventional wish for a wife he could get along with and for "a good crop of boys," he admits it is "beyond immediate possibility—I don't have plans for when I'm fifty." Brown does not have much interest in ordinary social affairs; he likes to dance, but he is poor at it and seldom attends dances. He does have occasional dates and goes to a cocktail party now and then. He is vaguely aware of a certain lack of knowledge and sophistication in himself, due to his pre-college background, and so would like to study, meet "smart people," and acquire polish in whatever ways he can.

It would be a mistake to leave an impression of Morris as a completely calculating person, either consciously or unconsciously, as some of the foregoing material may suggest. A final appraisal must mention his genuine desire to please, his fresh interest in people and things about him, his perennial good spirits, his willingness to help and to cooperate, and his quite charming naive frankness, without which it would not have been possible for the investigators to write this story of his life.

So ends the case history written in 1940. The next two chapters will present additional data on Morris Brown gathered at that time, to serve as illustrative material for a detailed consideration of objective and projective tests of personality.

So we sometimes espy a bright cloud formed into an irregular figure; when it is observed by unskilful and fantastic travellers, it looks like a centaur to some, and as a castle to others; some tell that they saw an army with banners, and it signifies war; but another, wiser than his fellow, says it looks for all the world like a flock of sheep, and foretells plenty; and all the while it is nothing but a shining cloud.

JEREMY TAYLOR. Holy Living and Holy Dying

CHAPTER 6
OBJECTIVE AND PROJECTIVE TECHNIQUES OF ASSESSMENT

N ow that we have a grasp of the main facts in Morris Brown's life up to the time of his formal assessment in 1940–41, we are in a position to appreciate the kinds of contributions to understanding him that both projective and nonprojective (or objective) techniques can supply. In the process, some of the general points about these types of assessment made in previous chapters may become more concrete as they take on relevance.

Objective Techniques

QUESTIONNAIRES

As we noted in Chapter 4, self-administering tests and inventories are a major resource of objective assessment. Eight such tests were taken by Morris Brown in 1940, a good sample of the instruments available at the time. Of these eight, we shall examine here only two, which are still used today.

The A-S (Ascendance-Submission) Reaction Study, by G. W. and F. H. Allport (1928), was one of the first trait measures. It has only moderate retest reliability (measured by a correlation coefficient of .74 for men), and the evidence for its validity is even weaker: Correlations of about .45 (but ranging from .29 to .74) have been reported, the criteria being ratings by self and others. It can hardly be regarded as a precise or highly trustworthy measuring stick for *ascendance-submission* (the tendency to dominate others or to give way to them), yet most of its content seems meaningfully relevant to that trait. Here is a sample item:

> You are at a mixed party where about half the people are friends of yours. The affair becomes very dull, and something should be done to enliven it. You have an idea. Do you usually
>> take the initiative in carrying it out———————————
>> pass it on to another to put into execution——————
>> say nothing about it———————————————

The subject merely checks the answer he considers most self-descriptive. Morris attained a score of +11, which the authors express as A2, or moderately ascendant, on a scale ranging from A4 through Average to S4. This score agrees reasonably well with the informal and clinical assessment of Morris, who was clearly not a shy or self-abasing person in most situations, particularly since he had begun to take on positions of leadership, to speak at meetings, and to work successfully at an occupation demanding a good deal of persuasiveness on his part. The score would be more valuable if there had been more work on norms (see page 124).

The Study of Values, by G. W. Allport and P. E. Vernon (1931), gives scores on half a dozen variables and is based on the theory of personality of the German psychologist, E. Spranger. In his book *Types of Men* (1928), Spranger proposed that six major foci attract the interest of adults: Theoretical, Economic, Aesthetic, Social, Political, and Religious values. Because these values represent relatively conflict-free areas of experience, in which defensiveness and concealment are not expected, the authors constructed a test of a few dozen transparent items relevant to these six categories of personal values.

The test has enjoyed wide use in research and, to some extent, in other types of assessment, such as vocational guidance and selection; in its recent revision (which will be discussed in Chapter 8), it has taken a new lease on life. The reliabilities of the six scores from the original form vary, but they are generally satisfactory: On retest after three months, correlation coefficients range from a distinctly poor .39 (Social) to a good .87 (Religious) and, for internal consistency, from .49 (Social) to .84 (Aesthetic and Religious). A respectable degree of validity is indicated by the differences between the scores of occupational groups; for example, ministers and seminary students do score higher on the Religious interest than men in general.

The test is ingeniously constructed so that it gives a purely *relative* measure of the strength of a person's values. Each item pits two to four values against one another, as in the following examples (taken from Lindzey's 1951 revision). In the first type of item, the subject is to distribute 3 points between two possible answers:

> Which of the following branches of study do you expect ultimately will prove more important for mankind? (a) mathematics; (b) theology.

By awarding 2 points to the first alternative, Morris contributed that much to his score on the Theoretical value; the single point for (b) was chalked up to his score on the Religious value.

In the second type of item, the four possible answers are to be ranked in reverse order. In the example below, Morris' answers are given, along with the value measured by each (which does not appear in the actual item):

> To what extent do the following famous persons interest you—
> a. Florence Nightingale (2) (Social value)
> b. Napoleon (4) (Political value)
> c. Henry Ford (3) (Economic value)
> d. Galileo (1) (Theoretical value)

In these answers, Morris indicated that his strongest interest was in Napoleon, the political figure, his least in Galileo, who embodies the Theoretical value.

As can be seen from the profile of values for Morris in 1940 (Figure 6-1), his strongest value was the Political, on which his score exceeds that of 90 percent of the normative group of college students. This finding implies a primary interest in power, not necessarily within the field of politics as such; it suggests that he is motivated by a desire to be a leader, to dominate others, and to gain influence and renown.

The next rank was shared by the Economic and Social values, both at the 70th percentile. The economic man, according to Spranger, is interested in what is *useful;* but the Economic value also includes self-preservation, all the practical concerns of business, and the gaining of wealth. The Social value was defined by Spranger as love for people in all its manifestations; it was the most diffuse of the values. The social man is kind, sympathetic, and unselfish; or, at least, someone with a strong Social value rates such qualities high as ideals.

The Aesthetic value, at the 20th percentile, was quite low; unlike Spranger's aesthetic man, Morris did not prize form and harmony above all

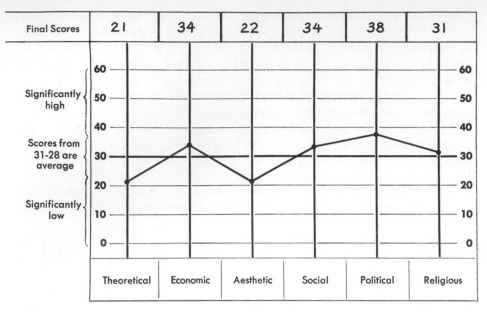

Final Scores	21	34	22	34	38	31

Significantly high

Scores from 31-28 are average

Significantly low

| Theoretical | Economic | Aesthetic | Social | Political | Religious |

Figure 6-1   Morris Brown's profile of values (Allport & Vernon, 1931).

else, nor did he tend to judge things in terms of grace, symmetry, or fitness. Morris' weakest value—the Theoretical—showed a slightly lower score, but was also at the 20th percentile. The dominant concern of the theoretical man, Allport and Vernon tell us, is the discovery of truth; his interests are cognitive, empirical, critical, and rational.

This ordering agrees well with the assessors' impressions on the basis of interviews and other data. To quote the original report: "One of them predicted at the beginning of the study, on the basis of only a few casual contacts, that the Political, Social, and Economic would be the leading interests." The Study of Values provided confirmation, true, but just what else did the test provide? In defense of the test's authors it must be added that their manual suggests only the following types of use with individuals: "to secure an initial impression . . . and as a basis for subsequent interviews."

INTELLIGENCE TESTING

Terman and Merrill's 1937 revision of the Stanford-Binet Scale was long the standard individual test of intelligence for subjects of all ages. (Today, as Chapter 8 will point out, the Wechsler Adult Intelligence Scale has supplanted it in work with adults.) In 1940, the Stanford-Binet existed in two forms (L and M), with unusually good alternate-form reliability (.91) and excellent stability over time. One group of 11-year-olds was retested after 1 year, 2 years, and finally after 6 years; the later I.Q.'s were correlated with the earlier set to an equally high degree (.93, .93, .92). As the direct lineal descendant of the original Binet test that virtually defined intelligence in 1905, the Stanford-Binet had almost unquestioned validity in 1940. It is heavily weighted with verbal skills and is a particularly good predictor of academic achievement, which is what Binet intended it to be in the first place. But the test also predicts life achievement; for example, children with I.Q.'s in the mentally defective range (65 and lower) can be expected never to enter college or to succeed in professional or managerial occupations, unless the I.Q. is temporarily lowered by an emotional disturbance that is later alleviated. Terman and Oden (1947) made a special study of those at the other extreme, following up 730 persons whose childhood I.Q.'s were 140 or higher. By age 40, they had published 67 books, more than 200 plays and short stories, and over 1400 professional or scientific papers; they tended to be in occupations with the highest levels of prestige and remuneration.

Form L was administered to Morris Brown in 1940 by a graduate student who had had enough experience to feel comfortable in giving it. Morris' I.Q. was determined to be 146, Very Superior; he was able to perform practically every task that was put to him. This score was a quantitative measure of considerable interest in light of Morris' tardiness in learning to speak. To be sure, that he graduated with honors from one of the country's most respected colleges suggests that he must have had at least superior intelligence, as does his history of rapid advancement in primary school and his early graduation from high school. Casual contact and even extended conversation, however, would not have led the investigators to predict such a high intelligence quotient. Despite his *cum laude*, Morris seems to have been somewhat of an underachiever for most of his college career and was still not using the full extent of his ability in his activities as of 1940.

CONSTITUTIONAL ANALYSIS

Somatotype   Morris' *somatotype* was determined according to the judgmental system of W. H. Sheldon and under his supervision. Sheldon took a standardized photograph, from which the somatotype was rated 4½ 5 1½. These numbers mean that Brown's physique was just above the theoretical midpoint of a 7-point scale of endomorphy, slightly higher on mesomorphy (which was thus the dominant component), and only a fraction of a point above the theoretical minimum for ectomorphy. This somatotype is a member of a family of rather common ones; Sheldon (1940) describes its closest relatives as follows:

> The 452 is the commonest of the overwhelmingly massive physiques . . . These are solid, heavy people, of great strength and energy [p. 201].
> The 451 is a massive, compact physique, of short stature [not true of Morris], and usually of tremendous energy. It is a body built for an active, strenuous life. The endomorphic 4 supports the predominant mesomorphic

5 to produce a highly efficient machine as long as the first component is kept in check by vigorous activity, but given an opportunity, the endomorphic 4 will produce a laying-on of fat which rises like the tide and soon swamps the athletic outline of the physique. . . . [Athletic slenderness] is predominant only as long as a vigorously active life is maintained, or a rigid diet established. Under ordinary circumstances, especially after marriage, the first component suddenly asserts itself and for a time seems to run rampant. These people can sometimes gain 30 or 40 pounds within a year. Likewise they can lose this weight relatively easily, if they are willing to diet rigidly, but usually they are not [pp. 212–13].

The 4 5 1 somatotype is illustrated in Figure 4-1, page 77.

Brown did not deviate markedly from the norms for his physique in the secondary variables, also rated on 7-point scales. His scores were gynandromorphy (resemblance to the other sex), 2; texture (fineness of structural detail), 2½; dysplasia (inconsistency between regions), 5 (Morris' rather moonshaped face, for example, made his head considerably more endomorphic than his hard-muscled legs).

Temperament Typing

Sheldon's method for the analysis of temperament is basically clinical: It relies upon interviewing and direct observation to collect facts, which are processed by means of ratings, again on 7-point scales. Temperament, Sheldon believes, is best conceived of as varying on three dimensions (or *components*), which are defined in terms of three somewhat heterogeneous lists of separately rated traits. The 20 ratings for each component are averaged to arrive at the final scores, expressed in a formula similar to the somatotype: 5 5 3.

Morris' overall rating of 5 on *viscerotonia* indicates a considerable liking for comfort, eating, and relaxation, with attendant good fellowship, and dependence on expressed affection, particularly when in trouble. This above-average rating also reflects warm and readily expressed emotions and the ability to get along with people easily and well. The equally high rating of 5 on *somatotonia* reflects Morris' characteristically high level of energy, activity, and exercise. The rating was earned also by his loud extroverted characteristics—his aggressive leadership, his insensitivity to others, and his maturity of appearance (one of Sheldon's odd variables of "temperament" that guarantee high correlations with measures of physique). On each of those traits Morris was moderately strong, and he was particularly strong on having "sharp cleavage between conscious and unconscious." He was rated below the midpoint on *cerebrotonia*, a tense, inhibited hyperattentionality that is revealed both physiologically and socially.

Sheldon's variables did not, however, fit Brown without internal contradictions. With his high degree of viscerotonia, he should have been a better sleeper and a more ceremonious person. Greater love of adventure and danger and a much more aggressive and active response to both trouble and alcohol should go with a rating of 5 in somatotonia. And, finally, Brown was more cerebrotonic than his 3 rating implied, in that he had difficulty making habits, resisted disease well, and was often rather tense.

A COMMENT ON THE OBJECTIVE ASSESSMENT
OF MORRIS BROWN

In spite of some attempts to interpret his scores on a few of the questionnaires, it can hardly be argued that the objective assessment, except for the I.Q., contributed very much to our understanding of Morris. With one further exception (see next paragraph), the objective assessment did not provide concepts that would help us pull facts together in ways that are not already obvious, nor does it deepen our sense of knowing him as a person. Even the quantitative precision apparently given by numerical scores is vitiated by their only moderate validities.

For the most part the scores could be taken at face value, and the test results seemed to make far better sense than might have been expected from the meager evidences of validity accompanying most of the questionnaires. Consider, for example, the Humm-Wadsworth Temperament Scale, a then-popular multitrait test that is no longer widely used; it brought out his lack of ambition, his deficiency in what Morris himself called "moral sense," and his tendency to be below average in fantasy, imaginativeness, and schizoid traits. His highest scores were on the "cycloid component" scales of both manic and depressive tendencies. This finding had the value of suggesting that his fluctuating moods—his generally high level of energy and cheerfulness, which were sometimes replaced by considerable self-doubt and feelings of uneasiness—could be seen as expressions of cyclothymic temperament.

A moment's reflection can provide us with a hypothesis to explain both the surprising "validity" of the tests and their failure to add much to the picture of our man. In both interviews and tests, Morris made a conscientious attempt to present himself honestly. Indeed, his only motivation—the wish to gain more self-understanding, perhaps in the service of self-control— operated to minimize conscious faking of any kind and helped to make the tests valid in his case. It is not surprising that a consistent picture emerged in both interviews and questionnaires—two types of assessment that had in common their directness of approach. Because the interviews were so comprehensive, the tests did not cover much new ground.

We have thus seen exemplified a point already made about inventories: If a subject is willing and able to describe himself truthfully, they allow him to present himself rather faithfully and efficiently (at least in terms of the investigator's time), even if in a less personalized and individualized way than the methods of direct clinical assessment permit. The main advantage these inventories have over free self-description is the opportunity they give for systematic coverage and interindividual comparison: It is possible to see to what extent other people have answered the same questions in a similar way. But *what* other people? It makes little sense to compare a 26-year-old college graduate with high school seniors on a questionnaire like the Wrightstone Test of Civic Beliefs (another test Morris took, which is now defunct), because even the data of that test's author showed that the average score on liberalism rises steadily during the high school years, and it might surely be expected to go up even more during the college years (as subsequent research has shown to be true; see Sanford, 1962). The moderately liberal Brown looked like an extreme radical in comparison to the only available norms.

Projective Techniques

By turning now to projective tests, which are widely used in the interpretive phase of clinical assessment, we can go beyond the point to which the objective tests have brought us. The Thematic Apperception Test and the Rorschach Test given to Morris Brown exemplify the uses to which these techniques can be put.

THE THEMATIC APPERCEPTION TEST

The TAT (Morgan & Murray, 1935) was devised in the course of a research program at the Harvard Psychological Clinic and was published after some years of development (Murray, 1943). The test consists of 30 pictures and a blank card, onto which the subject is encouraged to project his own imagined picture. The pictures are marked in such a way as to indicate four overlapping sets of 20 each: one for boys, one for girls, one for males over 14, and one for females over 14. Thus, card 6BM is to be used both for boys and for older males, 13MF is for older males and females only, and card 1 is used with all subjects. The subject tells a story about each picture, following instructions similar to those given two paragraphs below.

The investigators used a set of the TAT pictures that were then current, most of which were either identical with or very similar to the ones generally available today; see Figure 6-2 for two of the pictures. Being untrained and inexperienced in the use of projective techniques, they made just about every mistake possible in administering the test to Morris; nevertheless, they obtained a great deal of usable material. In three sessions, Morris told stories about 22 pictures; 7 of these stories are quoted below and 2 are summarized briefly.*

* In the old series, the first 10 pictures were used with all subjects; only one of these, card 1, carries the same number in the current, published test. The investigators also got Morris to tell stories about 9 of the 10 pictures used with men only (which were designated M-11 through M-20), and 3 of the 10 pictures for women (F-11 through F-20). To minimize confusion, the stories will be numbered here sequentially as they were given, and where possible the pictures will be referred to by their current code numbers.

Figure 6-2   Illustrative TAT pictures (numbers 8 and 10 in an unpublished series).

Administration   As it is used today, the TAT is introduced by instructions like the following:

This is a story-telling test. I am going to show you some pictures, one at a time, and your task will be to make up as dramatic (or interesting) a story as you can for each. Tell what has led up to the event shown in the picture, describe what is happening at the moment, what the characters are feeling and thinking; and then give the outcome. Speak your thoughts as they come to your mind. Do you understand? Here is the first picture.

The instructions given to Morris were essentially the same, except that they specified that the test was "a test of imagination, one form of intelligence." The examiner today records the length of time before the subject begins and the total time he takes for each story.

**Sample Stories
from Session 1**

1. [A young boy is contemplating a violin, which rests on a table in front of him.]

Probably this boy has just taken up the violin and is looking at it wondering how he is going to make anything out of it. His teacher wasn't very encouraging. It's not his first lesson, I see now—all this music, he wouldn't have it in the first few weeks. Could be Yehudi what's-his-name at the time he made his first concert appearance. Reminds me of a story about a boy who went to hear Kreisler, came home and broke his violin. Thereafter he wouldn't go watch good tennis.

5. [Card 10 in the present, published series: A young woman's head against a man's shoulder.]

Can you explain what this is? (points; E [Examiner] shakes head) It suggests something similar to the idea of *Ladies in Retirement*—the woman is similar to Flora Robson in that, or the servant in *Rebecca*. She's devoted her whole life to the boy; this is one of the few times she's let herself go. He's home from school on holidays, about 15 or 16. Thinking about how much she has and is going to do for him; her whole life is wrapped up in him, yet he's probably going to turn out something like the boy in *My Son, My Son*. (At this point Morris complains about how he keeps thinking about other books, plays, and so on.) I have seen that somewhere in some play. Anyone can see—it's obvious to look at the boy that he'll never be worth a damn—he's pudgy, soft, and sort of weak.

8. [See Figure 6-2.]

This could be in a primitive Indian civilization in Central America. It's hard to put in any specific atmosphere; faces are so different. (He may have said "indistinct.")

Down in Yucatan, Mayans or Incas—where family life was different from what we know—more like in India today, where marriages are apart from the wishes of the participants or anything like that, this young couple about 17–18 years old—the man's a very sensitive sort, an artist; therefore, he must have been . . . very much in love with this very charming girl. Since custom . . . Well, the idea is, somehow they got together, she had a baby—but since the marriage hadn't been sanctioned, the elders of the tribe were outraged. They couldn't have the baby, since they had violated all the taboos, etc. It would be taken by the boy's mother, who felt worst about it, to be reared by a priest in one of the temples. The couple were driven out of the place and were never heard of again. This is where the baby's being taken away. The girl's pretty much crushed; he'd like to do something about it, but there's nothing he can.

10. [See Figure 6-2.]

(laughs) It suggests Sinbad and the sailor—I could be very trite and tell that. I must have a very trite brain. (long pause; turns it several ways)

This is a copy of a drawing found on the wall of a cave in Arabia by Burton. He had the idea of getting down all the old Arabian legends. He went all over Arabia, eating their food, living with their women, trying to run down all the stories that were told by night around the fire. This was the first time anybody had heard of a cave in Arabia—why the mouth wasn't closed by sand, nobody could imagine. He went in, found the walls covered with drawings; there was a whole series of caves, and he could recognize a lot of the drawings because they illustrated stories he'd found. He went further back, found some he couldn't recognize; this was one of them. Then he noticed this same gaunt, weary figure was in many of the other pictures, representing many adventures this same man had gone through—trials and tribulations. Burton had found that opium smoking helped in this work so he decided to settle down and try it to see if he couldn't get some interpretation of the picture. They camped outside, and for the next week he spent 24 hours a day lying on a couch in the cave looking at the pictures. Gradually he saw in this gaunt old man a curious portrayal of all the difficulties the human soul must undergo. The idea of everyone bearing his own cross: Sinbad carrying this old man on his shoulders. When Burton got back to England after this, people found him changed. He had been knighted and had great honors. He was very different now, liked more and more to sit alone, smoke, and read. He was a man of great wealth and lacked for nothing. It came to be that he had to be watched, because his mind wasn't just right. He would wander around the room shaking himself as if trying to get rid of this burden. They say that when he died he was alone in his big old castle in an ornate room clutching at his throat trying to tear the old man's hands away.

It is usually not desirable to administer more than 10 pictures in one session, since the subject—particularly if he is as productive as Morris—is likely to become too tired to do the job properly. A new set of instructions was given at the second session one week later, in accordance with the procedure Murray recommended at that time. Current practice does not require different instructions.

Sample Stories from Session 2   Brown had a bad headache during this whole session. He was instructed as follows:

The procedure today is the same as before, only this time you can give freer rein to your imagination. Your first ten stories were excellent, but you confined yourself pretty much to the facts of everyday life. Now I would like to see what you can do when you disregard the commonplace realities and let your imagination have its way, as in a myth, fairy story, or allegory.

11. [6BM: A short elderly woman stands with her back turned to a tall young man. The latter is looking downward with a perplexed expression.]

(Before starting, Morris said that he could make up an unusual one, about murder, and also the obvious one. E asked for the latter.) The obvious thing is that this fellow has just told his mother that he is going away on a trip, won't be back for several years; she's obviously all broken up about it, thinks it's not necessary, is foolish. His mind was made up; nothing she said or thought could change it, so he's getting ready to go. There's nothing especially dangerous, about where he's going—just different sort of work. She doesn't like to see the settled order of their life broken up. This is the end of a couple of weeks of talking and worrying about it; he has told her what he's going to do; they've had a lot of trouble about it.

14. [12M: A young man is lying on a couch with his eyes closed. Leaning over him is another man, his hand stretched out above the face of the reclining figure.]

This is about a couple of roommates in prep school, one of whom thought he was pretty hot stuff as a hypnotist, other thought it was a lot of crap, that it was impossible for anyone to hypnotize him, for his will to be subject to another's. Wright explained that only a strong will could be hypnotized and then if he were willing, so they agreed to try it out. The picture represents just about when the subject is getting completely under the control of Wright, the other boy. Of course, there's no need for Wright to use his hands and gestures, it's not an essential part; but it fits in with the usual picture and he was that kind of fellow, wanted to be spectacular about it. The main reason Wright was interested in this work was he knew that in the state of hypnosis a subject will do nothing against his fundamental nature, and he wanted to find out a few things about his roommate. So as soon as everything was fixed he asked him to walk over to his—Wright's—bureau, take some money that was there, put it in his pocket, which Bill did. He came back and sat on the edge of the couch, took one of the pillows, put it between his legs and started screwing it, faster and faster until he went off and came out of the state of hypnotism at once. The problem is, whether the act was something repugnant to him or whether it was a reaction to his nervous state that made him snap out of it. This is a problem story, sort of like the Lady and the Tiger.

Came from a little incident I heard about 13 years ago; never thought of it since. A fellow in prep school hypnotized his roommate, had him screw a pillow; the fellow who told me about it was named Wright. From the general situation, I don't think it was a true story.

(Brown asked if it were true that one would do only what he really had no objections to; said he had learned about hypnotism only here and there, partly from Poe's story "Mesmerism.") I was brought up on five volumes of Poe—do you want them lurid? I could probably drag sex in by the heels all over the place, a few dead bodies and so on.

16. [17BM: A naked man is clinging to a rope. He is in the act of climbing up or down.]

The man is a eunuch in Ethiopia—I've just been reading in *Days of Our Years* a chapter about it. At 14, he was captured by a slave trader who at one blow cut off not only his balls but his prick—that's the way the Arabs liked 'em. He was bought by this Arab chief who very peculiarly had a castle—would have to because of the picture—and there this man Ahab, as he was called by the Arabs, lived for 20 years, as servant in the chief's harem. Surprisingly, instead of developing the usual lackadaisical castrated attitude that comes to eunuchs (laughs)—oh, yes!—this Ahab was constantly tormented by the presence of all the women and his complete inability to do anything about it. Thinking the thing over, trying to reason it out, he decided he must escape, come what may. Since the harem was kept in the tower of this peculiar castle and he never did get outside for a minute, there was only one way to do it: by means of a rope. So early one morning just as the sun was coming up, he threw a rope out of the window, tying it to a post inside the room, and let himself down. As in most such rash acts, fate was against him. He got to the bottom; four of the servants of the Arab chief were there, ready to grab him. So Ahab failed in his attempt to gain freedom. He died in the most unique way the chief could think up. Do you want to know the way? They put him in a room with a couple of colonies of red ants: one of the quaint Ethiopian customs I've just been reading about.

Sample Stories from Session 3 A week after the second session Morris told stories about some more pictures to the other investigator. Two of these stories are summarized below.

21. [18GF: A woman has her hands squeezed around the throat of another woman whom she appears to be pushing backwards across the banister of a stairway.] "That's a beaut! Oh boy! One woman murdering another one." A younger woman served as personal secretary to an older one—"it's coming from a story," he interpolated—and they got involved in a lesbian relationship. The secretary eventually turned on her employer and choked her; the latter fell, hit her head, and died. "The girl had a good time on the swag she had gotten away with." Apparently pleased with his surprise ending, Morris remarked that it wouldn't do for Hollywood.

22. [13MF: A young man is standing with downcast head buried in his arm. Behind him is the figure of a woman lying in bed.] "I've got to cut loose on this one. Jesus, what a shape! Positively indecent! Looks like a Gibson girl!" His first thought was that the man was "going to the bathroom to make sure he doesn't catch anything!" He then said the scene was in Hawaii, where a man and girl were "sitting and drinking on a terrace." After "six drinks, they stagger upstairs and land on the bed"; a couple of minutes later, the man goes to the bathroom to throw up.

Inquiry One of the investigators conducted an inquiry into the sources of the stories, asking Morris where he got the ideas for each. For the most part, he attributed them to various books he had read; but the following responses (quoted just as recorded in the investigator's handwritten notes) are more personally revealing:

1. From a story he read in a tennis book. Tennis doesn't fit in naturally around here. Did want to be a famous tennis player. Never got any definite goal. Golf now. Either going to be good or leave it alone. Hates to think he is wasting his time.

5. Had a job figuring out the sexes. Came from the stories mentioned. Does think of himself as pudgy and soft as a kid; didn't then.

11. No special source. Ties back to own experience probably. Overdrawn. Resistance she didn't express.

16. Directly from *Days of Our Years*. Escape—something I've read somewhere—*Thief of Bagdad*—or Arabian Nights story where hero cut villain in two. (Couldn't believe Arab actually cut off members.) Escape, from *The Three Musketeers*.

The Process of Interpretation

How should one interpret a projective technique like the TAT? There is no one correct way. Experts differ in their procedures, and few of them use any formal system of scoring. Analyzing a TAT is not a complicated technical process of counting certain kinds of words or making quantitative ratings on many variables and entering formulas of any kind.

Rather, the general practice is, first, to approach the stories with a background of general knowledge about the person (the more knowledge the better), which helps orient the investigator to what is relevant and helps him to rule out various obviously inappropriate hypotheses that might otherwise cause him to waste time. To take an extreme example, there is no point in trying to figure out from a set of stories whether the author was a man or a woman; there are easier and more valid ways of finding that out. The task of the interpreter is to develop hypotheses about what caused the person to tell just these stories in just these ways—hypotheses about the determinants of all aspects of the test data—in order to help develop a picture of the storyteller's personality.

Second, as the skilled interpreter makes himself more and more thoroughly familiar with the stories, he begins to notice divergences from what would be expected on the basis of experience with the stories most people tell about any given picture and divergences from the subject's own baseline. Divergent material, which is unusual through being rare, or repetitive, or very intensely stated, or accompanied by signs of strong emotion, is the main basis for inferences, or interpretive hypotheses. After putting these hypotheses together and checking them against other evidence (which causes some of them to be dropped or modified), the interpreter finally writes his report.

In making his interpretations the investigator may use such procedures as *empathic perception, statistical inference,* or *inference based on theory.* Statistical inference simply means reasoning that if one aspect of a test has often been associated in the past with a personal characteristic, such as a kind of symptom, it will continue to have the same significance whether or not there is any intelligible connection between the two. In inference based on theory (or clinical inference), a theory of personality, or a more specific theory of a particular kind is used to establish a meaningful connection, which makes it understandable that some feature of a test performance is determined by some aspect of personality. These forms of inference are not mutually incompatible; ideally, a hypothesis suggested by theory is verified by statistical data, so that the interpreter can have a known degree of confidence in the inference.

Whatever the procedures the interpreter uses, they amount to *generalizing from particulars*. He translates the test responses as raw data into statements about aspects of personality, which he then treats as if they are characteristic. If he is prudent, he will use as wide a base as possible for such generalizations; therefore, he will test hypotheses from the TAT against other types of information.

By now it should be evident that projective techniques differ sharply from self-reporting questionnaires as techniques of assessment. It is misleading to group them all together as "personality tests," because they contribute to the assessment of personality in quite different ways. Projective techniques provide raw data of special value and richness, which the psychologist must then *interpret* before he can obtain measures of any variables of personality; the scores of inventories give immediate measures of personality variables. Thereafter, the psychologist may or may not decide to draw interpretive inferences from the profile, or configuration of scores, on a multidimensional test like the MMPI; in any event he does not have to. In a test like the TAT or Rorschach, however, the most commonly used scoring schemes merely count salient features of the subject's responses and are not direct measures of any one variable. It is impossible, therefore, to escape the necessity of interpreting projective test data. Some of the worst abuses of projective techniques have resulted from attempts to bypass clinical judgment and to use them as if scores derived from them were comparable to those of an inventory.

The lack of immediately meaningful scores also means that it is difficult to pursue the standard psychometric ideals, which presuppose such scores as the only yield of tests. That does not imply that reliability and validity are irrelevant. Validity remains an overriding consideration, and reliability concerns us in the following ways: We do not want to make the mistake of interpreting an aspect of a story in terms of some semipermanent feature of the personality if it actually resulted from a purely temporary mood (like Brown's headache) or a recent but unimportant experience like a movie the subject saw the night before. Furthermore, it is highly desirable for more than one assessor to be able to reach the same conclusions about the subject through interpreting his projective test results. The more the process of interpretation is structured and systematized, and the more common experience of training and working over the same data that two judges have, the better one can do in attaining reliability of this latter kind ("observer agreement").

The account given above deliberately avoids treatment of the more detailed steps, commonly found in texts on interpretation. Such accounts of orderly procedure give a false impression: Experts do not operate that way. ~~Interpreting complex qualitative data, like any other exercise of ex-pertise, is largely a tacit process.~~ The interpreter concentrates his attention on the *person*, trying to catch glimpses of him through the medium of his test responses, which are not of interest in themselves. Even less prominent in his awareness are his own methods of processing the data. To be sure, in the early stages of learning, things are quite different: Just as when you are learning to drive a car, you are vividly conscious of where you put your hands and feet at every moment and how you move them, so also when you are mastering the craft of interpreting clinical data you must do it with slow, awkward laboriousness. With practice and experience, performance of these steps merges into performance of the whole act and recedes from awareness, which makes it possible to become aware of much more about the person.

How Inferences	
Were Drawn	The most this account can do to illustrate
from the Stories	interpretation is to consider a few inter-

pretive hypotheses about Morris and relate them to the TAT data. Since Morris' stories suggest a tremendous number of possible hypotheses, let us concentrate on a few areas—the problematic ones raised at the end of Chapter 5 and restated below:

1. What had been going on in Morris during the years since college when he "turned inside out"?
2. What can we learn about his conflict over dependence and independence?
3. How can we understand his problem of controlling himself?
4. What can we make of his confused sexual adjustment?

From each question, we hope to learn something of the *unconscious* meanings of these conscious conflicts by the indirect method of the TAT. The underlying assumption is that the same unconscious needs, anxieties, and defenses that shape a person's everyday behavior will affect his cognitive products during the test in such a way that they can be discerned through interpretation. The very indirectness of the approach—the fact that the subject himself was in the dark about the personal significance of his stories, beyond the superficial parallels to his experience he pointed out in the inquiry—means that if dynamic factors within the subject did in fact determine the test responses, they were unconscious ones.

Inferences about sexual adjustment. To take these questions in reverse order, let us see what light the stories can throw on Morris' sexual problems. Why was he so little interested in girls? Why did he get involved in homosexual contacts? What did it all mean to him? An answer to any such focused set of questions requires that we examine all the stories that contain direct or circuitous reference to sex and to intimate relationships between actual or possible sexual partners. In doing so, we will be guided by certain normative expectations: To most people, the scene shown in picture 13MF (story 22) is an overtly sexual one, although many will knowingly avoid this interpretation of the relationship in their stories. Number 8 in the old series (Figure 6-2) had at least as strong a "pull" for a heterosexual interpretation. But tender and intimate relations between partners are also commonly seen in picture 10 of the present series, so we should examine story 5 as well. Since the other pictures do not directly suggest anything heterosexual, a story told about one of them should be examined with particular interest if erotic material crops up (see stories 10 and 16). The only picture that is at all often responded to as if there might be a homosexual relationship between the characters is 12M (see story 14; in the old series the characters' ages look more comparable than they do in the present, redrawn version); the emergence of the homosexual theme in story 21 is therefore of particular note.

One noteworthy element that is common to stories 8, 10, 16, and 22, where there is heterosexual content, is that they all take place in remote locations—Hawaii, Arabia, Ethiopia, and even ancient Yucatan. A fairly conservative interpretation would be that Morris found it difficult to imagine or at least to describe a sexual involvement with a girl in a "here and now" setting. Perhaps that would be so close to home as to make him anxious. Another possibility is that his heterosexual desires are repressed and thus can find only relatively remote expression. By contrast, note that the one explicitly homosexual theme (in story 21) and the implicit one (in story 14) came out in settings that seem to be contemporaneous and American.

In story 22, there is no suggestion of love, nor of any relationship at all other than a strictly sexual one, which takes place in a virtually anesthetic state of intoxication. The pseudo-enthusiastic exclamation about the woman's exposed breasts ("Positively indecent!") is a curious mixture of pleasure and rejection, and disgust with heterosexuality is strongly suggested by the man's throwing up. This reaction, however, could have been anticipated from Morris' remark about disgust and shame after heavy petting (see Chapter 5, page 112); the question remains: Why did Morris feel this way? The story contains two hints in associations he tossed off at the beginning and did not develop: first, that the woman looked "like a Gibson girl"—the equivalent of a pin-up girl in his mother's generation; and second, that the man might be afraid of venereal disease. From these hints come two possible inferences to be checked against other data: Morris may have been inhibited heterosexually (1) because a girl was unconsciously equivalent to his mother and (2) because he feared damage to his genitals. These are familiar elements of the Oedipus complex; psychoanalytic experience has taught us that a boy often develops a homosexual orientation because of the incest taboo and castration anxiety. Neither of these themes is at all directly expressed, yet the symbolic translation used here is not a far-fetched one in psychoanalytic practice.

As it happens, however, one of Morris' stories (16) does contain an unusually graphic and explicit reference to castration—and it is a story that also contains heterosexual material. This story is an interesting combination of common and unusual, original and borrowed elements: The interpretation of the picture (Daumier's lithograph "The House Painter") as one of a man escaping by climbing down a rope is quite usual; most of the rest of the content stands out by being highly infrequent, if not unique. Although the immediate source of much of this shocking content was a current best-selling travel book, the story is twisted around to highly personal ends. The fact that Morris could so easily disavow responsibility for having made up these improbable events undoubtedly made it possible for him to talk about them without anxiety—indeed, with a teasing kind of relish—for surely the events had nothing to do with *him*.

An interpreter of such a story always looks first at the central character (usually the one depicted in the picture), or *hero*, and makes the trial assumption that the teller expresses various feelings about himself through what he says about the hero. Moreover, older male figures—particularly those in positions of authority—are often symbols of the subject's father. Adopting these two assumptions, we can translate the underlying theme as an unconscious fantasy that says something like this: "Father castrated me and made me a powerless slave because he liked me better that way; if I showed sexual interest in mother or sisters [the chief's harem], with whom I was forced to be in close contact, he would torture me to death—escape would be impossible."

Before we turn to other stories for corroborative evidence or refutation, notice that the reaction of the hero to the (presumably sexy) women of the harem was not disgust but a tormenting conflict between sexual desire and "complete inability to do anything about it." Perhaps the attitude of disgust (which Morris consciously felt, for example, about prostitutes) was a cover for a more terrifying unconscious feeling of impotence, a fear of being castrated if he should make a move toward *any* woman (for, in Ahab's world, all the women belonged to the powerful father-figure and were thus taboo), or a feeling of already having been castrated. Indeed, Morris was impotent on his first visit with Henry to the brothel. Too much, however, must not be made of this as corroborative evidence for the deep and complicated interpretation being developed here, since for many reasons boys quite commonly react with both impotence and disgust on a first encounter with prostitutes.

Picture 8 (Figure 6-2), which virtually guarantees a story with sexual content, is the one that Morris made most remote, placing it in the Yucatan and verbalizing a feeling that the people were entirely alien ("faces are so different"). The embarrassed, almost euphemistic tone and the lack of any direct reference to sex are in striking contrast to the crudity and Anglo-Saxon explicitness of story 16, told when he was urged to let himself go. Moreover, in story 8 Morris spoke about love, the love of a man for a "very charming girl." Though the lovers had their baby taken away and incurred the wrath of all the parental figures for their explicitly taboo relationship, their punishment was to be banished and "never heard of again." The contrast of attitudes expressed in these two stories is an ancient one in Western culture and a familiar one in this case history: sacred love versus profane sex, the madonna versus the prostitute. In the dream about Ethel Merman (Chapter 5, page 112), as in this story, sacred love led to consequences Morris experienced as unpleasant, but not to any of the agonizing fates imagined in story 16.

The other stories mentioned above contain bits of corroborative evidence. In picture 5 (10 in the present numeration), typically seen as an embracing, mature couple, Morris saw a mother and a son with whom he identified. Notice that he did not refer explicitly to an embrace or to any feelings; it would have been helpful if the examiner had asked what he meant by saying "she's let herself go." Morris did mention the mother's devotion and all that she had done and would do for the son. Again, he could conceive of a tender relationship with a woman, but only a maternal (tabooed) one, and his conception primarily emphasized getting, not giving.

This picture is the only one in which Morris misperceived the sexes, but he got them both wrong, seeing the upper, comforting (male) figure as the mother and the soft, feminine, lower figure as the boy, whom he took to be much like himself at age 15 or 16. This misperception is a formal aspect of the test that strongly suggests a confusion in Morris' sense of sexual identity. That inference is quite consistent with his feeling of having been castrated in some sense, which was inferred from story 16.

In story 10, the hero is said to have sought to learn the Arabs' culture by "eating their food, living with their women" (note the close relation of these two ideas). Morris tossed off this remark in a casual, man-of-the-world tone, as if for him sex was a gratification to be taken as lightly as a good meal. Yet at the end of the story, we see that this same hero comes to a very bad end: For unexplained, mysterious reasons, he loses his mind and dies under the delusion that he is being choked by "the old man"—another unmistakable father figure. In Morris' story, the Old Man of the Sea (Morris was correct in so identifying him, for the picture *was* an illustration for *Sinbad the Sailor*) becomes a symbol of the conscience; the religious metaphor (the cross) strengthens this interpretation. Psychoanalysis teaches us that the main constituent of the conscience is an image of the punishing father and that this superego is the source of self-punishment, the burden of guilt, and the inability to enjoy worldly success. Perhaps the unconscious message here is: "If I gratify my desires with other men's food and women and if I pry into secret cavelike places, that bad, punitive father will eventually kill me, even if he is far away or dead, for I carry him around inside me."

Story 14 is not obviously homosexual, but one boy has an orgasm while performing a sexual act in the presence of his roommate, who has him in a hypnotic state, which is conceived largely in terms of dominance and submission. This is about as thin a disguise for a homosexual fantasy as one could hope to find. The story is further notable for its curiously illogical quality; it remains unexplained why Bill started acting out a sexual impulse after having been told only to take some of his roommate's money. Morris apparently felt a need to explain this non sequitur by the reference to an allegedly true story, but that did not succeed in making his own story plausible. It is as if the sexual fantasy stirred up by the dominance-submission relationship clearly stated in the picture had to break through, following an associative link that makes sense only in terms of unconscious (anal) symbolism.

Morris managed to put story 21, which does contain an explicit homosexual reference, at some distance from himself by describing a relationship between two women. Note that, as in story 14, there is a close relationship between stealing and homosexuality; and again he had to push the theme away from himself by parenthetically noting, "It's coming from a story." Interestingly enough, guilt seems connected with heterosexual activity (disgust or drastic punishment), but not with homosexuality; the initiators of the latter relationship in both stories come through unscathed, and only the partner gets hurt.

Summary of additional TAT interpretations. Limitations of space make it impossible to continue to present the process of interpretation in this much detail. The interpretive summary that follows draws on all the stories (not just the ones quoted above) and uses their formal aspects and the subject's behavior during the test as well as thematic content, which has been heavily emphasized up to this point. This summary also continues to make frequent use of the historical data from Chapter 5.

It seems that Morris as a little boy may have been confused about the sexual identity of his parents and at times may have conceived of his mother as the one who wore the pants. He may also have been sexually attracted to his father and frightened by closeness to him. His parents conveyed to him a strong incest taboo and castration anxiety, not necessarily by overt threats but more likely by their own emotional attitudes. As a result (and, of course, because of his father's absence), he lacked a strong sense of masculine identity at a time in adolescence when he was overweight and was far outstripped by his older classmates in physical, athletic manifestations of virility. The blow to his self-esteem was so great that at age 26 he had not yet gained an inner sense of being an adult, competent man, but unconsciously doubted his capacity to cope successfully with life's demands. Heterosexuality was altogether too frightening; but he was quite ambivalent about homosexuality too, for that threatened to undermine his feeling of manliness.

The unconscious picture of Morris' father that emerges from the TAT stories is a split image of a remote, terrifying castrator and a lovable, harmless man who, however, could not inspire respect. Perhaps quite early in

Morris' life Mr. Brown was impatient and punitive with the demanding, poorly controlled infant, and at a later stage he seemed more appealing but fumbling and ineffectual.

An equal degree of ambivalence, or simultaneous positive and negative feelings, about his mother may be inferred from Morris' stories. A rejecting conscious attitude of impatience with her covered a deeper feeling of dependence and respect for her strength and competence. He saw her as having considerable influence on his father and as having done a great deal for himself; she was someone whose strength and generosity he could rely on, without having to give much love in return.

Lacking a strong sense of identity and inwardly confused and insecure because of an identification with both his father and his mother, neither of which was integrated with his conscious picture of himself, Morris did not have a firm inner base of operations for self-control.

An important sub-issue of self-control was what Morris felt to be a lack of moral sense in himself. Signs that he had not achieved a well-integrated conscience (superego) are plentiful in the TAT: On the one hand, he portrayed self-destructive behavior and severe, cruel punishments for relatively slight offenses; on the other hand, more serious crimes went unpunished in some stories. He seemed preoccupied with thoughts about crime and troubled by the feeling that he had a hidden, immoral self. It would be easy to infer from these signs that the internalized parental images that make up the core of the unconscious self-regulating agency, the superego, were too harsh and punitive to be of much help in controlling his day-to-day behavior and would operate only to make him dissatisfied and self-destructive; compare the classical pattern of the "criminal out of a sense of (unconscious) guilt" described by Freud (1916).

But this pessimistic formulation would overlook several important, common-sense facts: Morris was quite self-critical without being self-defeating in any obvious way—he was not accident prone, nor addicted, nor involved in serious crime, but was *actively striving* to gain self-control. The TAT shows us what he had to fear in himself—the temptations and dangers from his own superego if he yielded too much; the stories tell little about his everyday behavior, especially those of the second and third sessions, when he was urged to let his fantasy roam as unrealistically as he liked. When a person is in conflict, as Morris Brown was, it is not unusual for apparent contradictions to result from analyses of data about the conscious and the unconscious levels of personality. This very lack of internal consistency and integration is an important fact about Morris in 1940; neither the apparent adjustment of his manifest behavior nor the indications of strong impulses for immediate gratification with only ineffective and oversevere superego controls on the unconscious level give a complete picture, and neither level can be properly understood without the other.

The conflict of dependence versus independence looks somewhat different from the perspective of the TAT. According to his conscious picture of himself, Morris was already completely independent of parents and friends; he was an adult, on his own. In his stories, there is little evidence that he felt able to succeed unaided, even though his heroes do often lack support from others. When (as in story 5) a hero depends on a parent to do things for him, he turns out to be weak and worthless. Thus, though Morris had little confidence in his own ability to strive manfully and independently and little ambition to attain distant goals, his stories suggest a sense that he had to break away from his mother if he was ever to be a man. There are repeated themes of rebellion, revolution, and violation of the rules set by "the elders of the tribe," which are common in the TAT's of late adolescents who are trying to free themselves from the emotional hold of the family, which they feel to be infantilizing.

Morris wanted money, prestige, fame, and power; but these goals seemed impossibly remote, and at the time he took the test he was discouraged, tempted to chuck them in favor of more easily obtained immediate gratifications. Nevertheless, there were some slight signs of the beginnings of an identification with the positive and admirable aspects of his mother's personality. The stories do not suggest that he felt very close to, or dependent upon, friends, but that they were a natural part of his life.

We come now to the first question, concerning what had been going on inside Morris during his first five postcollege years. This actually requires an overall diagnostic formulation, which we will not be ready for until we have looked into the Rorschach Test and then back over all the data. Meanwhile we can examine the TAT for signs of possible psychopathology. Could it be that Morris' state of relative turmoil, inner confusion, and implicit reaching out for help (which may have motivated him to offer himself as a subject for study) was part of a decompensation ("breakdown") into a neurosis or other such condition?

In regard to his characterological diagnosis (also called ego structure and defensive style), Morris' TAT gives evidence of a primarily *compulsive* kind of organization: his attempts to infer the story from details of the picture, his frequent display of his large fund of general information, his marked ambivalence, his severe superego, and his use of isolation as a defense. Without the capacity to isolate feelings from ideas, Morris would never have been able to speak so freely about the deeply disturbing matters that occur in his stories. Indeed, he seemed relatively cut off from experiencing genuine emotions, despite the presence of superficial displays of shallow affect in his exclamations about the pictures, none of which was deeply felt.

Morris' way of handling emotions at times went beyond isolation and suggested the callous, flippant, avoidant style of persons with a character disorder. Such people have little tolerance for anxiety or inner tension; they keep themselves busy (by "acting out") rather than permit themselves any moments of introspection and self-scrutiny. Consistent with this pattern was the teasing, tantalizing role Morris tended to play during the test, using trick or puzzle endings and attempting to shock or upset the examiner by "dragging in sex by the heels, a few dead bodies" and other sadistic details. Despite his attempts to be cooperative, Morris was evasive; and running away or escaping (as a way of reacting to an unpleasant conflict) is a frequent theme in his stories.

Nevertheless, Morris' generally good contact with reality and orderly thinking, together with his ability to flaunt conflict-laden ideas without getting noticeably upset, would be very surprising characteristics in a seriously disturbed man. Despite his insecurity, he did not appear especially anxious or on the verge of a breakdown.

THE RORSCHACH PSYCHODIAGNOSTIC
INKBLOT TEST

Rorschach's test (1921) is the oldest and most widely used of projective techniques. The subject's task is to look at inkblots on 10 separate cards and say in each case everything that the blot could resemble. The examiner then conducts an inquiry in which he asks enough questions about the responses to enable him to score them in terms of location (where seen on the card), determinants (the aspect of the blot that suggested the content, such as its shape, color, or shading, or an impression of movement), and the accuracy of the forms. Even when fully scored, however, this test—like the TAT—cannot be used without expert interpretation. The responses to the blots, which may be seen in as many ways as Taylor's "shining cloud," betray the perceiver's interests (as the seventeenth-century divine surmised) and a good deal more.

Morris Brown's
Rorschach Test Protocol

Two years after his initial assessment, the Rorschach Test was given to Morris by a graduate student of psychology who had had only a year or so of training and who wanted to supplement her experience with the test. She was kind enough to make the data available, even though the original case study had been finished. Because the tester was a Swiss girl whose English was somewhat imperfect, the following scored protocol, taken from her notes, is almost certainly not a verbatim transcript of all that Morris said; but it is good enough for our purpose: to illustrate the type of data this technique of assessment provides and the general procedure of interpretation. (The scoring symbols, in the left column, will be explained shortly.)

	Responses	*Inquiry*
Card I. 5″ *		
W F+ A P	1. This looks like a bat, prehistoric.	
W M+ (H)	2. Fantasia monster, hands upraised; early crude attempt at flying, tying bat wings to his body. That's about all.—1′30″ [total time]	2. Belt and clasp; hands and arms and bat wings attached. Smooth brown umbrella-silk material.

* The subject's reaction time, from presentation to first scorable response.

Card II. (laughs) 10″

W MC+ H P   1. Can-can dancers playing pattycake.   1. Cigarette; hairdo. Fluffy
                      Peculiar kind of head-dress and red   petticoat business down
                      stockings . . . That's all. That's just   here.   Impressionistic.
                      very queer.—50″   Gaité Parisienne satin
                                                                    dresses.

Card III. 5″

W MC+ H P   1. Two waiters bowing to each other.   1. I always go back to con-
(FC′ tendency)   Each one carrying a basket of candy   crete things I have seen.
                      or something. . . . They have high   White wing collar, high
                      heeled shoes on. The rest doesn't   shoes.
                      seem to be important.—1′5″
                                                                 2. [an additional response
                                                                    made during inquiry]
W M± H   ∨ * Aviator with gog-
                                                                    gles, upraised hands.

Card IV. 7″

W FCh+ Ad P   1. Bear skin rug.—30″   1. Fuzzy side turned back
                                                                    on edges.

Card V. 7″

W′ F+ A P   1. Same as first one. Some kind of a
                      bat or an insect with antenna up
                      here and leg down to the side.
D F+ Hd   2. A girl's leg minus the foot over here,
                      her knee here.—1′35″

Card VI. 5″

D FCh+ Obj   1. The only thing I see in that is a   1. Woven rug.
                      certain Navajo Indian design and
D FCh+ Ad P   2. bear skin underneath—that's—that's   2. Peculiar skin of an ani-
                      all.—1′30″   mal at the top; it got
                                                                    woven.

Card VII. 5″

D M+ H P   1. Little boys making faces at each
                      other.
D F± Map   2. All four of these upper bodies look
D F± Map   3. like a map of South America.
W M+ H   4. Two women with hairdo gadget in   4. Nondescript gray clothes
(FC′ tendency)   back looking at each other . . .   on.
                      Curved back chair, curving in the
                      back. Sitting perhaps with their
                      knees touching.—1′35″

Card VIII. 5″

Ws MC(C)— H   1. Fu Manchu: Tartar with a beard and
                      a triangular hat on with his bloody
                      hands raised like this. A fur collar
                      on. Some kind of chain around
                      his neck. Looks pretty, disemboweled
                      himself.

* The subject may turn the card any way he wishes; the position of the card when he
gives a response is indicated by this ∧-sign, the point indicating the top of the blot. Unless
specifically indicated, the blots were upright, as presented.

D→W FM+ A P	2. > Perfect little mammal of some kind, a weasel or mountain animal jumping from one cliff to another on different ledges of rock.	
Dr→D F(C)± Hd, Obj	3. < Eurasian with fur cap, mouth wide open, short nose. An arrow has just been shot into his mouth. I don't know why I didn't think of turning them around like this.	3. (part of blue and darker center Dr).
Ds FC± At (CF tendency)	4. ∨ Vertebrae—skeleton of a woman's body; these are the 2 lungs and the vertebral column all through. —4′15″	4. pinky, fleshy mass (lungs).

Card IX. 20″

D F+ Ad	1. ∨ Elephants with their trunks together.	
D F± Pl (FC?)	2. Some trees.	
S F± At	3. In between, a skull.	
D F± Obj	4. In the center is an elephant hook. < ∧ Those same eyes I noticed the other way in the skull.—50″	
D M+ H P		5. [additional] Two old Chinamen with long fingernails looking at each other.

Card X. 10″

D FMC+ A	1. (laughs) Couple of mice holding up	1. Sort of mouse color.
D F+ Pl	2. a corn stalk.	
D F± Ats	3. Down here a section of a large intestine. < (laughs) These could be a whole bunch of medical diagrams:	3. (in area usually seen as a green worm)
D F+ Obj	4. Wishbone,	
Dr F∓ Ats (FC?)	5. Liver,	5. Doesn't look so much like a liver (side red)
Dr F∓ Ats	6. Appendix.	6. (tiny detail, outside lower end of worm)
D F± A	7. Double bodied caterpillar.	7. (green worm)
D F+ A (FM?)	8. Sheep—a ram with his horn, sitting down. ∨ That's about it. [E did not record the total time for card X.]	8. (upper green)

Morris' final comment on the test was: "It let me down completely. I thought I was not being original; annoyed me. I didn't see anything."

Scoring and Interpreting the Rorschach

The responses have been scored in the left-hand column of the protocol above according to the system worked out by Rorschach himself, as revised and extended by Rapaport (Rapaport, Gill, & Schafer, 1968). Though the scores are not necessarily the most important features of

Table 6-1   *Rorschach Summary ("Psychogram")*

Locations			Determinants			Content			Popular (P) Responses and Ratios	
W	8 ⎱ 9		F+	7		A	6 ⎱ 9		P	9
Ws	1 ⎰		F±	7		Ad	3 ⎰		(1 on each card except X)	
D	16 ⎱		F∓	2		H	7 ⎱		P%	29
Ds	1 ⎱ 18		F−	0		Hd	2 ⎱ 10			
D→W	1 ⎰		Total F	16		(H)	1 ⎰			
Dr→D	1 ⎱ 3		FM+	2		Obj	3 (4)		Other Ratios	
Dr	2 ⎰		M+	6 ⎱		Map	2		M:ΣC = 8:2.5	
S	1 (3)*		M±	1 ⎬ 8		At	2 ⎱ 5		F%	52/100
	31		M−	1 ⎰		Ats	3 ⎰		F+%	87
			FC+	(3) ⎤		Pl	2		A%	29
			FC∓	1 ⎬ 1 (5)			31		H%	32
			FC−	(1) ⎦					AT%	16
			FCh+	3					W%	29
			F(C)+	1 ⎱ 1 (2)					D%	58
			F(C)−	(1) ⎰					DR%	13
				31						

R (total number of responses) = 31

*Parenthetical numbers indicate frequency of secondary determinants. Thus, the MC(C)− on card VIII is tallied as M−:1, but also as FC−:(1) and F(C)−:(1).

KEY TO SYMBOLS

Locations

W   Whole blot
D   Large, common detail
Dr   Rare detail
S, s   White space (large or small portions)

D→W   A response primarily based on one detail but extended to include the entire blot

Dr→D   From a small part to all of a large, common detail

Determinants

F   Form
FM   Animals seen in movement
M   Human movement

C   Chromatic color
C'   Achromatic color
Ch   Chiaroscuro (gray shading)
(C)   Shading in a chromatic area

Note: Form may be combined with the color or shading scores, the order of the symbols indicating which predominates in determining the response. Thus, in FC the form is definitive; in CF form is vague and the color impression strong; and in C form plays no part.

Form Level (accuracy of match between the subject's concept and the blot area he chooses)

+   Sharp, accurate match between concept and blot, easily seen by E
±   Reasonably good fit with some weakness of perceptual organization (included in F+%)
∓   Poor match but with some redeeming features
−   Arbitrary response with little or no convincing resemblance between concept and blot

Content

A   Animal
Ad   Part (detail) of an animal
H   Human being
Hd   Part of a person
(H)   Quasihuman beings (monstrous, mythological, or the like)

Obj   Object
At   Bony anatomy
Ats   Soft anatomy
Pl   Plant

DR%   Percentage of all responses to unusual areas (including *Dr* and *S*)

AT%   Percentage of all anatomical responses (including both *At* and *Ats*)

F%   The first figure is the proportion of all responses determined by form alone; the second is the proportion of all responses in which form is predominant.

M:ΣC   This ratio of the number of *M* responses to the weighted total of color responses is always written thus, not as a percentage. FC responses are weighted ½, CF 1, and C 1½.

the responses, they form a conventional starting point for the interpreter; Table 6-1 summarizes the scores in what is usually called a *psychogram*.

There are 31 responses, fewer than might have been expected from Morris' very superior I.Q. and his verbal productiveness in part of the TAT. But Morris is an extrovert who does not feel particularly at home in tasks requiring imagination; for example, his final, self-critical comment about his lack of originality is similar to complaints in the TAT ("I must have a very trite brain"). Actually, the responses are an interesting mixture of the original and the banal. He is capable of such a well-observed, integrated whole response as the second one to card I and of a couple of highly original but pathological-sounding ones (card VIII, 1 and 3), yet he seems to push himself to produce, and often comes out with relatively "cheap" responses, giving a rather high proportion (about 30 percent) of interpretations that are very commonly seen, or *popular* (scored P). This mixture parallels the pattern that emerged in his TAT stories, and represents the quality of Morris' thought rather well. He certainly has the common touch, which is probably more important for his work than creative originality. And the accuracy of his form perception ($F+\%$ of 87) implies good contact with reality.

Location. The first letter in the string of symbols that constitutes the full score of a response (W, D, Dr, and so on) indicates where Morris saw whatever he reported. On the first four cards, he responded only to the whole blot (W), which is not uncommon for people of his intelligence who are not highly productive; when he got the idea that he could use the large, easily segregated details (D), he responded mostly to them, and occasionally to rare details (Dr) or parts of the white space (S). The distribution of his location scores altogether is not remarkable, being roughly within average expectations; perhaps the 13 percent of all rare details he reacted to is enough above the average expectation (about 5 to 10 percent) for a record of this size to lend weak support to the TAT indication of a basically compulsive defensive style. This interpretation is based on statistical inference as well as on theoretical expectations: Part of the compulsive style is meticulousness, a concern for fine points. Although that quality is not obviously characteristic of Morris, it is present to a noticeable degree if one looks for it; recall his tendency to pick out details of the TAT pictures and infer story content from them, as in his first story, and his detailed expense accounts (Chapter 5, page 109).

Determinants. The second group of letters in the full scores represent the determinants. Half the responses were determined by form (*F*) alone, which is somewhat below the average; on the other hand, there was not a single response in which form or shape was not the primary determinant. Otherwise put, Morris described only things that have definitive shapes, instead of including vaguely shaped content like clouds or blood spots, or offering amorphous responses like "sky" or "springtime," in which color or some attribute of the blots other than shape sets off the association.

According to the tradition of Rorschach interpretation, Morris' pattern suggests tight control under an appearance of easy responsiveness. Again, we know this to be characteristic of him: Morris was much concerned about self-control and the task of striving for it, despite a superficial appearance of easygoing, ready responsivity. Such an effort for control is another Rorschach indicator of a compulsive ego structure, and his large number of human-movement (*M*) responses supports the inference. When Morris responded, with moderate frequency, to the color of the blots, it was only in a controlled way; the color impression was subordinated to and controlled within the framework of a definitive form (*FC*). This suggests a socially adaptable, compliant, and cooperative person; again, no news, but what we know of Morris supports the traditional interpretation. The fact that two of his five *FC* responses were inaccurately seen is consistent with the occasionally forced quality of his social adaptation.

Content. The third column of symbols consists of abbreviations for content, the general class of things seen. The most frequent content category in Morris' responses is the human (*H, Hd,* and (*H*) for the monster on card I); a third of his responses are of this kind. The implication here is congruent with his fairly high score on the Social value (Allport-Vernon): He is strongly interested in people. Other frequent scores are for animals (the percentage of *A* is 29, about average) and for anatomy (16 percent or more—some would include two extra scores on card VIII). The rather high *AT* percentage suggests an underlying bodily concern, which is given particular point by the content of three responses that did not happen to be scored either *At* or *Ats* (hard or soft anatomy)—the "girl's leg minus the foot" on card V, a classical symbol of castration anxiety, and the two gory images of deadly wounds to human beings on card VIII, the first of them self-inflicted.

Sequence analysis. Let us consider the series of responses to card VIII in a little more detail and sequentially, a technique of interpretation called *sequence analysis.* Card VIII presents the first blot to be made up entirely of colored inks; it therefore produces a strong visual impact. The prevailing assumption is that people tend to react to such a vivid, "compelling" stimulus in the same way they cope with the inner impact of impulses and affects. Morris was not slowed up; his excellent intellect immediately supplied him with a highly original, strong, though quite inaccurate, integration of the disparate parts of the blot. Fu Manchu, a fictional character in a series of novels, represents a literary association that has a distinctly lower-middle-class flavor and thus reflects the intellectual limitations of Morris' precollege milieu. This rather frightening, sinister figure with upraised bloody hands was controlled, not realistically (the form level is minus), but in a way familiar to us from Morris' TAT—by being put at a great distance in terms of geographic location, ethnic identity, and level of reality.

Then an even more pathological-sounding defensive attempt ensued: Morris saw the sinister figure as just having disemboweled himself. This sequence is reminiscent of his own development from an aggressive, pugnacious child to a timid older boy who turned his aggression against himself. The inappropriate attempt to laugh it off ("Looks pretty") has the same quality as his laughter in story 16 of the TAT, where the hero was also the victim of bodily mutilation; again, this reaction suggests a defense that protects Morris from fully experiencing his own affects.

Despite his poor control of this masochistic response, Morris was able to make a quick recovery and give a good popular response, which he obviously enjoyed. Immediately afterward, he returned to the realm of pathological fantasy, using again the defense that made the person he visualized— a Eurasian with an arrow shot into his mouth—quite remote from himself. This third response, like the first one, is strikingly original; but it is better justified by the form of the blot, and it was handled more calmly. It suggests an underlying homosexual preoccupation as well as the same self-directed aggression; this interpretation is somewhat supported by the final response, a safely intellectualized and disguised image of aggression turned against a woman. There is, of course, nothing about lungs or vertebrae to indicate sex, yet he said that they were part of a woman's body. (Perhaps it is relevant to note here that the examiner was a very attractive young woman.)

Another point that is well to keep in mind, particularly with reference to responses 1 and 3, is that the Rorschach was given just before Morris was inducted into the armed services, at a time when America was involved in a bloody war that was precipitated by an attack by an oriental power. The thoughts of young men of draft age at that time often dwelt on the possibility of severe bodily injury.

An Overview of the Rorschach

Some of the main ways a Rorschach is interpreted have been exemplified above. Clearly, when the responses are treated as if they were comparable to dream symbols, as was just illustrated, speculation may soar. So long as it is regarded as a source of hypotheses to be checked against other data, such speculation can be useful to an assessor of personality. He must guard, however, against a tendency to become enchanted with his own ingenuity and to treat such shaky extrapolations as true findings.

On the whole, the Rorschach furnished many bits of evidence corroborating points inferred from the TAT. Most of what it rather directly suggests is confirmed by the case history and the other tests; but it adds little that is new, at least on the issues of major interest. What shows up more clearly here than in the TAT is the somewhat sloppy cognitive style that limited Morris' intellectual achievements: a quality of slipperiness, a slight fluidity, and an occasional tendency for ideas to interpenetrate (for example, the two responses to card VI—or is it just one?), all of which made it difficult to pin him down precisely. From the perspective of the test alone it is difficult to evaluate this quality of cognitive style properly, but it contributes to the impression given by many of the responses, when closely examined, that the subject was to some extent seriously disturbed.

FREE ASSOCIATION

The therapeutic and investigative technique of free association, developed by Sigmund Freud, can be a valuable form of assessment, though it is rarely used outside the context of professional psychoanalytic treatment. With some stretching, it may be classified with projective techniques because many of the interpretive principles and methods used in the analysis of free associations, TAT stories, and Rorschach responses are the same. The procedure is deceptively simple. The subject is asked to stretch out on a couch in a softly lighted room; the examiner sits out of his line of sight. The instructions to the subject are to let his thoughts move freely and to say everything that comes to mind, without censoring it on any grounds.

Many psychoanalysts use the first session of psychoanalytic treatment for purposes of additional diagnostic assessment (beyond the appraisal of the patient that always precedes the start of treatment).They rightly object to the use of free association by psychologists who have not been trained in psychoanalysis, because it may release powerful emotional reactions with which the examiner is unprepared to deal as a therapist may. In the case of Morris Brown, the investigators' very ignorance encouraged them to try it; and they were fortunate in that Morris was able to go through two such sessions of approximately an hour each without becoming particularly upset and without the development of unmanageable emotional reactions to themselves.

**Examples of Data
and Interpretation** The data (which were written down in longhand notes as faithfully as possible) are not presented here in full; but certain passages can provide corroboration of hypotheses drawn from the TAT stories.

In the first session, Morris moved from thinking about the process of free association to the idea of being able to read minds: "It would be an awful power, wouldn't want anyone to have that power over me. (pause) Something in the sex business is sort of funny." He related a conversation he had had with a busboy at a bar, about (hetero-) sex, adding two thoughts about him:

1. Raise his sights a little, get him a good job; 2. If I wanted to make a pass at him I could—comes up when I've had about 5 drinks—never done anything about it, never would. Because if I had inclinations I think I sometimes have on that stuff I wouldn't hesitate. Conscience stirring within you—two weekends ago, up at the cabin—it would have been so damn nice to have Alison there. When I get it built I've got to get a woman for it: after finishing the cage, get a bird for it. Do you ever do any sailing?

He then spoke about a recent sailing trip: "Don't know why I got so seasick. I came close to chucking up" (laughs).

Notice here that the theme of power and domination makes him think of sex and a homosexual impulse he has been restraining. It is closely related to a nurturant, parental kind of concern for a younger man. Then his conscience objects and he thinks (presumably as he knows he should) of Alison, the focus of his distant, romantic ("sacred") love fantasies, but he comes back to the theme of domination in the metaphor about the bird and the cage. The next thought concerns a physical manifestation of disgust. (Compare this sequence with the similar one in TAT story 22.)

A similar sequence of themes came out toward the end of the same session:

Morris first spoke of a man he knows: "just got married—birth control—cesspool," whereupon he sat up and said loudly, "Boy, if you tie those up you're a hot one!" After a pause, he mentioned "sugar" and some other kinds of food, then: "playing tag at the 'Y' pool. Jim, hot shower Saturday night. Swimming practice. George, poor guy, what a damn fool he was when he married."

The close association of heterosexuality with the disgusting image of a cesspool (perhaps mediated by the "messiness" of birth control) was too obvious for Morris himself to miss, but he reacted as if it were only a surprising concatenation of unrelated ideas. An oral wish then obtruded itself, followed by an indirect (perhaps sublimated) homosexual thought about one of his favorite activities, where he sees many men in the nude. The reversion of thought to marriage was followed once again by a strongly rejective sentiment.

In the second free-association hour, Morris' thoughts were preoccupied with two seemingly unrelated topics—money and sex (but see TAT story 14); he also mentioned travel several times. On this occasion, there was much less evidence of homosexual desires; the relations with men he mentioned were competitive and unsuccessful. As in the second TAT session, he had a headache. He seemed to feel under considerable pressure about his debts (a theme that had appeared in the earlier hour) and cast about for a source of funds:

> "So much money—Red Cross—no. Blood transfusion—no, last one hit me. Home." A moment later, "where you gonna get any money this time of year. I don't know. Communism—amputation." After more stewing about possible securities sales: "That's the trouble—I sit around and think about the big clients I could get instead of getting out and working my ass off."

Although the themes of money and of girls who might be possible sexual objects wove in and out throughout this session, it is hard to see just how they were connected in his mind; perhaps it was through the common theme of *getting* something. The experience of being pressured by external demands on him for money may have stirred up aggressive feelings, which were then turned against himself (the headache and the castrative theme of an amputation), because he was feeling a lack of self-confidence and competence. He was struggling with a conflict between the knowledge that he should force himself to go after some big deals and the frequently expressed wish to travel—to escape into irresponsibility.

A COMMENT ON THE PROJECTIVE ASSESSMENT OF MORRIS BROWN

The case of Morris Brown is an excellent example of what is at once a characteristic strength and weakness of projective techniques: They tend to highlight pathological trends. At times, that is a useful property, particularly when an attempt is made to diagnose a person who is very guarded but is suspected on other grounds of being seriously maladjusted. At other times, however, this property can lead to serious overestimation of the degree to which a person is disturbed, especially if diagnosis is based entirely on projective tests analyzed without the benefit of a clinical history.

In this instance, the facts as they could be learned through extended and fairly intimate conversation and through objective tests were deliberately presented before the projective techniques. Treated in this order, these techniques can contribute a useful increment of hypotheses, and other knowledge can act as a protection against jumping to conclusions that the subject must have been very "sick" at the time.

In the presentations of the objective tests used with Morris Brown, quantitative data were given on the reliability and validity of their scores, but no such figures appear in the sections on projective techniques. One reason is that the scores themselves play a much less prominent role in the latter; another reason is that both scores and qualitative data lend themselves to a great range of interpretations. Properly speaking, each interpretive principle or inferential hypothesis used to interpret the TAT and the Rorschach should be the subject of a validation study, but obviously such research would be difficult (see, however, Lindzey, 1952). Without some sort of time machine we cannot get direct observations to verify some of the developmental hypotheses, and it is virtually impossible to get direct data for the many interpretations that deal with unconscious configurations. The best we can usually do is to look for the convergence of independent sources of data, as in the parallels between projective test data and free associations that have just been pointed out. Seeking such convergences is the first step in the *synthesis* of a case history, to which the next chapter is devoted.

He . . . overhauled his room, wrote out resolutions, marshalled his books up and down their shelves, pored upon all kinds of price lists . . . tried to build a breakwater of order and elegance against the sordid tide of life without him and to dam up, by rules of conduct and active interests and new filial relations, the powerful recurrence of the tides within him.

JAMES JOYCE. A Portrait of the Artist as a Young Man

CHAPTER 7
THE SYNTHESIS OF DIVERSE DATA ON PERSONALITY

N o matter how large a file of tests, personal documents, interviews, and what-not is compiled on a person, and no matter how well the sources agree, the data do not pull themselves together. To synthesize such materials is something of an art, and doubtless always will be.

How Data on Personality
Are Synthesized

The basic procedure is to look for agreements and disagreements on the level of primary inferences from the various individual procedures. When agreement, or convergence, emerges, our confidence in the validity of the indicators increases. When there are seeming contradictions, we may first examine the validity of the conflicting indicators with a skeptical but open mind; occasionally we will simply discover that one is right and the other wrong. More usually, both will be partly right, but they may be operating under the confusing influence of some condition that we had not paid enough attention to before. Or other kinds of hypotheses may suggest ways to reconcile both points of view in a larger synthesis.

As we start our synthesis, we enter the realm of *secondary inference*. We are no longer reasoning directly from test scores or the subject's statements but from our previously (although tentatively) established primary inferences about his personality traits. The process of fitting the pieces together shows us gaps to be filled by going back to the raw data or by making changes in some of the more dubious primary inferences, so that they fit the emerging schema. If the synthesis is well done, a very high proportion of the primary inferences can be used directly or can be fitted in, sometimes in surprising ways.

Of course, it takes more than cleverness to develop a schema of secondary inferences: The process must be guided by a theory of personality. Of currently available theories, psychoanalysis is the richest with relevant principles and generalizations; it is the theory that will be drawn on most heavily in this chapter.

What follows is a synthesis of the case of Morris Brown, in which we may be able to see how the data and inferences developed to this point from both objective and subjective procedures can be put together. Although many of the formulations will be more or less factual, and although others will come from the confluence of several streams of evidence, this sketch is still largely constructed of hypotheses. Some of the most important ones, in terms of their function of bringing together several disparate kinds of facts about Morris and making common sense of them, will be plausible speculative constructions for which there is no *direct* evidence. But that is the nature of personality assessment: At best, it is a matter of obtaining a closer approximation to a receding, never securely attained truth.

An Integrative Summary
of the Case of Morris Brown at Age 26

THE RAW MATERIALS

Physique
and Constitution   One of Morris' great assets is his tough, solid, manly, and well-coordinated body. Morris' constitutional endowment seems to include natural athletic ability as well as sheer strength and sturdiness, and great energy and endurance. He was thus automatically protected from many of the troubles that beset boys with weaker frames. He appears to have been naturally resistant to most diseases and rugged enough in bone to have gone through a good deal of rough and tumble without incapacitating accidents. In general, he was endowed with natural competence in bodily matters, and as he was neither strikingly handsome nor ugly, he was spared the problems that accompany a very deviant physical appearance.

Abilities　　In regard to the most important ability, general intelligence, Morris Brown was also well endowed: His I.Q. of about 145 easily surpasses that of 99 people out of every hundred in the general population. This intellectual gift supplemented his outstanding physical abilities as a guarantee of competence; it assured him educational and vocational success, unless he were seriously crippled in some other way.

Morris had no other obvious and outstanding abilities or talents, nor was he notably lacking in any special ability that might have played a role in his general adaptation.

Temperament　　Temperament is considered to be a person's largely innate endowment of emotional and energetic characteristics. It is difficult to summarize because just what personal qualities constitute this endowment has not yet been determined. Nevertheless, Sheldonian analysis and some of the questionnaires agree in finding the cycloid (or cyclothymic) characteristics typically associated with his kind of physique: He tended to be outgoing rather than withdrawn, extroverted rather than introverted, and in general exuberant, energetic, and buoyant, but he also suffered periods of mild depression. His friendliness, readily available warmth, and emotional display, though they seemed shallow, were all cyclothymic qualities. Morris' temperamental (as well as constitutional) qualities seem definitely masculine. Certainly his mother's description of his stubbornly persistent, aggressive, and generally rambunctious behavior in his preschool years is that of a very boyish little boy.

Cultural Tradition　　The raw materials for the formation of a personality that are contributed from cultural sources are among the most elusive to a person working within the same culture. We know, however, that Mrs. Brown had a sense of identity with "a fine old family," that she treasured certain ideals of gentility, *noblesse oblige,* integrity, and altruism. It is clear that she struggled to maintain these ideals and to prevent Morris from slipping in the class hierarchy as he grew up in a deteriorating neighborhood. That he was a WASP Yankee was an important fact about Morris in the same kind of quiet, almost negative sense as was his freedom from serious medical problems: For a boy growing up in a small city in eastern America, it was the least troublesome kind of ethnic and cultural identity to have.

Mrs. Brown's marginal position and her fight against downward mobility, however, inevitably contributed to a conflict between the boy and his mother and caused her to try constantly to block his natural social impulses, which were to play with and identify himself with the children in the neighborhood. Moreover, in grade school Morris' self-esteem probably suffered more than it was enhanced because of his cultural identity: His Polish-

American classmates rejected him for belonging to a group considered socially "superior" to them.

Family Members   It would be ideal to have direct information about Mr. and Mrs. Brown instead of having to rely on what can be pieced together from their son, who certainly could not be disinterested or impartial. Fortunately, the very circumstances of their lives tend to confirm most of what Morris said directly or indirectly about their personalities.

The major facts about the father were that he was so unreliably present for Morris' first eight, crucially formative, years, and that he thereafter deserted the family. Information available only recently reveals that he was brilliant: He earned a Phi Beta Kappa key at a fine university and graduated later from an equally well-known Protestant seminary. Yet the elder Brown refused both a fellowship for advanced study and a congregation; he was a YMCA secretary for a number of years but tended to drift from job to job. His marriage to Morris' mother seems to have been motivated by expediency on both sides rather than by any depth of love; they needed each other for external reasons rather than for what they could give each other emotionally. The father, at least, seems never to have been deeply committed to the marriage or to his children. His image is that of a self-centered seeker after easy money and direct gratifications.

The following is a list of his father's traits that also seem to have been present in Morris at age 26:

> Enthusiastic, impatient, independent, lacked closeness to family, little capacity to give love, tended to avoid difficulties, footloose (loved travel), disliked long-term planning, self-centered, highly intelligent.

In addition, Morris was struggling to control the following tendencies, which were prominent in his father's personality:

> Impractical about money, speculative, undependable and irresponsible, unconscientious (hated routine).

Mrs. Brown was an anxious, hard-working, often tearful woman who was forced to bear heavy burdens and who must have had extraordinary inner strength to persevere and achieve as much success as she did. Despite poor health and three children to care for, one of whom (Morris) was difficult to manage, she supported the family by converting her home into a rooming house. She provided private schooling for the girls, gave Morris as many cultural advantages as she could to afford him contact with his peers of a class higher than that in the neighborhood, put him and the younger of his two sisters through colleges with the highest prestige, and in general kept up appearances despite many rebuffs to her self-esteem and to her feeling of being lovable. She seems to have possessed a unique mixture of masochism and strength, which may have been transmitted in subtle ways to her son.

The following traits, clearly discernible in the Morris Brown of 1940, he shared with his mother:

Concern about money, concern about appearances (present in Morris' projective tests though not superficially obvious), insecurity, sensitivity to rejection, anxiety about maintaining status identity (in Morris' case, about how to avoid having other people think he was Jewish).

GENETIC HYPOTHESES

If we put the elements above together, guided by what we know from the historical facts in Chapter 5 and the insights afforded by the interpretation of clinical data such as the TAT, it becomes possible to construct some plausible theories about what caused Morris to develop as he did. For lack of adequate data, it will be necessary to pass much more quickly over the earliest years than psychoanalytic theory would suggest.

The Maternal Relationship   The very fact that Mrs. Brown made so many careful entries in Morris' baby books and that she kept them so long are evidence both of her compulsiveness and of her devotion. It is easy to imagine how precious the first months of nursing and of Morris' complete dependence must have been to this woman, who for years may have longed to have a baby and who probably had given up even the hope of marriage. His delay in talking suggests that this early *symbiotic* relationship (that is, one of great mutual involvement and dependence) was unusually prolonged by her slavish devotion. This hypothesis would also help account for his pattern of resisting his mother and trying to push her away, which began early and was still strong at age 26.

Yet by satisfying his wants so completely in the first period of life, Morris' mother laid the foundation for his sense of basic trust (Erikson, 1959), his feeling that the world is ultimately a pretty good place and likely to yield satisfactions. We can never know how much of Morris' optimism and energy is attributable to this good start in the oral phase and how much is genetically determined, but surely these qualities go back very far. The history also shows us that from the beginning he had strong oral needs; apparently the basic mode of *getting* was strongly reinforced and pervaded much of Morris' subsequent life.

At a fairly early age, Morris began to have tantrums. A small child's tantrums are an exhausting ordeal for him as well as for his mother. In light of this fact, Mrs. Brown unwittingly failed Morris by her inability to cope with his tantrums and to give him an external model of control and calmness, from which he in turn could borrow strength. His tantrums and their consequences probably laid a foundation for Morris' fear of his own anger and for his inability to let himself go in later childhood when he could have gained self-respect by becoming the rugged scrapper he was otherwise cut out to be. These hypothetical constructions also help us to understand better the projective test indications of a savage, primitive superego and unconscious masochistic fantasies in a man of 26 who was still struggling to complete the task of getting control over himself: If a child's tantrums are uncontrolled, the exhaustion and pain that result forcibly demonstrate that when anger is aroused it turns against oneself.

The Paternal Relationship

Mrs. Brown's intuitive feeling that her husband should have been more active in controlling Morris may have been correct. As Morris grew older and needed to develop more of a sense of what it was to be a male person, his father was simply not there enough to set the example of strong masterfulness that our culture calls for a man to aspire to.

According to Morris' conscious recollections, his father was easygoing, companionable, certainly not punitive. And yet his projective test productions consistently present images of frightful, remote, overwhelmingly evil father figures, which one would expect to be the residue of terrifying experiences of sudden, arbitrary, and severe punishment in early childhood. If we consider what we know about the father—his self-indulgence and disinclination to accept the more distasteful aspects of familial responsibility— it is easy to understand how he must have resisted being the awesome authority figure who meted out just punishment for the day's sins when he arrived home each night. But is it not also probable that such a man would have had little patience with a demanding, noisy, highly active, and headstrong little boy during the second and third years, when Morris had less inner control and a more effective motor apparatus for causing trouble than most boys his age? Although Morris himself did not remember such experiences, the unempathic Mr. Brown may well have lost his temper easily, doling out unpredictable cuffs and slaps, which might have hurt all the more coming from a father who was seldom around.

Undoubtedly, one of the most important events in Morris' life was being abandoned by his father. It must have been a major blow to his developing a feeling that he could be loved, a traumatic experience that was rekindled with every subsequent rejection by anyone he cared about. Each such episode thus became an occasion of poignant grief. To take the place of a man about whom he had mostly fond conscious memories, he started turning to father substitutes: the Sunday school teacher who was his hero, the boys (generally older than himself during adolescence) on whom he had crushes, and finally, at about the time of the assessment in 1940, a Catholic priest with whom he had many long talks. (Curiously, though he mentioned a recently developed strong interest in Catholicism, he did not at that time tell the investigators about this "father.") The urge to travel may have been in part an identification with his father and in part an effort to find him (which he actually succeeded in doing on one occasion). It is worth mentioning in passing that he had no living grandfathers, and none of his several uncles assumed a supportive paternal role that might have substituted for the loss of his father.

Sexual Behavior   During the preschool years, Morris was in a dangerous situation: He was the dominant member in a household with three females, where the father's presence was unpredictable and infrequent. Proper as she was, Mrs. Brown must have transmitted the incest taboo clearly enough, discouraging too intrusive or bodily a closeness but at the same time inevitably trying in subtle ways to make her son stand in the place of his father. Ideally Morris would have given her great quantities of devoted but quite desexualized affection to help fill the void left by her uninterested husband. Instead, it seems likely that he fought off her enveloping tenderness and showed some openly sexual interest in her and in his sisters.

We do not know the timing of Morris' two operations, for tonsils and adenoids, but if either of them happened to come at a time of awakened sexual intrusiveness, which is normal in little boys, it might very well have been the sort of real event that can leave the lasting scar of castration anxiety.

From what we know of it, Morris' sexual behavior in childhood seems to have been normal, with enough emphasis on peeping to suggest that his sexual curiosity was quite active. Psychoanalysts generally find that when people easily recall having seen their parents in the act of intercourse during childhood, as Morris did at age 8, the memory is a screen for an earlier, repressed, and more traumatic instance of this *primal scene*. The feeling of not understanding what was going on, attached to the conscious memory, may be a displaced and toned-down version of a more intense bewilderment and anxiety from an earlier exposure. Memories of such episodes, according to psychoanalytic clinical observations, may often cause the later behavior of mutual display. In addition, the child typically interprets the memories in sado-masochistic terms; that is, he believes that the parents are hurting each other in this strange act. This interpretation can cause considerable fear of heterosexual intercourse and of the intimacies leading up to it.

From these speculative inferences, it is possible to formulate the following theory about the development of sexual patterns in Morris. His native endowment seems to have been essentially masculine; his lack of effeminate prettiness or weakness of frame and his temperamentally active and hardy bent for such manly activities as sports may have saved him from becoming a confirmed, overt homosexual. Yet there are strongly feminine elements in his make-up, derived from identification with his mother in the absence of his father. At the same time, Morris became fearful of making sexual approaches to girls because of the combination of fearing his father's unpredictable wrath, learning that the women of the family were all sexually taboo (despite the seductiveness implied in his mother's need for him and in his sisters' playing doctor with him), and developing a deep anxiety about bodily mutilation that unconsciously probably meant castration.

Although it is not known at what point Morris learned to control his temper, it was not a secure control that enabled him to use aggression in the service of manliness. In fact, his struggle to control his anger seems to have ended in his turning it against himself. One result was probably a generalization to heterosexual impulses of the anxiety Morris felt about hostile impulses. The lack of easy opportunities to be with eligible girls and the availability of boys helped to initiate his pleasurable sexual activity with persons who were reassuringly like himself in having penises.

During childhood Morris' superior intelligence undid the advantage his superior physique might have given him, pushing him ahead so that for a time he was no match for his classmates either physically or socially. His inferiority and anxiety, both bodily and social, caused him uncharacteristically (though temporarily) to become a sissy and to withdraw socially at around the time of his father's final departure. This pattern, and the fact that he had been somewhat isolated from other children, prevented him from developing social skills.

Not to paint too black a picture, we should keep in mind that Morris' feeling of worth and competence must have been bolstered by the recognition he no doubt received for being a good student most of the time. And with adolescence, his bodily prowess began to assert itself, so that he was able to attain even more self-respect and esteem from others through his outstanding performance in sports. He still had a strong need for autonomy, which helped him fight back against feelings of desertion by going places quite on his own.

MORRIS BROWN'S PERSONALITY PATTERN
(AS OF 1940–41)

Defensive Organization
("Ego Structure") Morris' major defenses are a variant form of obsessive-compulsive reactions. His main goal was self-control; and he was beginning to attain it relatively late, using compulsive, ritualistic devices to aid himself, just as Joyce's hero did in *A Portrait of the Artist as a Young Man*. Because of his ability to isolate feelings from ideas, Morris was able to talk easily about very disturbing matters. His unusual defense against homosexuality also relied on isolation: He knew what homosexuality was, he knew its socially condemned status, and he knew what kinds of acts he had performed with men; but somehow he was able to keep these pieces of knowledge rather confusedly unintegrated, so that he never looked squarely at the total pattern and hence never saw himself as a homosexual. His emphases on reason and rationality

and on using his good mind to collect information were parts of an intellectualizing and rationalizing defense.

There were, as we have seen, paradoxes and inconsistencies in his use of these defenses. Certainly they were not developed to a high degree of elaboration: He was not erudite, ruminative, rigid, or especially orderly. The compulsive's concern with time and his proclivity for delaying gratification did not fit in with Morris' impatience for quick action in sexual contacts and his wish to get rich quick by speculation. Moreover, his style of intellectualizing was somewhat roughhewn, not what one would have expected of an average Ivy League graduate; he would have liked to seem an urbane intellectual sophisticate and occasionally made some efforts in this direction. These intellectualizing aspects of the compulsive ego structure had developed late in Morris, for he had not grown up in a home that especially valued ideas, conceptual and verbal precision, and subtle distinctions. As a result there was some strain and inappropriateness in his efforts to be *au courant* culturally.

Part of the reason for the atypical organization of his compulsive defenses was the early development of another, somewhat contradictory, set, based on his physical attributes rather than on his mental prowess. In adolescence, Morris found that he could escape anxiety and boredom through action, especially adventurous activity that took him into the teeth of the dangers he feared. He had a capacity for introspection but tended to turn away from it, to rely on his extroverted interest in the actual world of things and activities to take him out of himself. The result was a mixture of acting out, counterphobic defense (mastering anxiety by taking pleasure in what had been feared), evasion, and avoidance, which together tend to eliminate the subtleties and depths of emotional experience in favor of immediate excitement. His self-centeredness, his tendency to be flippant or inappropriately jocular in the face of unpleasant feelings like sadness, and his inclination to exploit others while giving little in return, all fitted in with the acting-out defenses to suggest the personality pattern of someone with a narcissistic character disorder. Yet none of these trends were very strongly developed or rigidly applied.

Thus, two antithetical defensive organizations were present in Morris, alternating in prominence. The second, narcissistic pattern stressed quick gratification of rather selfish impulses (getting something for nothing), cynicism about moral values, an avoidance of anxiety, and evasion of responsibility. The first pattern, which seemed to be in the ascendant, included a conscientious effort at self-improvement and hard work, an attempt to prevent anxiety by organizing his life, an effort to work out and live up to a rational moral code of his own, and a seeking of responsibility. It is tempting, though perhaps oversimple, to connect the compulsive pattern to his identification with his mother, the narcissistic to his paternal identification.

Finally, some signs of a cyclothymic ego structure are evident—in his temperament, in his rather strong defense of denial, and in his tendency to turn aggression against himself. The latter defense did at times produce some depressive symptoms, but his tendency to deny depressed affect produced a generally prevalent *hypomanic* pattern (manic-like cheerfulness, energy, and activity, but within normal limits).

Organization of Thought and Speech   Though covered to some extent in the preceding section, Morris' cognitive style has some further features. He gave no sign of obsessional thinking; his thoughts tended toward the practical rather than toward highly abstract concepts. His thinking was for the most part orderly; but under the pressure of anxiety or conflict it often became somewhat fluid and elusive, and his use of words could become mildly confused and momentarily incoherent (apparently as part of a defensive maneuver to keep himself from confronting the source of his anxiety). He could at such times become aware of surprisingly gory, unrealistic ideas derived from unconscious sado-masochistic fantasies, taking rather gleeful pleasure in shocking others by means of them.

His style of talking was casual and informal to the point of occasional coarseness and poor taste; his conversation included a heavy admixture of slang and a light peppering of words from the upper reaches of a superior vocabulary. He did not use the latter in a pretentious way; because he knew them more from his reading than from conversation, such words not infrequently came out haltingly and mispronounced. Brown's speech tended to be rapid, often trailing off into swallowed or dangling phrases, spoken in a light baritone voice of mellow, rather than deeply resonant, timbre. But he had a ready flow of ideas and words, so that he could be persuasive with another person and effective as a public speaker. He was a pleasant if not a remarkable conversationalist.

Affects and Impulses   Morris readily displayed cheer and extroverted friendliness. He could—as his work required—easily meet people and impress them as "a good guy," normal and easygoing. He was, however, unwilling to take the risk of a full emotional investment in a close relationship. The fact that obligingness was a deliberate policy with him gave his adaptability a forced quality. For the most part he expressed appropriate feelings in predictable ways, while giving the impression of a somewhat limited emotional range. He would occasionally act out impulses, yet on the whole kept himself under rather tight control.

Motives   Morris had not yet made a number of important choices as far as his principal conscious and unconscious goals were concerned—another indication that he was in a transitional phase of development. Much as he strove to please and to be liked by everyone, he seemed to be leaning toward recognition, power, and money as substitutes for love. Voyeuristic conflicts and fixations in childhood sometimes stimulate an adult drive for learning and discovery; sometimes, however, they stimulate more of a concern about appearances, prestige, and status in the eyes of others—the outcome in Morris' case. Yet, paradoxically, his interest in recognition and acquisition did not result in a strong need for achievement. Perhaps the lack of a family tradition along these lines—that is, his father's spotty and erratic career and his mother's contentment in maintaining the status quo rather than advancing toward a higher status (directly or vicariously through pushing her son)—accounted for Morris' never having developed the typical businessman's insatiable drive.

As he saw it, Morris' main motive was to gain control over himself— a kind of power drive turned inward. His sexual drive was, as he recognized, stunted. He had an above-average urge to travel and seek adventure and excitement, which fitted in well with his constitution (though his degree of castration anxiety probably restrained him from becoming markedly counterphobic and going in for such dangerous thrills as skiing, shooting rapids, and the like). His urge to engage in vigorous bodily activity seemed a natural outgrowth of his physique, and in the direct competition of tennis and golf he found an adaptive outlet for his generally closed-off aggressive needs. Perhaps these needs were also expressed in the form of dominance in his drive to assume positions of leadership and to exercise his organizational talent. They contrasted with his interest in music and his enjoyment of nature.

Attitudes and Values

Like the great majority of his contemporaries, Morris was not ideologically committed. Nor was he actively engaged in working out a conscious philosophy of life for himself. He had liberal attitudes on most social issues, although he was sufficiently identified with the commercial world to have fairly conservative attitudes as well (for example, he opposed increased governmental control over business). He belonged to no political party, no religion, no organized social movement of consequence. In general, the Allport-Vernon test summed up his values rather well.

Relationships to Principal Figures

On the surface, Morris was impatient with his mother and felt like pulling away from what he considered to be her wishes to control and change him. But there are other signs of considerable underlying respect and affection for her and a growing identification with her. The letter written from camp when he was an adolescent (quoted on page 109 in Chapter 5) gives evidence of more positive feeling than he would have verbalized as such; he usually thought of her consciously in terms of what he could get from her. But in his mid-20's, Morris was beginning to assume for himself her role of controlling and attempting to improve him.

By this time, he seemed to have recovered from the wound of losing his father, who receded into a shadowy, still wistfully admired and pitied figure. Morris was more empathic and more willing to understand and forgive his father than a more bitter man might have been. In addition, he was no longer obviously seeking father substitutes. Though his occasional homosexual contacts may still have had some unconscious meaning of a search and propitiation, he was beginning to adopt a more parental role (recall the combined nurturant and sexual interest in the busboy, brought out in the free-association interview).

Morris' relationships to male and female peers have already been touched on; they were friendly, somewhat competitive, and occasionally exploitative, but not intimate.

Identity   Who and what was Morris in 1940? It is not possible to give a very clear answer to such questions, because he was not sure himself. At the root of his insecure sense of identity was his confused sexual identification. In addition, he had little feeling for his home town, where he had few friends, and he had no regional loyalty to speak of. In his latest locality, he had no roots, was only on the fringe of the academic world, and had not yet established a place for himself in a circle of friends.

His concern about being taken for a Jew signified a lack of a firm self-definition in ethnic, religious, or cultural terms; his family's marginal status, their clinging to the remnants of a lower-upper- or upper-middle-class position, which might be lost at any time, left him a heritage more of insecurity than of positive identity. As an outstanding young leader in civic affairs and in the business community, he hoped that others regarded him with respect, but he felt too newly arrived to believe in himself. He felt like an impostor with a secret, dirty, and shameful self—"if they only knew!"

Yet he believed in his athletic talent; his conception of himself as a good, perhaps someday an outstanding, golfer was a source of considerable self-esteem. It probably did not contribute much to his sense of maturity, however. Inwardly, Morris remained an adolescent at the age of 26, still on the threshold of the adult world, wondering if he had what it took to be accepted among the mothers and fathers, and half ready to cut loose and move on rather than let himself get thoroughly committed to anything.

Diagnostic
Formulation   The state of confusion and turmoil Morris was in does not approximate any standard diagnostic category, but it brings to mind the kind of condition described by Erikson (1959, 1963) as a *postadolescent identity crisis*. Morris was chron-

ologically in the time of young adulthood when his peers were rapidly finding life partners with whom to share an intimacy for which he was not yet ready, partly because he lacked an inner solidity from which to reach out to another. Instead, he was still grappling with the task of self-formulation his peers had mastered in adolescence. As Erikson and Anna Freud (1958) have taught us, a young man or woman who develops outside the mainstream in this way may go through a period of upheaval in which alarming signs of serious pathology are likely to appear—antisocial acting out, self-damaging sexual escapades, the temporary emergence of depersonalization and other near-psychotic symptoms, all of which may get the youth into serious trouble. Yet these same young people, if properly treated or if merely given a moratorium from having to assume the burdens of an adult role, may straighten out astonishingly well.

Morris' conflicts were typical of this condition: dependence on his mother versus rejection of her, need for the approval of others versus fear of involvement, resistance to external constraint and a deficiency in moral restraints versus a seeking for his own form of self-control and morality, and a deep confusion about himself growing out of his basic uncertainty about his sexual identity—am I a man? a woman? some kind of sexually deficient eunuch? All these problems were, as he vaguely realized, related to "growing up." And there was intuitive wisdom in his own sense of the priorities: It did make most sense for him to concentrate on getting himself in hand by building up his compulsive defenses before thinking about long-term goals and plans.

We should remember, too, that the historical era was one of considerable uncertainty and growing uneasiness for young men. World War II was a year old when our study of Morris Brown began; at the time he was given the Rorschach Test in 1942 America was already involved in the war and he himself was waiting until some minor medical matters were taken care of so that he could join the Navy as an officer candidate. These were troubled years, not a time when a physically fit man in his 20's could realistically plan many months ahead. The prospect of active participation in the war was something unknown, with great potentialities for making or breaking him, or even snuffing him out completely. Small wonder that Morris was inwardly at sea and rather desperately groping for the tiller!

This summary completes the first assessment of Morris Brown. The next two chapters will pick up his story and the evaluation of his personality after a lapse of 26 years.

Mankind is made up of inconsistencies, and no man acts invariably up to his predominant character. The wisest man sometimes acts weakly, and the weakest sometimes wisely.

LORD CHESTERFIELD. Letters to his son

CHAPTER 8
RECENT DEVELOPMENTS IN NONPROJECTIVE ASSESSMENT

During the past two decades—the period of clinical psychology's most dramatic growth—a number of new, nonprojective approaches to the assessment of personality have been developed by research psychologists in an effort to broaden the scope and to improve on the validity of existing tests. By mid-1964, there were at least 800 English-language tests in print that were of interest to assessors of personality. In addition to hundreds of tests of intelligence, other abilities and aptitudes, and vocational interests, there were 312 personality tests, of which about a third were projective techniques (Buros, 1965).

Among the nonprojective personality tests developed since the first assessment of Morris Brown were questionnaires such as the MMPI, the Eysenck Personality Inventory, and Lindzey's revision of the Study of Values; among intelligence tests, the Wechsler Adult Intelligence Scale. Tests of cognitive style (for example, leveling-sharpening and field articulation) and new types of rating scales such as Gough's Adjective Check List and various types of Q sorts (a rating technique described later in this chapter) also appeared. In contrast to the earlier tests, which were often put into use before being carefully appraised, many of the new instruments have received a sophisticated evaluation with respect to reliability, norms (the average performance of large, unselected samples of people), and to some extent, validity.

New Tests in a New Assessment

In this chapter, each of the techniques listed in the paragraph above will be described in some detail. Recently gathered data from a follow-up reassessment of Morris Brown will be used to illustrate some of the problems involved in evaluating the test results. First, however, an explanation should be given for the resumption of the case study of Morris Brown 26 years after the first assessment.

Shortly after World War II, Morris reestablished contact with one of the investigators * by means of Christmas cards, which were exchanged off and on thereafter. Notes on these cards related that Morris had seen combat in the Pacific with the Navy, had returned to the same city and the same securities business, was now concentrating on selling mutual funds, and in spite of one intense involvement had remained a bachelor. When he went into politics, he sent a piece of campaign literature, on which the smiling, plump face looked much as it had before the war. It seemed at the least that he had attained enough success and was now sufficiently well adjusted to be able to undergo an unusual experiment in self-confrontation.

Early in 1966 the investigator proposed that it would be fascinating for him and perhaps of interest to Morris if he would cooperate once again in an assessment of his personality. He would be given new tests and some of the old ones, and they would have long talks; he would see what was written and of course would have to give his approval before anything was published. Morris responded with alacrity and enthusiasm and evinced some of the old curiosity to see what he could learn about himself. He completed the inventories and questionnaires and mailed them before flying in for a weekend of intensive clinical assessment.

With his unusual pattern of assets and liabilities, which might have resulted in either good adaptation or severe maladjustment, Morris exemplifies Lord Chesterfield's remark: His inconsistent performance on the new tests and procedures is such that it is difficult to describe him or fit him into any general set of types.

The attempt made below to relate Morris' test findings to the standard procedures used in evaluating them will bring out quite clearly some of the weaknesses as well as the strengths of the nonprojective techniques, and the problems in interpreting them. The discussion starts off with the MMPI and some of its modifications and focuses attention on general problems in interpreting even the most intensively developed objective tests, when they are used in accordance with recent practice. Each of the other new techniques will then be examined in turn.

* That investigator is the author of this book.

Personality Questionnaires

THE MINNESOTA MULTIPHASIC
PERSONALITY INVENTORY

The MMPI, by S. R. Hathaway and J. C. McKinley (1943), is the most widely used of all personality questionnaires today and has been the object of extensive and continuing developmental efforts. As was pointed out in Chapter 4, the original MMPI has four "validity" scales and nine clinical scales concerned with pathological trends. Many of the approximately 1400 titles that would appear in a complete bibliography of this test report the development of new scales; over 200 are current, and more are being produced every year.

The MMPI's original claim to attention among inventories purporting to measure several traits (hence, "multiphasic") was the nature of its scales. They were derived by the method of empirical keying described in Chapter 4 (pages 68–70). Their names (see Figure 8-1 suggest direct and simple diagnostic use: Presumably, if the scales had been well constructed, a known schizophrenic's profile would peak at the *Sc* scale, and conversely anyone whose highest score was *Sc* (and was 70 or over) would be found to be a schizophrenic. What is more, since the items in any one scale were derived purely empirically and were embedded in many diverse statements, the test should give a correct diagnosis despite the efforts of subjects to put up a bold front or to conceal their true feelings. It was hoped that the correction keys would compensate for whatever the indirect method of empirical keying did not accomplish. The problems of interpretation will be treated below. First, however, let us take a look at Morris' profile so that reference may be made to it as we proceed in the chapter.

Morris Brown's
MMPI Profile

Morris took the group form of the test, following the standard printed instructions. His answers on the four validity scales, the nine clinical scales, and three additional scales were then scored by the use of punched answer keys. The results were plotted as *T* scores on the profile (see Figure 8-1). *T* scores are standard scores obtained by converting the raw scores into deviations from the mean of the original normal group (in this case, predominantly rural Minnesota men and women who were visiting relatives in hospitals). On these scales, scores of 70 (two standard deviations above the normal mean of 50) and over are considered of pathological significance.

Because research has not given strong support to the MMPI's attempts at spotting invalid records, the validity scores of *?*, *L*, *F*, and *K* will not be described in more detail than was devoted to them in Chapter 4 (pages

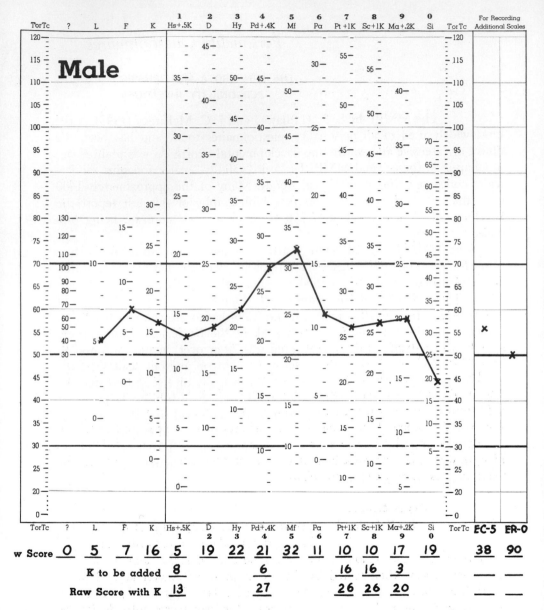

TorTc	?	L	F	K	1 Hs+.5K	2 D	3 Hy	4 Pd+.4K	5 Mf	6 Pa	7 Pt+1K	8 Sc+1K	9 Ma+.2K	0 Si	TorTc	EC-5	ER-0
w Score	0	5	7	16	5	19	22	21	32	11	10	10	17	19		38	90
K to be added					8			6			16	16	3			—	—
Raw Score with K					13			27			26	26	20			—	—

Figure 8-1 Morris Brown's MMPI profile (Hathaway & McKinley, 1943).

Key to Symbols

T or Tc	The T scale of standardized scores. (Tc means T score with K correction.)
?	The "Can't say" validity scale (number of omitted items).
L	The "Lie" validity scale (denial of trivial faults and symptoms).

F	The "False" validity scale (admission of rare, serious symptoms).
K	Correction score added to certain clinical scales to compensate for defensive understatement.

Clinical Scales

1	Hs	Hypochondriasis—multiple complaints of somatic symptoms without organic basis.
2	D	Depression—a sad, self-disparaging, apathetic, even suicidal, state.
3	Hy	Hysteria—a neurosis characterized by anxiety or blandness, naiveté, ready displays of emotion, and certain bodily symptoms.
4	Pd	Psychopathic deviate—a character disorder with impulsive, antisocial acting out.
5	Mf	Masculinity-femininity (based on responses of male overt homosexuals).
6	Pa	Paranoia—a rigid, suspicious, vengeful condition, which at its psychotic extreme includes delusions of persecution or of grandeur.
7	Pt	Psychasthenia—obsessive-compulsive neurosis, with vacillation, indecisiveness, over-conscientiousness, overintellectuality.
8	Sc	Schizophrenia—the most common psychosis, marked by withdrawal, inappropriate-ness, peculiar thinking, even delusions and hallucinations.
9	Ma	Mania—an overactive, excited, elated, driven condition; at its psychotic extreme, often alternating with depression.
0	Si	Social introversion.
	EC-5	Ego control (Block, 1965), the first factor in analyses of all scales.
	ER-0	Ego resiliency (Block, 1965), the second factor. (See text discussion of these two factors, page 73.)

71–72). Suffice it to say that Morris' validity scores are safely within normal limits, allowing the rest of his scores to be interpreted according to usual principles.

If we look at the profile quite naively, we notice that most of the pathological scales (even *Ma* and *D*) are less than one standard deviation above the mean and hence are not interpretable. Only *Si*, social introversion, is slightly below 50, indicating a moderate degree of extroversion. We should, therefore, disregard all the clinical scales except the high scores on scale 5 (*Mf*, masculinity-femininity) and scale 4 (*Pd*, psychopathic deviate). The MMPI manual tells us that "males with very high *Mf* scores have frequently been found to be either overt or repressed sexual inverts," though it goes on to warn that homosexuality must not be assumed without independent confirmatory evidence. Scale 4 (*Pd*) "measures the similarity of the subject to a group of persons whose main difficulty lies in their absence of deep emotional response, their inability to profit from experience, and their disregard of social mores." These statements are reminiscent of rather well-established features of Morris Brown as we knew him in 1940: Certainly he was inclined to seek overt homosexual experience, seemed relatively shallow in his emotional experience, and was prone to disregard social mores if they seemed silly or pointless to him. If he still had these characteristics, we might be tempted to conclude as well that he was not susceptible to learning from experience. The manual warns, however, that the scales should not be interpreted so simply and directly. Let us see, then, what other interpretive approaches add.

Pattern analysis. Research and clinical use quickly showed that the MMPI did not work as simply as originally intended. Its authors and proponents have been forced to abandon the attempt to make diagnoses by a literal interpretation of the scales and to adopt the configurational approach—that is, they now say that the profile must be taken as a complex piece of clinical information consisting of patterns to be interpreted only by someone with professional experience and trained judgment. There has come into being, therefore, a kind of "MMPI expert" who can at times perform dazzling feats of describing an "entire personality" on the basis of the profile alone. These clinicians generally report that they interpret any one scale quite differently in different contexts (that is, when certain other scale values are high or low), though there is little hard evidence that they actually do so in practice (Goldberg, 1968).

The development of profile interpretation has brought about a rather anomalous and unstable situation. The one great advantage of the MMPI is that it takes little of the clinician's time and requires no judgment to obtain a fully scored profile. Moreover, the original aim was to reduce psychiatric diagnosis to a simple clerical operation, eliminating the need for clinical judgment in the test's interpretation also. Yet after much initial work with the MMPI, its proponents declared that it had to be clinically interpreted, in a way much like the "scatter analysis" of Wechsler's intelligence tests (to be discussed later in this chapter) or the interpretation of a projective technique's quantitative scores.

Objective rules and ratios. In their research, Meehl and Dahlstrom (1960) have pursued the original goal of eliminating the need for clinical judgment. They sorted through the test profiles of hundreds of diagnosed mental-hospital and clinic patients and devised a set of objective rules and ratios by means of which a file clerk could classify an MMPI profile as psychotic, neurotic, or indeterminate, in about a minute. When cross-validated on 988 male patients, this procedure yielded a total correct classification of 53 percent, which is significantly above chance (50 percent) but not impressively so. If one disregards the 30 percent of profiles that were indeterminate, the rate of success ("hits") was 76 percent. It is especially noteworthy that these rules worked better than the pooled weighted judgments of 29 Minnesota clinicians who used all their skills at pattern analysis.

These rules, however, classify Morris Brown's profile as psychotic— an implausible diagnosis. Clearly, such a system is not suited for clinical use with individuals if any better method is available.

The "cookbook" approach. Halbower (described in Meehl, 1956) developed an original approach to interpreting the MMPI without clinical judgment. He constructed what he called a cookbook with four recipes; the recipes correspond to four of the five most common types of MMPI profiles. More than half of the patients seen at the Veterans' Administration Mental Hygiene Clinic in Minneapolis, where the research was done, fell into one of these four categories. From these patients, he selected 9 from each profile type and asked their therapists (or another qualified clinician who knew the case well) to describe each subject on a 154-item Q sort made up of statements taken from diagnostic reports. The 5 subjects in each group of 9 whose Q sorts intercorrelated most consistently were taken as representative; their Q sorts were averaged to get a description of the personality type represented by that MMPI profile.

The next step was to select 8 new patients, 2 with each of the four types of MMPI profile. Their therapists described them by means of the Q sort, providing a criterion. When the Q sort description from the four-recipe cookbook was correlated with the criterion sorts, the results were quite good, for the median (validity) correlation was .69. Moreover, when clinical psychologists who were quite experienced in the use of the MMPI described the same patients on the Q sort after studying their MMPI profiles, their validities were significantly and impressively lower; not once did the clinical integration of the profile information produce a correlation as good as that of the cookbook. (We shall return to the implications of this finding and other aspects of Halbower's study in Chapter 10.)

Again, however, this approach yields nothing of value for our understanding of Morris Brown. It may persuade us that there probably is little to the claims of the enthusiasts for pattern analysis of the MMPI, but Morris' profile is not one of the four described in the "cookbook." Instead, his is quite an unusual collection of scores: for example, profiles like Morris' with the highest scores on Mf, followed by Pd, occurred among only 1.5 percent of a group of 136 midwestern male adults. There was not a single similar score among 100 male Iowa college students, and only .7 percent of 2551 North Carolina prisoners produced this type of profile (Dahlstrom & Welsh, 1960). Consequently, it will be a long time before enough data have accumulated for statistical analysis to provide a ready-made interpretation of even the most outstanding parts of Morris' profile.

Development of new scales. Another line of research, unlike the studies just described, has not assumed that the original nine clinical scales are necessarily the best way to score the MMPI. These researchers assume rather that, using the same basic questionnaire, or pool of items, more directly meaningful scoring keys could perhaps be devised. A number of new empirical keys have been developed, some of which have attracted wide interest and are widely used—for example, Barron's Es or ego-strength scale (1953), originally made up of the items distinguishing patients who improved after brief psychotherapy from those who did not.

Other psychologists have used factor analysis to clarify the nature of the existing scales and construct new ones. Welsh (1956) is one of over a dozen workers who have factor-analyzed the original empirical scales, and several others, and have found that only two main factors account for most of the information in the profile. For a while, many psychometricians (such as Jackson & Messick, 1958) tended to assume that these factors were themselves mainly measures of response sets (see Chapter 4). Block (1965) has recently shown, however, that these same two factors emerge even when the scales are first purified by (1) eliminating items that are contained in more than one scale and which thus produce spurious correlations, (2) eliminating the effect of any tendency of the subject to agree or disagree with an item indiscriminately (the *acquiescence* response set) by including in each scale equal numbers of items keyed positively and negatively, and (3) suppressing the *social desirability* response set by excluding all items with too obvious a degree of rated desirability or undesirability.

The first factor Block calls ego control (*EC*), a measure of how tight, constricted, and overcontrolled a person is, rather than being loose, impulsive, and undercontrolled. He calls the second factor ego resiliency (*ER*); high scorers seem to bounce back after frustration or stress, and low scorers admit to having many neurotic and other symptoms. Most of the traditional clinical scales (and Barron's ego strength) are heavily loaded with *ER*. Block also reports independent data from the clinical assessment of several samples of subjects in the form of correlations with ratings, which tend to support the validity of his interpretations based on the content of the items. As Figure 8-1 shows, Morris scored just above average on both *EC* and *ER*. He could be described as being slightly on the reserved side and as admitting to about as many symptoms as the mean of several groups of healthy men considerably younger than himself.

Improvement of scales by means of factor analysis. It seems wasteful to ask a subject to respond to 566 items to get measures of only two constructs. Surely more than this meager crumb of information about rather general traits is contained in so many responses. Block himself points out that the factorial structure of the MMPI is much more complex if one begins with the intercorrelation of items, not scales; unfortunately, even with the aid of modern computers it is difficult to work with the entire pool of items at once.

Several researchers (such as Comrey, 1957, 1958) have factor-analyzed the intercorrelations of items *within* scales and have found each scale to contain two or more quite independent clusters of items. This is not surprising, because coefficients of internal consistency for the empirical scales have been reported to range all the way from $-.05$ (for *Pa*, the paranoid scale) to .81 (for *Pt*, the psychasthenia scale). These analyses tend to separate the "obvious," face-valid items from the subtle and indirect ones contributed by empirical keying; one study (Dempsey, 1964) suggests that the direct admission of relevant symptoms may be the principal determinant of the test's validity. The shortened but more useful scale for depression (D) resulting from his factor-analytic investigation consists entirely of items like "I cry easily" and "I wish I could be as happy as others seem to be." With the help of factor analysis, it looks as if shorter but homogeneous and more easily interpretable scales may be developed, which may considerably enhance the MMPI's usefulness.

Construction of scales other than by empirical keying. Might it not be that some other strategy of building scales to summarize the answers to many separate questions would yield better results than has empirical keying? Hase and Goldberg (1967) decided to compare several strategies of constructing inventory scales, using the item pool of the California Psychological Inventory (Gough, 1957) and working with the test responses of 201 freshman college girls. (The CPI is an attempt to modify the MMPI for use with normal college populations; of its 468 items, about 200 are drawn from the MMPI.) Since Gough's manual describes 11 scales built by the method of *empirical keying,* they constructed three additional sets of 11 scales each, one by *factor-analytic* methods (based on item intercorrelations) and two by other methods that they call intuitive. One intuition-based method involved the judgments of three advanced graduate students, who constructed *theoretical* scales by selecting items that seemed to measure 11 of Murray's needs (1938). The other method, used in making *rational* scales, also involved judgment: One person selected items that seemed to measure various traits; then, by statistical means, inconsistent items were eliminated. In addition, for a baseline against which to evaluate the validity of the other scales, Hase and Goldberg used 11 measures of the response sets of social desirability and acquiescence (in various combinations) and 11 purely random scales of 25 items each, selected and the direction of scoring keyed by use of a table of random numbers.

The scales were tested for reliability by the usual psychometric measures of internal consistency (fairly good for the four major strategies, fair for the response-set, or "stylistic," scales, and nil for the random ones) and by retest after a four-week interval. The four main strategies gave mean repeat correlations of from .81 to .87, which is satisfactory and slightly better than the usual retest reliability of MMPI scales; the two sets of control scales made a distinctly poorer showing.

To test validity, Hase and Goldberg put together 13 criteria, which included behavioral measures of social conformity, peer ratings on five traits, objective measures of academic achievement and dropping out of college, and so on. Several ways of analyzing the data all led to the same conclusion: Scales made by the four major strategies *all performed equally well* (with mean validity correlations of approximately .30) and significantly better than the stylistic and random scales, which did not differ from each other.

Another finding by Hase and Goldberg constitutes impressive evidence that much of the psychometric ingenuity that has gone into such complex strategies of scale construction as empirical keying has been wasted. The subjects' self-ratings on such traits as dominance, sociability, and femininity were *better* predictors of their friends' ratings than the most elaborate statistical manipulations of any CPI scales. This is not an isolated finding; Peterson (1965) and Carroll (1952) report the same superiority of simple, direct self-ratings over inventory-scale scores.

It seems, therefore, that the vaunted method of empirical keying has not made any special contribution to the measurement of personality by means of self-report inventories. It still remains true that a good deal can be learned about a cooperative person by asking him directly to tell you about his usual behavior, express his agreement or disagreement with statements of attitudes, rate himself on various traits, or the like. In the absence of frankness and some insight, no amount of manipulation of numerical scores can extract much useful information from an inventory.

In summary, the MMPI is a collection of many interesting and potentially useful items; the study of these items, however, has been too much neglected in favor of the nine empirical scales, which have not stood the test of time very well. There is no convincing proof that they are highly valid measures of anything very meaningful, and they will probably give way to other, more directly intelligible ways of summarizing answers to the items.

THE EYSENCK PERSONALITY INVENTORY

The inventory by H. J. and Sybil B. G. Eysenck (1963) is a recent offshoot of a long-established line of screening devices for neurotic tendencies, stretching back to Woodworth (see page 65) and World War I. The Eysenck inventory is brief and to the point; its 57 questions give stripped-down but reasonably reliable and statistically independent measures of Extroversion and of Neuroticism, a rather generalized willingness to admit symptoms of no great severity. These variables are the cornerstones of Eysenck's theory of personality, as they are the persistently recurring pair of independent dimensions that crop up in the great majority of self-descriptive questionnaires. The test itself is a recent, only slightly modified version of the Maudsley Personality Inventory (Eysenck, 1962), which has had retest reliabilities of from .70 to .90 and internal-consistency coefficients ranging between .75 and .90. The few figures on reliability available on the present form are of the same order of magnitude. The test incorporates a brief *L* scale adapted from the MMPI, which is intended to detect invalid records. Eysenck has done a great deal of work on the construct validity of the two factors measured by these tests; this work is impressive but difficult to summarize.

The results of Morris' test (Table 8-1) show us that he still comes across as a clear-cut social extrovert, and that he is below average on

Table 8-1   Morris Brown's Scores on the Eysenck Personality Inventory

Scale	Score	Classification
E (extroversion-introversion)	18	93rd percentile
N (neuroticism)	7	41st percentile
L (lie)	1	negligible; valid result

neuroticism. Eysenck's test admittedly has little clinical use, and for our purposes its contribution is minimal. Nevertheless, it is fair to say in summary that its aims are modest and its performance good within those limitations.

A STUDY OF VALUES

The revised form of the Study of Values (Allport, Vernon, & Lindzey, 1951) was given to Morris partly to see how closely the 1966 profile would correspond to the 1940 profile (described in Chapter 6). The revision is a better test; its items are more discriminating, it is more reliable, and the Social value has been redefined and sharpened. That value is now restricted to altruism and philanthropy, rather than taking in all manifestations of

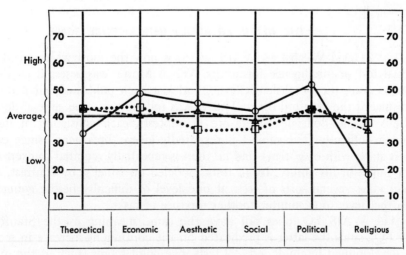

Figure 8-2   Value profiles (Allport-Vernon-Lindzey, 1951).

○————○ Profile for Morris Brown, 1966

△------△ Average profile for male students at Morris' college

□•••••□ Average male profile

affection for people, as before. Internal-consistency correlations now range from .73 (Theoretical) to .90 (Religious); repeat reliability after one month, from .77 (Social) to .92 (Economic). The old and new forms are reasonably equivalent for the Economic and Religious values (inter-form correlations are .74 and .75); as would be expected, the Social value shows the poorest correlation between the two versions (.31), and the others are only fair, ranging from .45 to .55. Just the changes in the test itself, therefore, might give rise to a good deal of the difference in the two profiles.

Compare Figure 8-2 with Figure 6-1, on page 120, and you will quickly see that there are at least two points of similarity: The Political and Economic values are still the two strongest. His scores on those are quite significantly above those of a group of 264 students who attended the same college (but who were about 20 years younger than Morris at the time of testing). The greatest rise has been in the Aesthetic value (as it later turned out, this is attributable almost entirely to Morris' love for music, which had grown considerably since 1940); though the Theoretical value has risen, it is still below average. The Social value is down, but it rests at just about the general mean. The big drop has come in the Religious value, which is extremely low by any standard. Recall, however, that in 1940 Morris had recently been under the influence of a Catholic priest; and even though his Religious value was not strong then, it may have been temporarily inflated. At any rate, Morris' 1966 value profile is that of a secular man of affairs; it is not unusual for a businessman.

So much for questionnaires; the other nonprojective instruments used with Morris at the time of the reassessment were of several different types— an intelligence test, self-rating devices, and tests of cognitive style.

Intelligence Tests

THE WECHSLER ADULT INTELLIGENCE SCALE

David Wechsler's WAIS (1955) is now the most widely used individual test of intelligence for adults. When Morris was assessed in 1940, its predecessor, the Wechsler-Bellevue, had just been published but had not yet displaced the Stanford-Binet. The WAIS follows the same general design as the Wechsler-Bellevue: There are 11 subtests, each consisting of items graded in difficulty. The subject is repeatedly given "breathers," since each subtest starts with easy items, and he then is repeatedly required to exert the upper limits of his ability. In all tests modeled on Binet's, by contrast, the subject takes several sorts of tests at one level of difficulty before going up to another level to encounter another mixture of tasks.

The WAIS I.Q. does not have the same meaning as the Stanford-Binet I.Q., since the latter is predicated on the continuous increase in scores with development in childhood. All tests give point scores (such as the number of items passed); to compute a Stanford-Binet I.Q., this score is converted into a mental age—that is, the score is expressed in age units that serve as the numerator of the I.Q. formula

$$I.Q. = \frac{Mental\ age}{Chronological\ age}$$

By the same reasoning, Wechsler argued, the denominator could be viewed as the expected or average point score expressed in age units. But if the numerator was kept a point score, rather than translated into age units, the I.Q. would have the same meaning if the denominator was the one translated—that is, converted into the expected point score for the person's age. This ingenious argument is the basis of his tables for converting raw (point) scores into I.Q.'s. Since there are separate tables for ages 20–24, 25–34, and thereafter for decades until ages 65–69, 70–74, and over 75, a person's Wechsler I.Q. tends to stay constant despite the tendency of point scores to decline after about age 30.

Correlations with other tests of intelligence range from the .50's through the .90's, depending partly on the adequacy of the other tests. The WAIS also meets the standards for a valid intelligence test set by other available criteria (correlation with ratings, appropriate age curves, selection of mental defectives, and differentiation of occupational groups). The split-half internal consistency of the total I.Q. (in which scores on half the test are correlated with scores on the other half) is .97; its repeat reliability has been reported to be almost as good—.90. The individual subtests have poorer reliability, and the reliability of differences among them is even worse, a point that has often been raised in criticism of scatter analysis (interpretation of the pattern of abilities measured by the different subtests). Curiously enough, however, this same point never seems to be raised in criticism of profile interpretation on the MMPI, the component scores of which are hardly more reliable than WAIS subtests and are about as highly intercorrelated. Nevertheless, unevenness in the pattern, when interpreted by an expert, often gives diagnostically useful leads (see Rapaport et al., 1968). Morris' pattern, or scatter, was not particularly noteworthy, except for a weakness in the Picture Completion subtest.

In clinical use, the importance of the WAIS goes beyond its quantitative scores. The verbalization of answers, qualitative features of the subject's approach to the tasks, and his behavior during testing are all recorded by the well-trained examiner and are weighed along with other qualitative data in the interpretive phase of clinical assessment. Though the contribution of the WAIS is not singled out in the next chapter, it did play a part in the clinical assessment in 1966.

To save time, and because Morris had been given the same test several years before, some results of which were available, he took only 7 of the 11 subtests. His estimated total I.Q. from these subtests taken in 1966 is 145, well up in the top 1 percent of men Morris' age. This figure happens by chance to coincide almost exactly with the Stanford-Binet I.Q. of 146 obtained in 1940. Measurement of this sort is not usually that exact, and the shift from one test to the other ordinarily results in greater discrepancies, even when they are taken in immediate succession. The correlation between the two tests varies with the samples, but it is generally about .85.

Self-Rating Devices

THE ADJECTIVE CHECK LIST

This instrument, by Harrison Gough (1960, 1965), takes us back to self-description as a means of getting data for assessment, but with a difference. In the earliest type of inventory, the subject's self-report was taken at face value, and the trait measures were built directly on the answers to questionnaires, which were treated as valid reports of behavior. Our examination of the MMPI has shown that this direct approach has considerable value if the subject is motivated to reveal himself frankly; but if he is not, any such technique of assessment is hazardous. The Adjective Check List is presented as a way of getting at the subject's self-concept rather than as a way of measuring 300 traits; because it is self-description taken as such, it can be presumed valid unless there is reason to believe the subject is motivated not to reveal what he actually thinks of himself. This technique of measurement is simplicity boiled down. The test consists merely of 300 adjectives, and the instructions are: "Please put a check by each adjective that applies to you."

The Adjective Check List has been extensively used at the Institute for Personality Assessment and Research at the University of California, where Gough developed it, and elsewhere. It has proved empirically valuable in that independently defined groups of subjects differ in terms of the frequency with which their members check different adjectives. For example, results of one experiment singled out a group of subjects who were easily swayed by group influence, and another group who stuck to their guns despite the (manipulated) consensus of a group. The yielders significantly ($p = .01$) more often checked the adjectives *optimistic, kind, obliging,* and *patient,* and also *determined* and *efficient.* The uninfluenced subjects (at the same level of significance) described themselves as *artistic, emotional,* and *original.* These findings contributed to a meaningful picture of the self-concepts of people who are and are not easily swayed by a group, a picture that fitted well with other data on their personalities (Barron, 1952).

The terms Morris chose to describe himself are grouped below into clusters, which have been numbered and arranged to bring out apparent relationships; the arbitrariness of such grouping is obvious. Words in parentheses indicate other possible classifications.

    1. adaptable, capable, versatile, practical, realistic
    2. alert, curious, interests wide, sensitive, clear-thinking, thoughtful

3. active, adventurous, enthusiastic
4. cheerful, contented, optimistic, good-natured
5. appreciative, friendly, generous, sympathetic, understanding, warm, outgoing (thoughtful, tolerant)
6. cooperative, dependable, loyal, responsible, honest, sincere, tolerant, steady
7. informal, natural, unaffected
8. independent, individualistic, unconventional
9. attractive, good-looking
10. healthy, robust

Whether or not Morris really *is* as he describes himself, the self-descriptions above provide quite a lot of information and in many ways reinforce what we already know about him. Groups 5 and 6 perhaps contain the most surprises, for they suggest that he has taken a definite turn toward close and friendly relationships with people (instead of holding back from involvement) and toward morally proper behavior. The markedly favorable tone of the adjectives chosen indicates that he feels generally good about himself. We might expect, therefore, that the internal confusion Morris so freely expressed in 1940 has been replaced by a good deal of self-acceptance.

At least one negative fact ought also to be brought out: The total check list contains 14 adjectives expressing shades of hostility ranging from *cruel* and *aggressive* to *stern* and *intolerant*, but Morris did not check one of them. The preceding sentence provides an example of what Gough calls analysis by means of rational scales; it is also possible to make use of empirically derived scales. For instance, the assessment staff of the Institute for Personality Assessment and Research described 40 graduate students in various fields, half of whom had been chosen by their departments as outstandingly high, half as outstandingly low, on research originality (Gough, 1960). The assessors checked the following adjectives significantly more often to characterize the *more* original students:

adventurous	fair-minded	original
alert	foresighted	quiet
civilized	imaginative	rational
clear-thinking	intelligent	reliable
clever	interests wide	responsible
curious	inventive	shy

These adjectives significantly characterized the *less* original subjects:

confused	prejudiced	stubborn
conventional	restless	suggestible
defensive	sentimental	thrifty
emotional	simple	trusting
polished	slow	

By assigning a plus to every adjective in the first list and a minus to each in the second, we get an empirical scale ranging from $+18$ to -14. Morris' score would be $+6$, from which we could conclude that his self-concept tends to resemble the personalities of graduate students who were considered original, although he did not describe himself as *original*. In these ways, a great variety of rational and empirical scales can be derived from the Adjective Check List.

Such an all-or-none judgment as a check by an adjective is, of course, crude. Though psychologists have sometimes used the Adjective Check List to record an assessment staff's judgments, they usually prefer to rate on a scale with more than two points (that is, more than a Yes and No). For example, on the MMPI, Morris said True to, "I get mad easily and then get over it soon." Assuming that this is an accurate self-observation, if he were asked to rate his temper on a 10-point scale, how would he weigh the two considerations of threshold and duration of anger against each other? And they are only half the considerations here. Logically, a person should be higher on a scale of temper (1) if the trait has a low threshold—if he gets mad easily, (2) if the trait is extensive—if he loses his temper in a wide variety of situations, (3) if the trait is intensive—if he typically explodes instead of getting moderately annoyed, and (4) if the trait's operation is prolonged—if his temper is slow to subside rather than, as in Morris' case, likely to simmer down quickly.

There are even further complications to rating traits. As another example consider the trait of adventurousness. The daily life of Morris, like that of most people, offers fewer opportunities for him to act adventurously than to act, say, irritably. This fact would make it difficult to compare these traits on the same kind of rating scale; it also raises the question of the time period when the trait is displayed. Morris went rock climbing in the West ten months before he described himself as adventurous, and it is quite possible that he had not done anything equally bold and exciting since then. Should he have checked the adjective or not? Most of us would agree that he should have; but what if the last opportunity for adventure had arisen ten years earlier instead of ten months? Even though a person had seized the opportunity eagerly then, we would hardly think that he was being accurate a decade later to continue to describe himself as adventurous.

The issue of absolute versus relative measurement as determined by one's reference group also comes up in ratings: A member of a parachute-jumping club knows that his occasional weekend adventures are tame compared to the activities of the professional stunt man in the movies, yet they are enough to make him outstandingly adventurous compared to the population as a whole. But is that the proper base for comparison? There is no easy answer. Surely we should try to find out what a person's reference groups are, for his self-ratings to be most useful. It is important to know whether a person tends to compare himself primarily with people in general, members of his own occupational group, fellow townsmen, others in a close but extended family, people with the same ethnic or religious background, or what not. Everyone belongs to many groups simultaneously, and his status may change drastically as he goes from one to another. To anticipate his recent history a bit, Morris is an outstandingly successful politician in the small town where he lives, having been elected the equivalent of mayor for a dozen years; but the year he lost his reelection to the state legislature he was a small frog in the large pond of state politics. To rate himself well in relation to any group means also that a person has to be able to assess the same traits equally well in himself and in others.

Because of these vexing problems in *normative* rating (using other members of a group as the standard), many workers in personality assessment have begun using *ipsative* scaling—rating a trait high if it is outstanding or important for the subject compared with his own other traits, not with the same trait in other people. To be sure, all the other problems of rating remain, but this device has the important advantage of enabling the assessor to consider only one subject at a time. In addition, the frame of reference for self-ratings and ratings by experts can be kept the same more easily in this way. This feature of ipsative scaling is part of a special technique of rating traits known as the Q-sort technique and will become clearer as we proceed.

THE Q-SORTING METHOD

The particular form of Q-sorting technique used with Morris was the California Q Set (Block, 1961). It consists of 100 statements printed on separate cards. When it is used for self-description (as was done with Morris), the subject is instructed to sort through the randomly ordered cards and make a preliminary decision about each statement, putting it in one pile if it seems to describe him, in another if it seems wrong or misleading as applied to him, and in between if it does not apply at all. Then he reexamines the cards in the first pile and picks out the five that seem most to hit the nail on the head and bring out the main points about him: These cards are called 9's. From the remainder of this pile, he selects the eight cards that best describe him (called 8's), and then the next twelve (7's); at this point, he may find it easiest to go to the group of uncharacteristic statements and select the five that are most wildly off the mark (the 1's), then another very uncharacteristic group of eight (2's), the next twelve (3's), and so forth. When he finishes, he should have nine piles with the distribution shown in Figure 8-3.

This forced distribution is usually approximately normal, as in Figure 8-3, but it can be any shape that an investigator chooses. The great advantage of the forced distribution is that it controls such response sets as hugging the mean or giving extreme ratings and thereby eliminates a good deal of unwanted variance. Its disadvantage is that it forces every subject into the same mold, regardless of how well it fits: Some subjects complain, for example, that they cannot find exactly five statements that are highly apt.

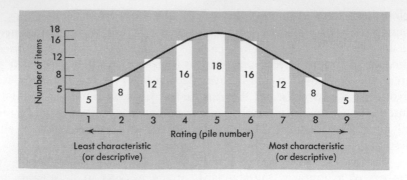

Figure 8-3   The California Q-Sort distribution, with a normal curve superimposed.

The California Q Set is not so much a test that could have reliability, or validity, as it is a language for describing a personality. As such, it is quite useful to assessors, who can use it to record a first impression or a more considered set of judgments. It was used in both ways with Morris: Two of the staff of the New York University Research Center for Mental Health, who had only brief encounters with him while administering some of the tests of cognitive style, Q-sorted their impressions, and the investigator close to Morris used the Q sort after having studied *all* the assessment data. The procedure also makes it easy to correlate two or more sets of ratings on the same person, as shown in Table 8-2.

Table 8-2   Correlations Among Q Sorts by Morris Brown, Raters, and Psychologists' Consensus on Optimal Adjustment

| | MB | Raters | | |
		RRH	DW	NI
RRH	.52	x		
DW	.33	.33	x	
NI	.32	.45	.31	x
Optimal Adjustment	.68	.39	.32	.35

Another feature of the Q sort is that it can be used to develop scales of various types, with which a subject's sort can be correlated. For example, Block had nine clinical psychologists describe "the optimally adjusted personality" by means of the Q set; he then made up a composite sort based on their ratings, which can serve as a standard with which to correlate other ratings. Thus, the bottom row of correlations in Table 8-2 may be taken as measures of how closely this conception of the well-adjusted man corresponded to Morris Brown's self-description (MB), and to the description of him given by the psychologist who knew him best (RRH) and by the other two assessors (DW and NI). The *absolute* sizes of coefficients like the ones in the table are not particularly meaningful, since they depend a good deal on the properties of the Q set. The ratings by the three judges do not appear very reliable, but it is surprising that the agreement is as good as it is, considering that judges DW and NI saw Morris for less than an hour each and had virtually no opportunity to talk with him. Block reports that well-trained observers who have had the opportunity to study a person can attain good agreement, with "typical reliabilities of .8 or .9 [Block, 1961, p. 91]."

Table 8-3 lists the 13 items Morris considered most characteristic of himself and the 13 items he considered least characteristic. These items, together with the Adjective Check List, give a good picture of his *self-concept*; by comparing his ratings with those given by the psychologists we can form some hypotheses about the nature of his insight.

Of the five most characteristic items (pile 9), only item 3 was given particularly discrepant ratings by Morris and by the psychologists. The two who had had brief contact with him had little basis for any direct knowledge about the breadth of his interests; the other psychologist's rating may have been affected by normative considerations: Knowing many people who have even broader interests, he may have been influenced to rate Morris lower than he deserves. Yet it is also possible that Morris considers this one of the most characteristic things about himself in part because he *values* breadth and would like to think of himself as more universal in his interests than he actually is.

This example brings out one of the ambiguities of ipsative scaling. What does it mean to say that items 19 and 96 are both true of Morris, but that the latter item, dealing with valuing independence, is more "characteristic" than the former, the issue of seeking reassurance? As we have just seen (page 180), there are many ways in which a behavioral tendency can be considered "strong," and they apply just as much to intraindividual comparisons among traits as to interindividual rankings or ratings.

When items are rated according to their *salience*, as Block calls the ipsative dimension, psychologists are likely to emphasize any items dealing with inferred inner constructs that seem to have explanatory relevance (such as item 86: "Handles anxiety and conflicts by, in effect, refusing to recognize their presence; repressive or dissociative tendencies"—rated 9 by both RRH and NI), even though—as in this case—the item may not precisely formulate Morris' individual blend of defenses. The subjects themselves, on the other hand, are likely to emphasize items that *describe* behavior or inner feelings to which they have direct access. Notice, for example, that all three psychologists put item 14 near the middle of the distribution, because of his unusual compliance and willingness to do whatever was asked of him, whereas Morris himself gave it a rock-bottom rating—which is probably more valid.

Table 8-3 Items from the California Q Set
Sorted in Extreme Positions by Morris Brown

Most Characteristic (pile 9)

Item No.
- 3. Has a wide range of interests. (6, 7, 4) *
- 5. Behaves in a giving way toward others. (8, 4, 9)
- 8. Appears to have a high degree of intellectual capacity. (5, 9, 6)
- 35. Has warmth; has the capacity for close relationships; compassionate. (8, 6, 7)
- 96. Values own independence and autonomy. (9, 8, 5)

Highly Characteristic (pile 8)

- 2. Is a genuinely dependable and responsible person. (9, 8, 7)
- 19. Seeks reassurance from others. (8, 5, 7)
- 26. Is productive; gets things done. (7, 6, 8)
- 28. Tends to arouse liking and acceptance in people. (7, 6, 7)
- 44. Evaluates the motivation of others in interpreting situations. (5, 6, 6)
- 59. Is concerned with own body and the adequacy of its physiological functioning. (8, 5, 6)
- 77. Appears straightforward, forthright, candid in dealing with others. (9, 9, 8)
- 93a. *Behaves in a masculine style and manner.* (4, 5, 4)

Least Characteristic (pile 1)

- 14. *Genuinely* submissive; accepts domination comfortably. (5, 5, 6)
- 36. Is subtly negativistic; tends to undermine and obstruct or sabotage. (3, 2, 1)
- 48. Keeps people at a distance; avoids close interpersonal relationships. (3, 4, 3)
- 78. Feels cheated and victimized by life; self-pitying. (2, 7, 3)
- 90. Is concerned with philosophical problems; religions, values, the meaning of life, etc. (2, 6, 6)

Highly Uncharacteristic (pile 2)

- 6. Is fastidious. (5, 7, 4)
- 34. Over-reactive to minor frustrations; irritable. (4, 3, 2)
- 49. Is basically distrustful of people in general; questions their motivations. (1, 4, 1)
- 63. Judges self and others in conventional terms like "popularity," "the correct thing to do," social pressures, etc. (5, 3, 7)
- 68. Is basically anxious. (6, 7, 5)
- 80. Interested in members of the opposite sex. (1, 5, 2)
- 97. Is emotionally bland; has flattened affect. (3, 2, 4)
- 99. Is self-dramatizing; histrionic. (6, 1, 7)

* Numbers in parentheses following items (Block, 1961) are ratings given by the three psychologists; RRH's ratings are given first (see also Table 8-2). Italics used in items are Block's.

Only he himself knows how comfortable he is when accepting domination; apparently his very strong need for autonomy makes him not at all genuinely submissive. His warmth (35), helpfulness (5), and need to be liked (19) are so strong, however, that he forces himself to accept a certain amount of domination. This is a good example of the importance of getting the subject's own introspective point of view in any thorough assessment of personality. (For further discussion of these issues, see Holt, 1951.)

Some other items on which there are discrepancies seem more plausibly to represent limitations in Morris' insight. He thinks of himself as more masculine in his manner and style of behavior than do the psychologists, all of whom rate this item (93a) at or just below the midpoint. At the same time, it is noteworthy that the matter of his masculinity did not seem salient one way or another to the two observers who had had very brief contact with him and knew nothing of his sexual history. In three other items, discrepancies similarly arose because they deal with ways the subject comes across to an outside observer: Morris appears to be more fastidious and more conventional (items 6 and 63) than he realizes. And though he is a genuine person who does not appear histrionic in the sense of displaying phoniness or deliberate dissimulation, he does tend to dramatize himself (item 99) more than he is aware of doing.

Finally, Morris quite strongly rejects the conception of himself as basically anxious (item 68), although he endorsed several MMPI items that support the psychologists' judgments—for example, "I am anxious about something or other most of the time." His evident need to be liked would be interpreted by many psychologists (as it was by the three who rated him) as indicating a moderate degree of basic anxiety, in Karen Horney's sense of a fear of rejection. Perhaps if he had been given a definition of "basically anxious," he might not have rated it so low in his sorting. In all fairness, it should be pointed out that the California Q Set was not designed for the average subject to use for self-description, however helpful it proved in this case.

Tests of Cognitive Style

LEVELING-SHARPENING

The schematizing test (Holzman & Klein, 1954; Gardner et al., 1959) is one of the first measures to be used in the recently developed area of cognitive style, and it remains one of the most studied. (See Chapter 4, pages 82–83, for a brief description of the test.) For this test, Morris came to the laboratory of the Research Center for Mental Health, where he was introduced to the experimenter and was taken into a large room. He sat facing a screen, with a record sheet in front of him, containing spaces numbered from 1 to 75.

The experimenter gave the following instructions:

We're going to show you a number of squares on the screen and I want you to tell me how big they are. The squares may range anywhere from 1 inch to 18 inches. This doesn't mean you will necessarily get a square that is 1 inch or 18 inches, though you may. The squares will always be somewhere within this range. To help you judge the size of squares, we will show you what a 1-inch square looks like—the smaller end of the range—and what an 18-inch square looks like—the larger end of the range. [These two squares were then projected for about 3 seconds each.] You will see 75 squares, and you have 75 numbered spaces on your sheet. Write your estimation of the size of each square in its own numbered space. Thus, for square number 1, record its size in inches next to number 1, etc. You will see each of the squares for only a few seconds. Look at the square all the time it is on the screen and make your estimation when it disappears. The next square you see will be number 1.

At first, the squares were all near the smaller end of the scale. Soon, however, the smallest of the initial group of 5 was dropped out and a larger one was added; after the slightly changed group of 5 had been reexposed in random order, the smallest was again omitted and a slightly larger one added. As this process continued, the average size of the squares steadily increased until they were about twice the original magnitude. The test thus provides a measure of incremental error, which reflects how closely the subject follows the gradually changing sizes. Subjects who estimate accurately are called sharpeners; those who lag behind, paying less heed to the changes in the squares, are called levelers.

Morris' performance was an extreme example of leveling: Throughout the series of 75, he gave his judgments only in terms of 3, 4, or 5 inches. The mean of his final 15 guesses (3.87 in.) was just one-fifth of an inch larger than the mean of the first 15, although the last 15 squares were actually from 5.5 to 11.4 inches wide. This shows a truly extraordinary capacity to cling to a fixed conception despite the fact that the situation is undergoing drastic, though gradual, change. Morris remarked after the test that he thought he had fouled it up; he was vaguely aware that something had gone wrong, that he had gotten into a rut and did not know how to get out of it.

What does the test measure and what does such a performance mean? First, it should be realized that Holzman and Klein were not trying to develop a "personality test." Their aim was to explore consistencies in cognitive behavior, and this test proved to be one that successfully predicted other ways of dealing with sequences of stimuli. A factor analysis showed that a leveling-sharpening factor included, besides the scores from the schematizing test, measures of tendencies to overestimate the size of hand-held discs, to talk for a long time on one topic in free association before going to another, to be slow in recognizing the effect of special (aniseikonic) eyeglasses in distorting the visual world, and to be influenced by an interpolated weight (which is supposed to be disregarded) when judging which one of a pair of weights is heavier. As the experimenters summarized it, "In levelers, successive perceptual impressions were assimilated to each other, so that distinctions among them were blurred. Memories of past impressions were also less available to them, presumably because of the general lack of differentiation of their memory schemata [Gardner et al., 1959, p. 105]."

Several other studies have found a close relationship between leveling and a tendency to rely on the defense of repression, as judged from the Rorschach Test. This finding suggests that the process that allows someone like Morris to disregard changes in the external world is repression or is closely related to that defense mechanism. The analogue of repression, when applied to external stimuli, is the defense of denial; as we saw in the last chapter, Morris' cyclothymic (hypomanic) pattern included the tendency to use denial as a defense. The present finding connecting leveling and repression supports that interpretation, therefore. It also helps us understand Morris' relatively mediocre performance on the Picture Completion subtest of the WAIS: His defenses evidently interfere at times with his capacity to take in and to process information, especially visual information.

FIELD ARTICULATION

The Hidden Figures Test was given to Morris as a measure of the other widely studied dimension of cognitive style—field dependence versus field independence, or field articulation (see Chapter 4, page 83). The development of that concept and the methods for measuring it was the work of H. A. Witkin and his collaborators. Witkin developed what he called the Embedded Figures Test (Witkin, 1950) out of a demonstration of a *Gestalt*-psychological point by Gottschaldt (1929). This in turn was modified by Educational Testing Service, shortened, and made into a group test, which is used here.

A sample problem, like that given in Figure 8-4, can give a better idea of these tests than can mere description. The test presents 16 such problems, and the subject has 15 minutes to solve as many as he can; his score is the number correct. Morris got 10 items correct (and 1 wrong), which is a good enough score to put him in the field-independent classification.

In his original research Witkin found that his experimental measures of field independence, or psychological differentiation, were correlated with several general personality dispositions. Thus, Morris' performance on the test would lead us to expect him to be active rather than passive, not to be anxious about controlling his bodily impulses, and to have a high level of self-esteem. Those expectations seem to be consistent with the picture emerging from the other objective tests. Two other dispositions that would be expected of high scorers—an awareness of an inner life and a mature body image—were *not* characteristic of Morris, judging from his own description of himself as nonintrospective and from his rather crude and unelaborated figure drawings. He is not, therefore, a "pure culture" field-independent type, as might have been predicted from the fact that his score on this test was only moderately high.

But why was Morris able to do a better-than-average job on this test, if he is weak in "taking in and processing visual information"? Apparently that formulation was too sweeping; we must restrict our generalization to situations involving a gradual change in the stimuli or the detection of

This is a test of your ability to tell which one of five simple figures can be found in a more complex pattern. At the top of each page in this test are five simple figures lettered A, B, C, D, and E. Beneath each row of figures is a page of patterns. Each pattern has a row of letters beneath it. Indicate your answer by putting an X through the letter of the figure which you find in the pattern.

NOTE: There is only one of these figures in each pattern, and this figure will always be right side up and exactly the same size as one of the five lettered figures.

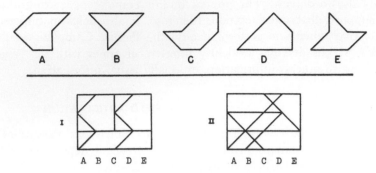

The figures below show how the figures are included in the problems. Figure A is in the first problem and figure D in the second.

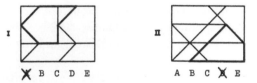

Figure 8-4   Sample items from the Hidden Figures Test. (From Messick, 1962)

something missing. (If Morris still has some unconscious concern about his own bodily integrity—castration anxiety—the Picture Completion task might be especially likely to arouse his defenses.) It will take a good deal more research, exploring the range of tasks that involve various kinds of visual processing, before we can be confident about just how far we can generalize. It has been demonstrated in several research studies (for example, Gardner et al., 1959) that leveling-sharpening and field articulation are separate factors, despite apparent similarities in the tasks, and Guilford (1967) indicates that many more independent factors exist in the content domain of processing information about visual figures.

Judging from the two samples of tests and other devices used with Morris Brown in 1940 and in 1966, nonprojective approaches to assessing personality have far more to offer today than they did 25 years ago. Especially good progress has been made in assessing the subject's self-concept and in developing cognitive tests—both of abilities and of the closely related area of cognitive style. The goal of a truly objective test of personality, which can be scored and interpreted by a clerk or a computer, as yet seems far away. Despite all the work that has gone into the pursuit of this ideal, it still takes a highly trained and intelligent person to interpret even the best of the currently available tests, if more than the simplest information is to be extracted from them.

Morris took a number of other objective tests and self-administering questionnaires in 1966, but they do not add a great deal to the information presented above. As was true of the 1940 assessment, it has been impossible to discuss even these nonprojective test findings without some exercise of clinical judgment or without drawing on some clinical observations. Let us see, then, how Morris appeared to the clinical eye in 1966.

To say that man is a compound of strength and weakness, light and darkness, smallness and greatness, is not to indict him, it is to define him.

DENIS DIDEROT. Supplement to Philosophical Thoughts

CHAPTER 9
THE MATURING
OF A PERSONALITY

After the tantalizing glimpse in the last chapter of a contemporary Morris Brown, so much the same and yet seemingly so different, the reader will probably want to know the intervening chapters of his life story and something about what the most recent clinical assessment reveals of its unconscious side. In the process of learning these things, we shall see some more facets of assessment in practice and find out what assessment can teach us about personal maturity.

Results of the 1966
Clinical Assessment of Morris Brown

In late 1942, Morris passed the Navy's medical examinations, went through communications training, and was put to work on the initial (or shakedown) cruises of small vessels destined for the European theater of the war. When the focus of the naval war shifted to the Pacific, he at last had a chance at regular sea duty and earned his battle star. He served honorably and well, staying in six months longer than required. Moreover, during nearly four years of active duty he developed an abiding affection for the naval service and a fondness for the sea.

On returning to the states, therefore, he decided to settle on the Eastern seaboard in a large city where he could be close to a weekend place on the water; Boston and Cape Cod seemed an ideal solution. He found a town on nearby Cape Cod—let us call it Inlet—which was convenient for both sailing and golf, and he bought several acres of land and a house there. Even with its very considerable growth since then, the town still has not exceeded a population of a few hundred and has remained off the tourist track. Morris spent his weekends in Inlet and the rest of the time in Boston, where he associated himself with a reputable securities firm and made an adequate living.

He started cultivating his golf game intensively. Golf is a sociable game, which mixes well with Morris' kind of business; he found that it brought him back into contact with a number of old golfing friends, some of whom had moved into the Boston area. Moreover, his prowess at golf gave Morris many opportunities to travel to invitational tournaments, and he saw a good deal of the South that way. More important, however, he became fast friends with a coterie of other good players and their wives, who followed the same circuit year after year. Through sailing, tennis, and bridge, he made still other groups of friends.

William Morris Brown (as he now regularly calls himself) rapidly became the best-known man in Inlet, where he had his legal residence. Soon he was elected to the local-government position equivalent to being mayor of a city, a post he has held for over a dozen years. He is particularly fond of this responsibility, for it puts him above the battle: He is responsible for chairing the town meetings and the sessions of the Board of Selectmen, where he casts a vote only in case of a tie. In each situation he tries to moderate disagreements and help disputing factions find compromise solutions. His is a middle-of-the-road political philosophy, with an emphasis on negotiating solutions and bringing warring parties together.

After several successful years in this role, Morris found himself (through a kind of "political fluke," as he put it) in the state legislature for a term. He enjoyed the one session in which he participated, but he disliked being forced to take a stand on every issue. Following a close defeat for reelection after a redistricting that forced him to run in an area where he was much less well known, Morris was happy to take a part-time civil-service job in the State House. This position keeps him in close contact with the legislature, but out of its hurly-burly, and enables him to continue to be well known to members of the lawmaking body. He now has political friends all over the state. He is being urged [as of 1966] to run again for state office, and he believes that his ever-widening circle of friends and acquaintances is a solid enough foundation for a fairly sure victory; at the moment, however, he is not certain that he wants the job.

The story of the last years of Morris' father has a touch of poetic justice to it. The elder Mr. Brown, alone and ailing, had again lost his speculatively gained substance and wrote to his wife asking if he could come home again. Certainly not, she replied; but he returned to the city anyway and took up residence in a nursing home. Several months later, taking pity on the feeble old man, now over 90, Mrs. Brown relented; he lived out his last six months in the same house where he had taken her as a bride. Morris had the opportunity to see his father again and to help his mother at the end.

After the war Morris and his mother had begun to be on increasingly good terms. Perhaps because she now accepted him as an adult (and a man of whom she could be proud), she made no efforts to interfere in his life. She continued running the rooming house, where she acted as informal foster mother to many a single woman. She and Morris began spending part of their vacations together, and he settled into a pattern of writing to her almost daily and talking to her by long distance every Sunday evening. When she died, a few years before the recent assessment, he could feel considerable satisfaction in the realization that he had been just the kind of devoted, good son she needed. He did not have to reproach himself, as did so many of his friends, for lack of consideration toward an elderly parent.

His stepsisters made good marriages to successful professional men and have families of their own with whom Morris keeps in touch. Nancy (the older sister) lives at some distance, but Marcia is close enough so that he has become her children's favorite uncle.

Morris has an unbroken record in the Naval Reserve; he has reported for summer training every year since his discharge and has carried through effectively every task he has been asked to perform. He is proud of the fact that he now has papers making him subject to call for active duty in an emergency; these papers are ordinarily held only by much younger men in the reserve. Moreover, through the excellence of his record and through friends now high in the Navy hierarchy, he has been called upon for special advisory assignments that have brought him into direct contact with famous persons in Washington and have given him very gratifying prestige.

The center of Morris' social life is his rambling Cape Cod house, which has been added onto so much it can now accommodate at least ten adults; a crib and a ready supply of disposable diapers are among its permanent amenities for family entertaining. In dozens of households all over New England and further south, people are accustomed to saying, "Let's run over to the Cape for a weekend at Morris' place." Uncle Morris is an almost legendary figure to the boys in these families—he swims and sails a boat as well as any teen-ager, licks most of them at tennis and all their fathers on the golf course, chops down trees, and is well-versed in the outdoorsman's lore of the Cape. The mothers are comfortable with him too, and his friends know that the latchstring is always out for them. Every weekend brings an interestingly different assortment: The husband in one couple was a member of Morris' old scout troop; another was a wartime buddy; there are always golfers when the weather permits a game (which is more than half the year in that location); occasionally a rebellious late adolescent will arrive without his family for a chance to have some long talks with a man who knows how to make him feel accepted for whatever he is.

Some of the younger members of his entourage became acquainted with Morris through his foster son Dave, now in his mid-20's. Morris had known Dave's father, who might have been a good golfer if alcoholism had not destroyed him. The widow found that she could lean on Morris and that her son took to him. Before she died, which was not long after her husband, she asked Morris to be the father Dave needed. Morris took him under his wing and feels that he helped get a rather mixed-up boy reasonably well straightened out. Although Dave is now on his own and lives in a different city, his relationship with Morris remains close.

Three years ago, Morris found that he was experiencing odd spells of fatigue and that he was losing much of his energy. He learned that he had diabetes.

Rather than make a more radical change in his style of life, Morris chose to lose 25 pounds and take insulin regularly. He can now eat anything he wants, but he has to keep his weight in the 170's. (His appearance is considerably the better for it; without the old rounded contours and with his now graying hair, his erect posture, and a spring in his step, he looks like a distinguished, vigorous executive.) The only way he could adhere to his new regimen was to give up his shared Boston apartment and constant commuting and live full time in Inlet. Morris proudly reports that his doctors have told him not 1 percent of diabetics hold to the necessary routines as well as he does, even though the patients know that carelessness will ultimately be fatal. Morris has gone into insulin coma twice, it is true, but he believes that he now knows the signs well enough to take the needed sugar promptly, and (to the relief of his friends) he has someone living with him—a foreigner who was offered a job in a city not far from Inlet but who had nowhere to stay. On hearing of the man's plight, Morris offered to take him in; though the two of them have no interests in common and virtually never converse, they get along amicably.

How should Morris' adjustment be described today? Is he happy? He surely seems to be; he claims to have found real peace since living in the country full time. In his own estimation, he has finally attained maturity since his mother's death. He sees himself as a contented man capable of frequent moments of high delight, even ecstasy:

> evenings of having the record player going and the dogs over in the corner and a good book to read and looking out and seeing all that snow and thinking, "Thank God I don't have to go anywhere!" Or now that it's getting to be spring, going out and chopping wood, staggering back and then taking a long hot shower, followed by a few beers. Those are the things that I love. And I really get ecstatic about 'em. The wonderful simple life.

At the same time, he noted that his (cyclothymic) mood swings have leveled out; both his highs and lows are less extreme.

In addition, he enjoys his work and is good enough at it to make a comfortable living. But he is content to work only enough to earn about $10,000 a year, and thus has more time for golf, sailing, tennis, and general outdoorsmanship than the great majority of more affluent men can enjoy. He is assured of financial security now: His savings, inheritance, and assured retirement pensions from the Navy, the investment firm, and Social Security enable him to look forward to a secure old age. In both work and sport he has attained positions of unusual recognition. He has hosts of friends, some of whom are young men who look up to him "as if I were Jesus Christ," as he puts it. He is fortunately situated where he can maintain a subscription to the Boston Symphony Orchestra and see his Boston bridge cronies regularly, while living the simple life in a rural community where he is the most respected of the town fathers. True, he has a chronic illness of some seriousness and a few other bodily complaints, but the diabetes is well controlled and on the whole his health and physical condition are far better than could be expected of the vast majority of men his age.

The one thing that is missing, as Morris himself is frank to point out, is love:

Whatever's wrong I have no idea, but people don't love me. They may like me very much—I'm not saying I'm a poor lost lonesome soul—but most of the people I know have somebody who is just absolutely wrapped up in them, and I never seem to have engendered that feeling. I have had plenty of gals who have made a first move. Maybe my trouble is I shove 'em away. I complain about not being loved but I'm not sure it's a complaint. Maybe I'd rather be more independent. . . . Is it possible that I'm so afraid of being hurt that I don't want to get involved?

So far in the second half of his life Morris' erotic life has remained fundamentally unchanged. He has had sexual affairs with both women and men, discreetly and rather infrequently, and usually without much tenderness and affection. His friends have for years introduced him to eligible and more or less attractive girls (by now they are mostly widows); he is polite, friendly, but rarely interested.

There was one major exception during a two-and-a-half-year period when Morris was about 35. His principal friends at the time were a group of men 10 years younger than himself, who were dating college girls; through them he met Sally, a sophomore at that time. When this beautiful young girl fell in love with him, Morris came closer to marriage than at any other time in his life. Yet, "as I finished with it, I was such an emotional wreck that I couldn't see, what is this business of being in love? I mean, it's just a torture—there was nothing good about it. We just badgered each other, killed each other—ecstatically happy for one moment and then made miserable for 24 hours. . . . There was just no peace in it," he concluded, observing that most of the happily married couples he is in constant contact with also have very little peace two-thirds of the time. He maintains that on a sexual level it was a highly satisfactory relationship, yet he spoke without nostalgia or any trace of unfulfilled yearning in his voice.

Recently, his main sexual contact has been with a younger man, who outwardly appears to be happily married but who has no moral scruples about taking any form of extramarital gratification he can get. Because he knows and likes the wife and children, Morris declares that he would have nothing to do with the man if he thought that there was any danger to the marriage. Neither man seeks the other out particularly; as Morris likes to put it, at times when they see each other something just happens spontaneously.

The encounter during the summer after graduation from college when he was a lifeguard (described in Chapter 5) is the only time Morris has had contact with an identifiably overt homosexual. There are colonies of such men on the Cape, but he avoids them; on the few occasions when he has been solicited, Morris says he has "run like hell in the opposite direction." He has thus managed to live a bachelor's life with only a minimum of gossipy suspicion and without a breath of scandal.

For the most part, however, Morris confines his sexual outlet to autoeroticism. Having close friends and much recognition, he has been able to renounce love without becoming a sexual prude. It is not an ideal life, but perhaps Morris has demonstrated (like many another unmarried man and woman before him) that it is possible to be reasonably well adjusted and socially effective without love, though cut off from the deepest of human satisfactions, which mature persons prize the most.

Some Reflections on Growing Up

Out of an unhappy family situation and a childhood most memorable for poverty and loneliness, we saw a confused young man grow, struggling to find himself and to control his impulsive, somewhat destructive behavior. A quarter of a century later, he had attained a large measure of happiness, peace, and adjustment, albeit in an atypical way.

Was he unusually slow to mature? Not nearly so much as one might think at first, for maturity is a continuous process rather than a state that should automatically set in at age 21 or any other time. Moreover, as White (1966) and Erikson (1963) tell us, maturation is a slower and more protracted process than is generally assumed, and many of the typical conflicts of adolescence do not subside in normal people until after the age of 30.

We should not, of course, overestimate Morris' achievement. His body is not functioning as well as could be desired; despite his good adjustment to the diabetes, it is a legitimate cause for anxiety. His sexual adjustment leaves a good deal to be desired, and there are other weak spots in his adaptation. The major problem of psychological interest, however, is how to explain his ability to get along so well by himself, quite without professional assistance.

The following explanation is a mixture of facts (elicited by interviews) and hypotheses, which are based on all the available data but especially on his projective test responses in the 1966 assessment.

HOW MORRIS BROWN ATTAINED MATURITY

The War Years:
A Moratorium

The Second World War, destructive though it was for millions of others, came at a fortunate time in Morris' life. It took him out of a situation containing almost as many temptations as supports and provided a temporary reprieve from his lonely effort to gain self-control. Such a period of time-out from the main game of life Erikson (1959) calls a *moratorium,* and he finds that it is often necessary for young people who are going through the kind of identity crisis Morris was enduring when he was first assessed. It takes off the pressure to make a major commitment, so that unconscious conflicts can simmer down and patterns of defense can be consolidated. The Navy replaced many burdensome responsibilities of civilian life with relatively manageable obligations within a tightly organized framework of external control. It was a common clinical observation during the war that military service was an unusually good environment for men who lacked inner controls, even for those with a psychopathic streak: The combination of absolute security, a strong institutional parent-substitute on which one could lean unobtrusively, and socially approved outlets for aggression provided a form of social control that allowed impulses to be expressed in acceptable ways. When Morris had to take command of a landing craft on its shakedown cruise, he could do it well (we saw in the preceding chapters that he had the necessary abilities) and therefore could legitimately feel he was becoming a man.

The service also gave him a sexual moratorium, freeing him from the social pressure to find a girl to marry while giving him occasional opportunities for condoned heterosexual adventures. And it threw him together with men in situations where his natural talent for friendship could manifest itself and his preference for close contact with men could be satisfied.

Thus, the war years took away opportunities for many elements of the more potentially pathological of Morris' two possible identities and ego structures to show themselves; and they strengthened important elements in the compulsive pattern. A major threat carried by the compulsive alternative was the danger of a predominantly feminine identity if he became too much like his mother. During the war and afterward, however, he was able to develop in himself the most adaptive and socially desirable aspects of his mother's heritage while being in many ways more masculine than his father had ever been.

Development of His Identity

When he first got out of the Navy, Morris experienced a short period of restlessness—he toured the national parks with four friends for several months before he settled down to work. During that period the paternal pattern seemed to be asserting itself one final time before subsiding. The strengthened compulsive defenses proved staunch, especially when Morris' athletic prowess began to emerge again. (Note that this important aspect of his personality owes little to either parent.) Thanks to his sturdy body and his extraordinary physical talents, Morris has always been outstanding in the "man's world" of sport. His travel in tournament competition seems to have satiated his wanderlust to the point where he seldom feels the old itch to get away.

But though he has been able to maintain an appropriately manly personality in many respects, it would probably have taken considerable psychotherapeutic help for Morris to have worked through the incest taboo, his anxiety about the masculine sexual role (basically, castration anxiety), and other unconscious hindrances to a sustained intimate relationship with a woman. Because that possibility was shut off, and because he had established a pattern of finding some sexual gratification with men, there was a distinct danger of overt homosexuality. In another situation and another vocation, and with various other changes, someone still recognizably similar to our man might have taken this route; but it was obviously impossible for

Morris. A political career, for example, would have been out of the question, as would many of the other important elements of his pattern of adjustment.

Thanks to Morris' unusual defenses—a blend of isolation, denial, and repression—he has been able to keep the door to sexual activity with males ajar, but not enough to bring against himself the accusation of being a "fairy," which he clearly is not, according to his own definition. Most people would probably agree. He has been able to develop an identity in which there are both masculine and feminine elements. And the latter are mainly qualities that were the source of his mother's *strength*—her moral backbone, her compulsive orderliness and organizing ability, and her kindly nurturance. The role Morris plays with so many of his young friends (and of course most literally with his foster son) is a parental one, just as his preferred role in politics is that of a just, impartial parent who empathically settles the children's squabbles without getting drawn into taking sides.

Morris' most recent projective test responses show none of the gory, self-directed destructive imagery that was so blatant in the Rorschach and TAT of 1940. The explanation may lie in one of Erikson's insights (1963): A strong sense of identity is a bulwark against the superego. As Morris grew more sure of himself and realized that he was a socially esteemed and estimable person, he was able to get control over the savagely self-punitive superego elements reflected in such images as the self-disemboweling Fu Manchu. The more his conscious values and role led to behavior that was acceptable to the primitive elements of his earliest identifications with his parents, the less unconscious guilt he had and the more he could consolidate a reasonable and useful nucleus of unconscious self-control. To be sure, this change, accomplished through the aid of more identification with his parents (particularly his mother), has also led to a degree of solidarity with all sources of authority that many would consider excessive. Morris feels so much at one with the controlling powers that he is overly ready to comply instantly with any authoritative requirement. At the same time, he has not developed an ideological authoritarianism; unconsciously, he seems to be more a good boy than a tyrant.

The Effect of His Environment

The importance of Morris' environment should not be overlooked as we try to understand how he made his adjustment. His being able to get away from the big-city pressure and competition to a small country town where he could live an outdoor life was a weekend safety valve for years, while he began to develop rootedness in the little community. His longtime position of public trust and leadership there has greatly strengthened his fatherliness and his sense of responsibility. It has made mature, moral integrity far more rewarding than any kind of opportunistic attempt at self-serving shortcuts could possibly be.

Morris Brown's life history is a good example of an important principle in understanding personality: Early traumas and other unhappy experiences and the growth of such defenses as isolation and denial do not necessarily imply a disturbance of the adult personality. These elements can constitute unsuccessful or successful personalities—people crippled by neurosis or solid citizens like Morris. Endowments of ability and strength (like our man's intelligence and physique) and how the person fits into his social setting probably tip the balance toward a socially desirable or undesirable personality.

Clinical psychologists and psychiatrists, who are accustomed to dealing only with people who have given up trying to make it on their own, often tend to overlook the positive role a defense like denial can play in a healthy adjustment. In some such colleagues, the presence of recognizably hypomanic elements in Morris' very happiness would bring on dark looks and ominously wagging heads. To them only this can be said: Let the one among you who is without this defense (or one of an equivalent and equally "pathological" type) cast the first stone. Good adaptation is not so much a question of the kind of defense as of the total biopsychosocial configuration in which it operates.

Concluding Thoughts
on Morris Brown's Assessment

It would be a mistake to leave the impression that this case study has been a typical application of personality assessment, or that it is being offered as a model for the practitioner to emulate. In many ways, it has been a unique opportunity and a special application of techniques. The very fact that so many hours were spent gathering and analyzing data of so many kinds makes this case history atypical. For most of the practical applications of personality assessment listed in Chapter 1, it would be a highly uneconomic procedure.

Much more abbreviated and limited approaches to personality assessment are not only more common but are more desirable, in a number of situations. When Morris served as a subject in an experiment, the quantitative data from objective assessment proved more useful than the qualitative understanding, for the group method called for uniform measures across all subjects. Most research projects are of necessity designed in that way, and if clinical assessments are to play a part they must be expressed in the form of quantitative ratings, like the criterion Q sort for Morris. The focused approach of objective tests of personality will continue to be the most useful one, particularly in research on the kinds of changes induced in personality by life conditions of stress or frustration, on the relationships between personality and ideology, and in general on any topic for which one (nonpersonality) variable must be quickly and accurately measured in large numbers of persons.

Let us turn, in the next chapter, to a reconsideration of the relative merits and uses of the two principal approaches to the assessment of personality.

He that judges without informing himself to the utmost that he is capable, cannot acquit himself of judging amiss.

JOHN LOCKE. Essay Concerning Human Understanding

CHAPTER 10
THE EVALUATION
OF PERSONALITY
ASSESSMENT

An attempt has been made in the preceding chapters to present research evidence bearing on assertions made there about personality assessment, but most of what is known about the topic, and about clinical assessment in particular, is the heritage of a tradition. Although this body of knowledge has been subjected to constant confrontation with empirical data and intermittent theoretical refinement, it remains true that assessing personality is the application of a science that is not yet fully developed.

One hallmark of a scientifically based discipline is that it tries to evaluate its practices as carefully and dispassionately as possible in a search not for self-justification but for the truth, which alone makes progress possible. Though there undeniably are elements of art and craft in assessment, its practitioners strive to put it on as sound a scientific basis as they can. In the course of this attempt, they have generated a fair amount of evidence, a large controversy, and some useful thinking about how so manifold an undertaking as personality assessment may be evaluated. This chapter is devoted to a survey of these topics.

How Should Personality Assessment Be Evaluated?

We have seen that the first types of formal assessment were clinical and that they were little more than an extended attempt to apply the methods of informal assessment with relatively little systematization (Chapter 3). These clinical methods were evaluated in correspondingly informal ways, usually without any focused intent to question their worth and effectiveness—that is, they won social and institutional acceptance, so that it became possible to earn a living by assessing personalities in the variety of settings we examined in Chapter 1. It is difficult to believe that specialists in assessment could have won and retained the respect of their professional colleagues if they actually had nothing valid to contribute.

A few notorious impostors have demonstrated that a charlatan can practice even so concrete a discipline as surgery undetected, for a while, with no assets other than an impressive, assured manner, an ear for shop talk, and some shrewdness and common sense in handling practical situations. The criterion of cure is much less clear-cut in psychotherapy, so that a private practitioner of this healing art may survive for years without any valid knowledge or skill, simply because his work is not observed and checked by colleagues and because people in need of treatment tend on the average to get better anyway. But a lack of clinical competence cannot be concealed for very long from anyone who has participated in the daily work of a "mental-health team" in a clinic or hospital. The method of evaluating clinical assessment implicit in such vocational success is sometimes called "clinical validation"; its evidence is surely fallible, and it would be dangerous to put sole reliance on it, but it is real and important evidence. The personality assessment practiced by psychiatrists, social workers, and other non-psychologists is generally subjected to no more searching evaluation than the judgment of colleagues that it is worthwhile.

The psychometric tradition has won a respected place within psychology, in part because psychometricians have stringently evaluated their own techniques and have produced both principles and methods for doing so. Their first evaluative ideals were reliability and validity, as we saw in Chapter 4. Today, it is being recognized that these touchstones are not as automatically applicable as had once been thought. A test should surely be reliable, but it is difficult to lay down any handy, generally useful set of guidelines. For example, a statement that "repeat reliability must be .85 or better if the test is to be used with individuals" must be hedged about by so many definitions, explanations, and exceptions that it is of very little value. There is no consensus among psychometric experts on the degree of internal consistency a test should have, and obviously a test that did not reflect a real change in a subject on being readministered would be "reliable" in the narrow sense, at the cost of usefulness—like a stopped clock that always tells the same time.

Nevertheless, the ideal of reliability is undeniably relevant both to the psychometric approach and to personality assessment as a whole. It is meaningful to ask how well assessors can agree among themselves when they examine the same person (consensus), how well each one can agree with his own previous conclusions when he reanalyzes the same body of data about a person after a lapse of time (stability, a form of repeat reliability), and how well various techniques of assessment agree among themselves or lead to common inferences (convergence).

Before these questions can be answered, two important limitations on their applicability must be stated. First, only by requiring assessors to express their statements about their subjects in a common language, preferably in the form of quantitative ratings, can precise information about each of these points be obtained. Since most professional practitioners of personality assessment do not use Q sorts or other forms of numerical rating but express their findings in verbal reports, and since they may use quite varied conceptual vocabularies, their routine work cannot easily be evaluated for any of these forms of reliability. Second, personality assessment is a sprawling, heterogeneous discipline, practiced by different kinds of people in different settings for a variety of purposes. It therefore cannot be meaningfully evaluated as a whole, just as we cannot sensibly ask, "On the average, how reliable are psychological tests?" We have seen in earlier chapters that some tests are highly reliable by several kinds of criteria, others seem worthless, and many others occupy positions all up and down the scale. In almost all branches of personality assessment, there have been reports that most kinds of assessment *can* be carried out with good reliability in all three of these senses. Most of the published evidence, however, suggests that although clinical assessors tend to agree fairly well with themselves over time (stability), they agree far less well with one another (consensus), and most of the evidence on convergence is discouraging (Goldberg, 1968).

With respect to the issue of validity the situation is even more confusing. Recent critics like Ebel (1961) and Vernon (1964) have seriously questioned the old dogma that validity—at least, as expressed in terms of correlation coefficients—is necessarily the most important criterion for evaluating tests. The traditional method of measuring validity assumes that there exists an intrinsically valid criterion against which a test score can be measured—when in fact such a criterion exists only in exceptional cases, and almost never in the general realm of personality traits. It is worthy of note, however, that those who have attempted to validate tests of personality have quite generally assumed that the best criterion available is ratings from intensive, multiform, clinical assessment. It is difficult indeed to imagine a wholly different and better approach to a criterion measure of traits.

In terms of the traditional approach to the validity of specific techniques of assessment (correlation with a criterion), the results are much the same as in the case of their reliability, except that correlations run much lower and the best are only moderately good. In place of reliance on "validity coefficients," Ebel suggests that the following list of criteria for determining the value, or quality, of a mental test or measurement procedure be adopted.

1. The importance of the inferences that can be made from the test scores [or, more generally, from the test data]
2. The meaningfulness of the test scores, based on
   a. An operational definition of the measurement procedure
   b. A knowledge of the relationships of the scores to other measures, from
      i. Validity coefficients, predictive and concurrent
      ii. Other correlation coefficients or measures of relationship
   c. A good estimate of the reliability of the scores
   d. Appropriate norms of examinee performance
3. The convenience of the test in use [Ebel, 1961, p. 646].

These standards were designed for the evaluation of tests, and they are not as directly applicable to entire enterprises of assessment. Nevertheless, they may be of some value as guides. Suppose we look back over the assessment of Morris Brown presented in earlier chapters and ask whether clinical or objective tests and methods were more useful in our attempt to grasp what sort of man he is and what sort of sense his life pattern makes. Judged in this way the clinical approach seems an easy winner. Such an evaluative approach is close in spirit to Ebel's first principle, for (compared with the objective procedures) clinical methods led to a wider range of inferences and observations, which touched on deeper and more important issues. Objective tests do tend to be more convenient (Ebel's third criterion) in that they take less time and skill to administer and score than projective techniques, and they have the advantage of yielding quantitative scores—which are necessary to make Ebel's second, complex criterion workable. A word of caution about the first criterion, however, is in order: The mere fact that it is possible to make inferences about important aspects of personality from the TAT, for example, does not mean that those inferences can be trusted, nor that they convey much useful information. Ultimately it remains necessary to find some external or independent way of evaluating the same aspects of personality, against which we can check interpretations based on any one test or procedure.

A simpler approach to validation has been proposed and has been widely accepted by psychologists. The ultimate aim of psychology is to predict human behavior, the argument begins; therefore, let us aim any particular method of assessment toward some specific behavioral *prediction* and judge the validity of that method according to just how correct the prediction is. Later in this chapter we shall take note of several ways in which this argument is not wholly acceptable and shall continue the discussion of how to evaluate approaches to assessment. First, however, let us examine in more detail the predictive approach—the controversy (clinical versus statistical prediction) it has aroused and the sorts of data it has generated.

Clinical Versus
Statistical Prediction

THE NATURE OF THE CONTROVERSY

A recurrent theme in the preceding chapters has been the objective versus the subjective tradition within personality assessment. It has surely become clear that this book has a bias—that personalities cannot be understood or even meaningfully measured without the necessarily subjective processes of the clinician as he perceives, empathizes, intuits, makes judgments, integrates and synthesizes information, and constructs a theory, or schema, of a person. It would not be fair to the reader, however, to imply that this view is widespread among American psychologists or to minimize the many important advances in personality assessment made by those whose ideal is objectivity and who hope eventually to eliminate the clinician altogether as an assessor of personality.

The origins of the controversy over prediction go back to the 1920's and '30's, when a small group of prominent psychologists challenged proponents of statistical methods to try to predict behavior as well as the clinical case-history method could do. It was said (for example by Allport, 1942) that statistical methods had severe, inherent limitations in their applicability to the behavior of unique individual personalities. This point of view derived from a number of fallacious theories about the nature of science as applied to personality (described in Holt, 1967) and perhaps also from an emotional rejection of the idea that mechanical systems could predict the acts of live human beings. These critics knew little about the refined techniques being developed by statistical workers, and some of the most vocal were not themselves practitioners of the clinical assessment they upheld.

It is important to realize that advocates of the clinical and the objective traditions of assessment have almost always been involved in rather different kinds of work. Clinical assessment is practiced predominantly in hospitals and clinics where the emphasis is on intensive study of individuals to gain an understanding of them that can facilitate decisions about how to help them and guide a psychotherapist in his initial approach.

Objective assessment of personality is the main work of a smaller number of psychologists, mostly researchers interested in developing tests, and it has been a sideline of persons interested in educational advisement, personnel selection, and criminology, who have relied for the most part on ability tests and measures not generally considered within the realm of personality assessment. The objective assessor is usually called upon to make a simple decision about accepting a person for some kind of education, training, or employment, or paroling a prisoner.

The clinical assessor does make similar judgments (for example, should a given patient be treated by a particular method or not?), but for the most part his task is the evaluation and understanding of a person's problems, his major patterns of behavior, and the nature of his development. In the normal course of events, therefore, there was little direct competition between these different approaches.

Behind the two traditions there is a good deal more, however. They are offshoots of different and conflicting ideologies and schools of psychology (and perhaps, ultimately, of different temperaments). Psychologists of personality generally respect the divergent ideals of scientific rigor and human relevance, but some emphasize the one, some the other. Despite the desire of many—perhaps most—people in the field to maintain some integration and balance between these often conflicting standards, there has been an escalating tendency toward dichotomous thinking. The resulting attitude has been this: If there are two ways of approaching the assessment of personality, one must be right or at least superior; therefore, let us pit one approach against the other and see which is better.

Clearly, there is no way of telling whether it is "better" to be a valued member of a clinical team or a successful constructer of objective tests. Some common ground had to be found on which the issue could be joined. That ground was the *prediction of behavior*, and the issue was formulated as "clinical versus statistical prediction." The result was a controversy that picked up steam right after World War II and has been one of the most conspicuous features of the psychological scene for over a decade.

SOME TERMS DEFINED

There is less agreement than one might expect on what is meant by the two types of prediction. As we shall shortly see, predicting behavior is a complicated matter that involves half a dozen steps, in any of which clinical judgment may play a role. But the prevailing tendency has been to focus on only the final step, when the data—however they may have been gathered and processed—are put together to yield an actual prediction. Sawyer (1966) says: "Whether *prediction* is called clinical or mechanical typically depends on how the data were *combined*." Meehl (1954) is somewhat more specific: "By *mechanical* (or statistical), I mean that the prediction is arrived at by some straightforward application of an equation or table to the data." This latter definition will become more meaningful after we have examined some concrete examples of how predictions are made by means of equations and tables.

Notice that clinical prediction appears to be defined residually; that is, it seems to be any kind of prediction that does *not* rely on mechanical rules and procedures. This failure to give clinical prediction as positive a definition as statistical prediction has introduced a subtle bias into the research on this topic: Almost anyone is considered a "clinician," whether he has any training in clinical assessment or not, as long as he does not follow some formula; and "clinical" has tended to become synonymous with "unsystematic," "casual," or "haphazard." It would seem a foregone conclusion that if predictions are considered "clinical" only when they are made by people who are selected without regard for their degree of clinical skill or training and who follow no definite procedures, the statistical approach will surely appear superior.

Nevertheless, the crux of the matter seems to be the degree to which objectivity is achieved by diminishing the role of clinical judgment, replacing it at the final stage by a set of predetermined rules that may be applied by a person with minimal training. If we consider stages other than the final one, the problem no longer looks so simple. Sawyer (1966) urged that we also consider whether a clinician was involved in gathering the data:

> Data collection is mechanical if rules can be prespecified so that no clinical judgment need be involved in the procedure. Thus, on the one hand are all the self-report and clerically obtained data: psychometric tests, biographical data, personnel records, etc.; on the other hand are the usual clinical interview and observation [and projective techniques]. [Sawyer, 1966, p. 181]

Further distinctions can usefully be made among other types of predictions, but in order to grasp them we shall first have to consider in more detail just what statistical prediction is and what some of its accomplishments have been.

METHODS AND ACHIEVEMENTS
OF STATISTICAL PREDICTION

From its beginning, the psychometric tradition has been concerned with prediction. Binet, you will recall, invented the first successful intelligence tests in what was essentially an attempt to predict educational achievement. In the next four decades, the predictive task widened from weeding out defectives in elementary schools to selecting students who would be most likely to profit from college or postgraduate education. One of the best predictors was essentially a descendant of Binet's test, via the line of group intelligence tests: the Scholastic Aptitude Test (SAT), developed by the College Entrance Examination Board. Its total score was correlated about .50 with achievement in freshman courses; average grades in secondary school also were correlated with the same target, or criterion, variable (freshman grades) at about the same level. A statistical combination of SAT scores and high school grades by means of multiple correlation was somewhat better than either alone, but more than half the variance in freshman grades remained unaccounted for.

Prediction by the Experience Table

During the decade just before World War II, sociologists and criminologists doing research on marital adjustment and on the violation of parole made active and successful use of a predictive device known as the *experience table*. This method is called *actuarial* because in setting rates for life insurance an actuary proceeds in much the same fashion. For this reason, the nonclinical approach in general has come to be called either actuarial or statistical prediction, the two terms being used interchangeably by most authors. Another commonly used synonym for statistical in this context is "mechanical."

An experience table is a summary of experience with a group of subjects, which is broken down according to background data, their answers to a questionnaire, or the like. The group should be as large as possible. For example, a criminologist may classify past parolees from a prison system according to a large number of available items of information about the prisoners, looking for those items that create a significant difference in the rate of parole violation. Thus, Burgess (1928) found that although the general rate of violation among 3000 men paroled from the Illinois prisons was just over 28 percent, the rate was less than half that among men whose records showed that they had worked regularly before imprisonment—a statistically significant finding. This then became one of 21 items associated with success, to each of which Burgess assigned a value of 1. He next tabulated the percentage of nonviolators of parole in 9 groupings of men according to their total scores on these items; the result of this tabulation is shown in Table 10-1.

Table 10-1   Rates of Success on Parole, According to the Burgess Experience Table

Experience Table Score Group	Number of Cases	Percentage of Nonviolators of Parole
A (16–21)	68	99
B (14–15)	140	98
C (13)	91	91
D (12)	106	85
E (11)	110	77
F (10)	88	66
G (7–9)	287	56
H (5–6)	85	33
I (2–4)	25	24

Adapted from Gough, 1962.

Two considerations must be kept in mind in evaluating any figures like those in Table 10-1, promising though they may appear. First, there is the problem of *cross-validation shrinkage*. This is a technical way of saying that one cannot expect everything to work out exactly the same with another group of subjects, and in fact if any of the original findings are attributable to chance (as they always are to some extent), cross-validating on a new sample will give poorer results. The larger the original group, the less likelihood there is that there has been much capitalizing on chance; but notice that although Table 10-1 is based on 1000 cases, the actual percentages in 5 of the 9 score groups are based on less than 100 men.

Second, there is the question of what is called the *base rate*—here, the proportion of persons who succeed in the total population of prisoners. Suppose that 95 percent of the men in a given prison tend to succeed in parole; obviously, we would very seldom be wrong if we *always* predicted nonviolation (assuming that the base rate remains stable, for variations in the base rate are one source of cross-validation shrinkage). Even when the base rate of violation is as high (28.5 percent) as it was in Burgess' original sample, Gough has shown that

> At only two cutting points, levels F and G, does the Burgess table improve over the flat assertion that no one will fail, and at the *optimum* point of dichotomy (predicting parole success for all men with scores of 7 or more) the error figure . . . is only 4.2 percentage points under that found when one simply forecasts that everyone will succeed [Gough, 1962, p. 563].

Indeed, Meehl and Rosen (1955) have shown that when the base rate of anything we are interested in predicting goes much above or below 50 percent, it is increasingly difficult to beat it. How can these statements be true, when it seems clear from Table 10-1 that if only those men with scores of 12 or more (groups A through D) were paroled, 9 out of 10 would be nonviolators? The hitch is that this is considering only what are technically called "valid positives" and "false positives," neglecting the "valid negatives" and especially the "false negatives"—in this example, the 338 men who would not violate parole if they got a chance but who would be refused it. Since almost as many subjects would be false negatives as valid positives (correctly predicted nonviolators) if the cut were made between D and E, this is a large group to overlook.

This example brings out another important point that has been learned from actuarial prediction: A predictor may be useful even when it has a relatively low validity, or success, rate attached to it, if the *selection ratio* is low—that is, if it is possible to skim off the cream by taking only the best applicants, or diagnosing only the clearest cases, or releasing only the best bets for parole. Where it is necessary, however, to predict for an entire population and to minimize both kinds of errors (false positives and false negatives), it becomes very important to know the base rate. "In order for a positive diagnostic assertion to be 'more likely true than false,' the ratio of the positive to the negative base rates in the examined population must exceed the ratio of the false positive rate to the valid positive rate [Meehl & Rosen, 1955]." This means that if only a small proportion of a total population actually belong to the predicted class (let us say, suicides), then if an indicator does not pick up virtually all of them (valid positives) and only a very small proportion of the great majority who are actually nonsuicidal (false positives), the latter will exceed the former. This is true whether the indicator is a test score, an objective fact of life history, or a clinical judgment by a team of investigators.

Prediction by Multiple Regression

Multiple regression is a complex statistical method of combining several variables in order to predict a quantitative criterion. It is an outgrowth of the method of correlation, a mathematical technique of expressing the degree of relation between two sets of numbers. If one set is a group's scores on a psychological test and the other set is their ratings on some kind of criterion behavior, a high correlation means that the first variable may be used to predict the second. Suppose that the same group has been given several tests, each of which is appreciably correlated with the criterion—how do we go about using all of them to improve the predictions that could be made with one test? If all the tests were measures of the same trait (for example, various intelligence tests), each would be highly correlated with all the others and any one of them would serve almost as well as the whole battery. But if the intercorrelations among the tests were low, there would be a good chance that they measured different traits and thus could supplement one another. Multiple regression is a statistical technique for extracting, from the web of interrelationships among a group of predictors and a criterion, a set of weights for each test score and a formula for combining them to yield the best possible prediction of the criterion.

This method will become clearer with an actual example. During World War II, the technique of multiple regression was brought to a high state of development in the Army Air Force. A battery of 20 tests (14 self-administering questionnaires and 6 tests requiring apparatus) was used to select men for the various jobs on a military plane—as pilots, navigators, tailgunners, and so on. Scores on the tests were put together by slightly different formulas for each aircrew job. When applied to new samples of recruits, these formulas repeatedly yielded predictions that correlated from .50 to .60 with passing versus failing the training course (DuBois, 1947).

How were such results obtained? (See the "pure actuarial" column in Table 10-2, page 215.) First, the army's psychologists made a "job analysis"—detailed studies of just what a pilot, for example, did and what the student had to learn. They next tried to determine what personal qualities—abilities, temperamental traits, and so on—a person must possess to carry out these functions. Assembling the existing tests of these characteristics, they made up others and put together a large battery, which was given to many hundreds of flight trainees. Records of these men's success or failure provided the criterion, with which every test's scores were correlated in a preliminary validation trial. Many tests immediately failed to show any promise and were dropped; others were modified, and the best were kept unchanged in the new battery. The statistical method of multiple regression helped the psychologists find the best ways of combining the separate test scores to predict a pass-fail criterion. Once the formula was found, it provided a statistical, or mechanical, rule for combining test data; the clerk who used it needed no special psychological knowledge. This formula was then put through further trial by cross-validation (being checked on a new group of subjects). The entire process was repeated until it looked as if the battery of tests had reached the limits of its effectiveness.

RELATIVE SUCCESSES
OF CLINICAL AND STATISTICAL PREDICTION

Emboldened by ignorance and by the encouragement of prestigious spokesmen, many clinical assessors of personality stuck their necks out in research projects that were set up—usually by the statisticians—to compare the "two kinds of prediction." The clinicians either did not notice or did not think it important that they were being asked to function in unfamiliar ways and to make statements about matters they understood poorly. Perhaps they thought there was nothing to be lost by such extra-curricular adventures, which were, after all, sidelines for them. Most clinicians spent by far the greater part of their time in diagnostic and therapeutic work with patients, where they earned their livings and made their reputations.

Results of Surveys   The highly influential book *Clinical Versus Statistical Prediction* (Meehl, 1954) was the first of several surveys of the comparative performance of clinical and statistical predictors (Cronbach, 1956; Gough, 1962; Sawyer, 1966). Meehl reported finding "from 16 to 20 studies involving a comparison of clinical and actuarial methods, *in all but one of which the predictions made actuarially were either approximately equal or superior to those made by a clinician* [1954, p. 119]."

Just over a decade later Meehl (1965) wrote that he had tallied 50 studies, in two-thirds of which the statistical predictions were superior and in the other one-third of which the two methods were substantially equal. He noted that the one exception he had found earlier demonstrated the apparent superiority of the clinician only by virtue of an invalid use of statistics, but he hailed a study by Lindzey (which will be described later in the chapter) as the first clear example in which the clinician was superior. Sawyer

(1966), in a slightly more recent survey tallying 75 comparisons in 45 different studies, is extremely discouraging in regard to both clinical measurement and clinical prediction: He reports *no* comparisons in which the clinical method was significantly superior to the mechanical (statistical) and many instances in which the latter approach *was* significantly more successful.

A Critique of the Surveys   Before looking at some of the successes of clinical prediction, let us note some of the flaws of these surveys. Meehl wrote in 1954:

> The ideal design [for a study comparing clinical and statistical predictions] is one in which the same basic set of facts is subjected on the one hand to the skilled analysis of a trained clinician, and on the other hand is subjected to mechanical operations (table entry, multiplication by weights, or the like) [pp. 89–90].

A good many other writers (for example, Hoffman, 1960; Gough, 1962) take essentially the same position. Note, however, that this design allows the clinician no data beyond a string of numbers, supplemented at best by a few simple objective facts like marital status. Only a clinical psychologist who had been trained primarily in the profile analysis of the MMPI would consider this to be material on which he could properly exercise his talents. With nothing more to work with, the clinician is perforce a second-rate calculating machine, and the only surprising result of such comparisons is that the clinicians occasionally do as well as the formulas. If there was any issue here, it is settled: In any situation where only objective data are available and statistical prediction is possible, there is no point in wasting clinical time and talent in an attempt to outdo statistical methods.

Second, both Meehl and Sawyer have apologetically included a good many studies in which predictions by multiple regression used statistical weights that were worked out and validated on the same group of subjects—that is, without cross-validation. Such investigations should be included only if the clinicians, too, have the benefit of seeing the answers and then revising their predictions accordingly. The invalidity of the latter procedure points up the inescapable need to carry a rational predictive study through all six steps outlined in Table 10-2. Even when the original sample includes more than 1000 subjects cross-validation is necessary, because there is no guarantee that the next group will continue to be similar: Unexpected sampling fluctuations do occur frequently when we are dealing with human subjects.

Third, as Meehl (1954, p. 122) pointed out, the researches he collated "all involve the prediction of a somewhat heterogeneous, crude, socially defined behavior outcome." That is to say, if a psychologist attempts to predict the usual criterion, like grades in some kind of school, the *behavior* being predicted is not that of the subject who has been tested, interviewed, or the like—it is grade-giving behavior by unassessed and unknown people. Moreover, they evaluate the subject's behavior in future situations unforeseeable at the time of the assessment (or even rate what they believe his behavior to be, which itself may be more of a prediction than an observation).

To a clinician whose idea of predicting behavior is anticipating patients' responses to psychotherapeutic maneuvers, the kind of prediction tested in the published research is more like prophecy. As Meehl demonstrates, the criterion in a typical predictive study is so complexly determined, being the cumulation of so many individual acts, that

> in order to predict this outcome by clinical understanding it would be necessary to formulate an extremely detailed conceptual model of personality structure [and of the situation, or "press"]. . . . Now it is obvious that in none of the studies cited did the clinician have an opportunity to "formulate the personality" or to determine the *press* in anything like the detail indicated [1954, p. 123].

But instead of concluding that the studies in question were not reasonable tests of the clinician's ability, Meehl indicates only that the latter should have refused to attempt nonstatistical predictions. He may be right, but judgment about when to cooperate and when to refuse is of a different order from that involved in combining data to make predictions and should not be confounded with it.

It is doubtful that much can be learned about the value of clinical assessment by having clinicians attempt to predict college grades, success in some kind of vocational training, violation of parole, officers' ratings of their men, the winning teams in football, or the number of live children that will be born to certain couples in the 20 years following assessment. Yet a majority of the studies tabulated in the most recent of the detailed surveys (Sawyer, 1966) used criteria of these kinds. It *would* make sense to try to predict some form of behavior or some behavioral outcome in which a major role is played by personality traits, motives, defenses, and other such inner dispositions of the kind clinicians are trained to assess, but very few studies have used such criteria.

Fourth, it is misleading to compare the effectiveness of clinical judgment with that of a mechanical rule at the final stage of combining data unless in all five of the preceding steps (see Table 10-2) the competitors are on an equal footing. And in none of the 20 studies Meehl cites was this requirement met. Instead, the statistical predictions were usually being cross-validated, and the clinical ones never were.

Most of the published studies pitted examples of *pure actuarial* against *naive clinical* predictions (Table 10-2; see also Holt, 1958). A pure actuarial predictive system is one that uses objective data to predict a clear-cut criterion with the help of statistics. The role of judgment is held to a minimum, and full use is made of psychometric know-how throughout the six stages.

**Table 10-2   An Outline of Three Types
of Predictive Systems**

Steps in Prediction	How Steps Are Carried Out in Three Predictive Systems		
	Naive Clinical System	Pure Actuarial System	Sophisticated Clinical System
1. Analyze the criterion (study what is to be predicted)	Omitted or left to guesswork	The criterion actually used to test predictions is studied, yielding a description of relevant kinds of behavior (job analysis)	
2. Discover intervening variables to be measured (personal and situational)	Left to intuition or guesswork	Often bypassed; sometimes done by factor analysis	Done by careful study of known criterion groups and of their working situations
3. Choose tests or other means of assessment	Interviews and/or projective tests are used (largely because of familiarity with them)	Objective tests (self-administering questionnaires or apparatus tests) are preferred; many are assembled or invented	Instruments (both objective and subjective) are chosen or devised in terms of their suitability for assessing the relevant variables
4. First stage of validation: preliminary trial	Omitted	All test scores are correlated with the criterion; those that do not work are dropped or modified; those that do are combined in a formula that "predicts" the criterion best	Where possible, the same procedure as in the actuarial system is used; also, qualitative data (such as from the interview) on known subjects are studied to see how they relate to the criterion, and scoring keys or manuals to guide analysis are developed and tried out
5. Final validation: Gather and process data for measures of intervening variables	Clinical experience and judgment are used exclusively to process clinical data	A relatively simple, routine procedure, done by subprofessionals who administer and score tests	A combination of the other two, plus specific guidance in making primary inferences, by prior study of known cases' data
6. Final validation: Combine data for crucial predictions and test statistically	Unguided intuition and clinical judgment are used to construct a schema of each personality, from which the clinician tries to guess the criterion	Statistics are used to combine scores mechanically (for example, by multiple correlation with the criterion), applying the same formula to all cases	Clinical judgment, disciplined by the previous steps, is used to construct a schema of each personality, considering its functioning in expected situations and ending with case-by-case quantitative prediction

In a naive clinical study, the qualitative data are processed intuitively by rule of thumb without any prior study of the criterion or of the relation of the assessment data to it. Clinical judgment is relied on from start to finish not only as a way of integrating data to produce predictions but also as an alternative to acquaintance with the facts.

Yet a third type of prediction is also possible: *sophisticated clinical* prediction. This approach tries to combine the best of both traditions. It uses the refinements of experimental design from the actuarial side, with job analyses, pilot studies, item analyses, and successive cross-validations; but it also includes a full use of qualitative data and the clinician's personal as well as intellectual resources. With the discipline of scientific method, the latter can be an even more sensitive instrument than he is when he is allowed to run wild, and he is surely more organized and balanced. It would be a perverse clinician indeed who claimed that a casual, informal, uncontrolled approach was necessarily better than a disciplined, unbiased one. It is not being "more clinical" to give tests in a slipshod fashion than to do so precisely and carefully. Why, therefore, should it be assumed that prediction is clinical only when the person doing the predicting does not have the benefit of well-organized procedures?

Table 10-2 makes it plain that clinical judgment can be used in the predictive process at any of several points, and each time in either a disciplined or an undisciplined way. Sawyer (1966) made a start in the right direction by tallying studies separately, depending on whether the measurement as well as the prediction was clinical or mechanical, but this classification is still a long way from being adequate. The three categories of naive clinical, pure actuarial, and sophisticated clinical systems are also far from exhaustive. The research literature is still too variegated and the different components of predictive systems are combined in too many ways for nose counting to be very meaningful.

The irony of these classification attempts is that some clinical research has been tallied as evidence for actuarial prediction. This was the case for the research of Wittman (1941), which shows what can be accomplished in selecting patients for shock treatment by applying clinical judgment to the qualitative information in case files in a systematic, controlled way. Here the measurement was clinical, and the data were processed subjectively by highly trained clinicians, albeit only to the point where the intervening variables were quantified by means of ratings, which were then added up to yield the predictive score. This score correlated well with response to shock treatment while the predictions of that same criterion made in routine case conference in a state hospital were ineffective. The study is therefore classified in all th surveys as evidence for the superiority of *statistical* prediction. The investiga tion does not fit readily into any simple category, but it is surely misleadin to tally it in a way that implies that clinical theories and techniques hav once again been shown to be invalid.

The case for prediction based on clinical assessment turns out to be not as bleak as the recent surveys would have us believe, if we look at the few studies of appropriate kinds of problems and note (as we have just done) where and how clinical judgment was used.

The kind of prediction at which clinicians are generally best is diagnosis, which is not "prediction" in the usual sense but generalization: From a relatively small body of facts about a person, a clinician infers the results of processing a large body of facts. Thus, from reading a few TAT stories, a clinician may attempt to infer the presence of overt homosexuality in the storyteller, which may be established by the scrutiny of a larger (or at least different) body of clinical observations.

Lindzey (1965) demonstrated that two experienced clinical psychologists who knew a good deal both about the TAT and about male homosexuality could distinguish homosexual from heterosexual protocols significantly better than chance. With a group of undergraduate subjects, the first judge made a correct diagnosis in 95 percent of the 40 TAT's, while an attempt to analyze the same data according to a list of signs that had distinguished heterosexual from homosexual students in previous research failed to do better than chance. It was possible to construct a formula that apparently did almost as well as the clinician (on the sample it was based on, it identified 90 percent of the cases correctly); but when it was cross-validated on a new sample, this time of 30 prisoners, the new check list did only slightly better than chance (57 percent accurate), a level that could not be improved by any after-the-fact juggling. The original judge performed at about the same lower level of accuracy (60 percent) with the prison subjects, but a second judge's accuracy was 80 percent. The study has some flaws; it does not, for example, consider the base-rate problem, for the subjects were matched pairs of homosexuals and heterosexuals; but it does demonstrate that trained and experienced clinicians can perform better than cross-validated "objective" processing of the same data.

Another investigation, aimed at developing methods of selecting men for training in psychiatry at the Menninger Foundation, attempted to make a fair comparison of all three types of predictive systems (Holt & Luborsky, 1958). In this instance, predicting success in psychiatric training was a reasonable undertaking for clinical assessment, because being a good psychiatrist involves much more of the personality than does learning to fly or getting good grades in college. Reasonable chances of success were assured also by the facts that the study was restricted to one large school in Topeka, Kansas, and the predictive judges all worked in this one setting and were acquainted with its intangibles.

The first system experimented with was a *naive clinical* design. Experienced psychiatrists and psychologists assessed the personalities of young physicians at the time they applied to the Menninger School of Psychiatry, without any prior job analysis, study of criterion groups, or the like. One of the advantages of this design was that the clinicians functioned in a routine fashion, using their favorite methods (interviews and diagnostic tests) in the usual way, with the opportunity to use empathy as well as inference.

Each applicant was interviewed by three psychiatrists and took a balanced battery of tests. After the hour-long interview, each psychiatrist wrote a qualitative report, rated the man on a 10-point scale, and recommended his acceptance or rejection for the training program. The clinical psychologist made similar ratings and recommendations after analyzing and writing a report on the Wechsler-Bellevue, Rorschach, and Word Association tests. An Admissions Committee made the final decision on each man after discussing the reports and ratings.

All these predictive decisions (those of the committee and of the individual assessors) had impressive and statistically very significant validities (p < .001) against the psychiatric profession's main pass-fail criterion—passing the certifying examination of the American Board of Psychiatry and Neurology. Out of a total of more than 400 subjects who were assessed from 1946 through 1952, twice as high a proportion of those accepted by the Admissions Committee (as of those who were rejected) had the Board's certification by 1956 (71 percent versus 36 percent).

These naive clinical evaluations were less successful in predicting relative standing within the group of accepted trainees. The predictive ratings of the tester and the mean rating of the three interviewers both had correlational validities of about .25 against ratings by the psychiatric resident's supervisors after two or three years of training. These validities are less significant; but from a practical standpoint, the important criterion to be able to predict is passing versus failing.

In a second experimental design, the Menninger team tried to make *sophisticated clinical* predictions. First, the experimenters made a job analysis of the work done by psychiatric residents; that is, they tried to specify the attributes of personality that would help or hinder a man in carrying out each of the psychiatric functions. They did so partly by collecting opinions from experts with long experience in training psychiatrists and psychoanalysts, and partly by making an intensive study of a small sample of both excellent and ineffective residents, using interviews and many types of tests. In an attempt to guide and objectify the analysis of projective tests and the interview, they prepared manuals listing cues that discriminated the best from the worst residents in the small sample; they then cross-validated these cues on one class with encouraging results, making revisions in an attempt to learn from the predictive successes and failures.

As a final step four psychologists acted as judges in a predictive study with 64 new applicants to the school. Each judge scored tests or interviews according to the manuals, but they also made free clinical judgments based on increasing amounts of data. The analyses were done "blind"—that is, from files of tests, credentials, and a recorded interview, with all identifying information removed. The manuals proved a disappointment; different judges using the same manual did not agree well, for a good deal of clinical judgment was still required to score them, and the validities were on about the level of the naive ratings. But the free clinical predictions yielded considerably better results, especially for the two psychologists who digested the entire file of data on each subject and then made predictions: Their validities against various criteria were at about the level of $r = .5$. Both judges were able to predict a sociometric criterion (the residents' ratings of one another's competence) better than they could predict the supervisors' evaluations; and in general one judge did somewhat better than the other. But both performed at a level considerably above that of either naive clinical prediction or the mechanical combination of clinically judged cues.

The exigencies of research may have caused the judges to approach each man's data in a more intellectual and inferential spirit than they would have shown in a normal clinical situation. Nevertheless, they did tend to develop some emotional reaction to the schema of a human being they built up out of the fragments of data; they recorded this in the form of a rating of *liking*, with the thought that it might be a source of error. Surprisingly, this rating turned out to be the best predictor of all criteria, yielding better validities (from .25 to .64) for both judges. In retrospect, this anomaly seems a reminder that the clinician's own affective reactions, of an empathic rather than an inferential nature, are one of his most valuable sources of information about another person. To be sure, this finding has to be used with great caution and cannot be taken simply as encouragement to allow one's prejudices to take over.

The *pure actuarial* approach to prediction failed completely in this study. A number of test scores were correlated with criterion evaluations of the residents in a group of 64; the scores that seemed most promising were the verbal I.Q. from the Wechsler-Bellevue scale, the Lawyer key to the Strong Vocational Interest Blank, and two scores from the Rorschach—the number of rare details seen and the number of human-movement responses. The multiple correlation of this group of scores was .56 on the original sample; when cross-validated on 100 new cases, the validity dropped to .13— completely negligible. Another actuarial prediction was made possible by the work of Strong and Tucker (1952), who developed a Psychiatrist key through a statistical analysis of tests filled out by thousands of psychiatrists certified by the American Board. This key failed to predict any of the criteria at a statistically significant or practically promising level. To be sure, greater effort over a longer period of time might have produced a slightly better actuarial system, but the conditions for successful actuarial prediction did not exist.

The first condition that is necessary is a
stable world, one that will not change in
relevant particulars. The fact that a statistical formula or actuarial table is
rigid is one of its merits: It plays no favorites, does not get sleepy or change
its standards, does not forget its principles or abandon them for some exciting new intellectual fad. But by the same token, it has no way of allowing
for the growth of a population, for changes in the meaning of test items, for
new institutional policies, for changed social conditions, or for anything else
that may affect part of the process. Such a system requires frequent revision,
therefore, if it is to be used for long.

Second, actuarial prediction demands certain *resources:* the development
of the system requires the services of a highly skilled technical staff and is
usually both expensive and time consuming. The payoff in potential applicability must be large to justify it as a practical matter. If the numbers of people
about whom predictions are being made in any one place are only moderate,
the negative consequences of failing to predict have to be severe, as they are
in situations where errors are costly in terms of money or lives.

Third, in order to establish an adequate statistical base, there must be
large numbers of subjects—preferably thousands of them, available in samples
of at least several hundred at a time and again not undergoing any important
changes. Otherwise, the originally obtained relationships between predictors
and criteria are likely to be misleading. Even a carefully developed system
could prove useless when put into effect if a different type of person presents
himself for testing, a type for which the previously established relationships
among variables no longer hold.

Fourth, in actuarial prediction there must be an objective, reliable,
and unvarying measure of the *criterion*—what it is you are trying to predict.
Passing or failing in a school or training program usually meets this specifica-
tion; but the faculty may suddenly change its standards with an increase in
enrollments or with the advent of a Sputnik. It would be difficult to set up
a statistical formula to predict the outcome of psychotherapy, since the only
criteria available are judgmental and are of unknown reliability, or stability
of meaning, when used by different judges.

In the Army Air Force example (see pages 211–12), all these conditions
were almost ideally met: For several years conditions were stable enough
and the numbers of men involved were large enough to make a very expensive system highly economical. The amount of money invested in each
man who was dropped from training was considerable, even if he did not
crash any planes and endanger any lives. The criterion (pass-fail) was objective, easy to obtain, and stable. And the whole process of training to this
point took only a few weeks. Compare this situation to medical school selection, for example: To find out whether the men admitted to medical
school make good doctors, it would be necessary to wait at least five years

while they got their minimal basic training, plus one to five more years for those who took advanced (residency) training. This is the point reached by the Army Air Force psychologists a few weeks after the subjects started training.

It may be objected that in both situations what is important is not just graduating from medical or flight training school but becoming a good physician or becoming an ace under combat conditions. Did the Air Force not care about predicting criteria like that? They did, but little is said about it, partly because good criterion measures proved hard to obtain and partly because the actuarial success story has such an anticlimactic ending. For *the composite test predictor that did so well in selecting men who could get over the first hurdle was totally unable to predict any criterion of competence under military conditions*—such as the number of missions completed, the number of enemy planes downed, or the number of decorations or promotions received. Of course not. The tests were carefully tailored to an entirely different criterion; it would have taken many more years to have gone through the necessary steps to develop accurate predictors of combat behavior. By that time the age of the missile and the helicopter would have arrived, and the whole process would have had to be revamped again.

By comparison with this failure, the modest success of the OSS (Office of Strategic Services) teams, who selected secret agents by means of clinical assessment, looks much more impressive. They had even more difficulty getting good criterion measures, but the average validity of their predictive assessments against independent ratings and other measures of success in the field was about .25, $p < .01$ (OSS Assessment Staff, 1948; see especially Table 31, p. 423).

It seems fair to conclude from the research on prediction that the six-step approach, developed in the statistical tradition, has proved its value and should be incorporated as much as possible into any serious effort to set up a predictive system. Should clinical judgment be admitted into the final process of combining data to generate predictions? If the necessary conditions for a pure actuarial system exist, that system should certainly be tried, for it has often yielded excellent results. If such conditions do not prevail and if good clinical talent is readily available, a clinical method should be tried. It may not always work, but often it is the only possible approach. Clinicians need not be intimidated when someone cites impressive figures attained by actuarial prediction where it has worked well; there are no necessary implications that what the diagnostic tester or the vocational counselor is trying to do could be accomplished better by a formula.

THE STATUS OF THE THEORETICAL ISSUES

Despite the many deficiencies of the surveys, all of which have been conducted by persons identified with the statistical, psychometric approach, it is nevertheless possible to reach some conclusions about clinical and statistical prediction. Only a few theoretical issues have been at stake in the controversy, though its practical, professional, and educational ramifications have been many and important.

The Epistemological
Issue
Does the clinician have some unique access to truth? The claim that individual behavior could be predicted only from qualitative case studies did lead to the hypothesis that clinical prediction would always be superior to actuarial, a claim that has now been decisively refuted. Whatever else one may think about the evidence, it has been clearly established that statistical prediction *is* applicable to unique individuals and that for many socially important kinds of "behavior" it can do as good a job as that done by trained clinicians, sometimes better.

Even so, the claim that statistical prediction is inherently limited is refutable on logical and philosophical grounds alone (Holt, 1961, 1967; see also the theoretical sections of Meehl, 1954). The theoretical position on which the hypothesis was based is held by few clinicians, and its demolition in no way undermines the logic of clinical assessment as presented here.

The Cognitive
Issue
Is clinical inference only informal statistical inference? This problem, most closely associated with the name Sarbin (1943; see also Sarbin, Taft, & Bailey, 1960), is even less related to data than the first issue. Sarbin claims that the clinical assessor can in principle predict *only* by statistical inference. He rejects the claim that building a theoretical schema is a genuinely creative act and holds that all expectations of the future can be nothing more than extrapolation from past experience. Since in Sarbin's original experiment (1943) the clinicians did not in fact do any better than systematically accumulated and statistically manipulated experience, he believed that his point was proved. Meehl (1954) adequately demonstrated that this was a non sequitur and that even when clinical predictions are incorrect, they do not necessarily consist only of informal statistical inferences, guesses, and speculations. (See the discussion of clinical and statistical inference in Chapter 3, page 57.)

The Conceptual
Issue
Are the clinician's concepts and theories any good? While this issue has not been explicitly posed by many writers on clinical and statistical prediction, it may well underlie a good deal of the heat that has been generated. Clinical psychologists tend to overlook the influence of the situation in determining behavior, and among determinants within the individual they tend to be most interested in unconscious needs, conflicts, fantasies, defenses, pathological trends, identifications, and the like. Since such variables are usually

assessed by means of indirect clinical inference and by methods (like projective techniques) that lack the usual psychometric credentials of demonstrated reliability and validity, many nonclinicians look askance at the whole enterprise of clinical assessment. They often feel that common sense, plus the application of the laws of learning, would probably do a much better job of psychodiagnosis and psychotherapy; and the simple, nontheoretical approach of statistical prediction appeals to them.

The major test of the usefulness of any theory is whether it contributes to man's knowledge of his world and his life and enables him to manage them more effectively through understanding. Yet there are too many other possible sources of error in the success or failure of clinical predictions for them to constitute a rigorous test of the clinician's theories. This does not mean that his concepts have too little relevance to reality, either. The concepts may be good, bad, or indifferent, but if a poorly trained person applies the measuring instruments ineptly, or if he lacks good normative information about how his tests operate in the population being studied, or if he makes incorrect assumptions about the situations in which future behavior will take place, or if he lacks information about some critically important ability—to give just a few examples—he may predict very badly. Likewise, he may predict correctly for reasons he does not understand, and he may erroneously attribute his success to a fallacious theory. It is impossible to conclude anything about the value of clinical assessment's conceptual underpinnings from the results of predictive studies.

The Real Issue: Not Theoretical but Emotional

There are probably no remaining theoretical issues to be tested by further competition between clinical and statistical predictions. Nor is it possible, in light of the many types and mixtures of clinical and statistical methods, to reach many meaningful conclusions of *any* kind from surveys of this highly miscellaneous literature. In the case of a particular predictive study, it is always possible to argue that different clinicians would have done either better or worse, since all studies show considerable individual variation in predictive ability, and that different formulas too could have performed either better or worse. What is being tested is "the state of the art" in two different technologies, and the procedure of simply tallying the studies that happen to have been published and discovered at some particular time is an extremely poor way of sampling the prevailing level of clinical and statistical prediction.

The argument that some empirical evidence is better than none, even though the sample is admittedly not in any way random or representative, is demonstrably weak. Before the scientific sampling of public opinion was invented, newspapers and magazines tried to predict American presidential elections by "straw ballots." One such magazine (the *Literary Digest*) collected literally millions of statements of voting intentions in 1936 and predicted

Roosevelt's defeat in an election that turned out to be the greatest landslide victory in United States history. This episode laid the *Literary Digest* to rest for all time and should have a similar effect on the notion that just collecting and tabulating available information is a reliable substitute for scientific sampling.

The competition between clinical and statistical prediction is both theoretically and practically useless. The main importance of the controversy is that the failure of clinicians to predict such complex social outcomes as school grades and success on parole any better than statistical methods has been used as a stick to beat the clinicians with. Because personality assessors have not surpassed statisticians on the latter's territory, they are being accused of incompetence in their own domain and are called smug and complacent when they fail to present convincing quantitative evidence that clinical assessment (and psychotherapy) is valid and effective.

The controversy has been going on during a time when clinical psychology has been coming under increasingly critical scrutiny. A widely publicized survey by Eysenck (1952) of research on the effectiveness of psychotherapy concluded that psychotherapists have not provided convincing quantitative evidence that their methods of treatment are effective. In the years following World War II, the number of clinical psychologists grew at a rate far greater than did the older, traditional branches of academic psychology; as a result, applied psychologists now vastly outnumber pure researchers and teachers. The latter group began to be distressed by the "professionalization" of psychology—by, for example, the need for the Central Office of the American Psychological Association and its officers and governing bodies to concern themselves increasingly with nonscientific problems and issues, mostly arising out of the work of clinical psychologists. Within the universities, too, there was rising dissatisfaction. Professors trained mostly in academic branches of psychology were called upon to train graduate students who wanted mainly to learn how to assess personalities and help troubled people. Partly, it was a clash of theoretical and pragmatic value systems, partly a matter of theoretical differences: As we have just seen, the theories that clinical psychologists tend to find useful in their work differ from those favored by experimental psychologists, who often consider the psychoanalytic, personalistic, or existentialist orientation of clinicians not really scientific.

There has, therefore, been a good deal of pressure on clinical psychologists to demonstrate the validity of their diagnostic and therapeutic techniques by the usual kinds of experimental evidence, or else to give up teaching and practicing a body of lore that for the most part is not even codified into the appearance of a coherent theory. It just happens, however, that there is hardly a research task within psychology so complex and difficult as the evaluation of assessment and treatment. In the judgment of most qualified members of the profession, there has never been a truly adequate study of either; a proper one would take great resources of money, time, personnel, subjects, statistical sophistication, and research creativity. The working clinician himself, spending most of his time trying to understand and to help people in distress, can hardly be expected to take careful stock of his theories and practices under such circumstances. As a result, the research that has been done has tended to be either what could be accomplished as a sideline by clinicians, or projects set up by persons more knowledgeable about experimental design than about the nature of clinical assessment and how it might be meaningfully studied.

Against this background, it is understandable how such excellent scientists as Meehl greatly overgeneralized the results of the surveys of research on clinical and statistical prediction and overlooked some of the data reviewed above (pages 217–19). Indeed, Meehl (1954) admits that his well-known conclusion—that the clinical psychologist should turn from diagnostic assessment to concentrate on therapy and research—"is my personal hunch, not proved by the presented data or strongly argued in the text [p. vii]."

THE PLACE OF THE STATISTICAL APPROACH
IN PSYCHODIAGNOSIS

Critics of clinical assessment often speak as if a great deal of the clinical psychologist's daily work consists of making predictions that could just as well (or better) be done by statistical methods. In a paper with a characteristically provocative title, "When Shall We Use Our Heads Instead of the Formula?" Meehl (1957) actually comes to a number of moderate and reasonable conclusions, but his very wording of the question implies that clinicians are frequently faced with such choices. In fact, however, "the formula" remains to be worked out in all but exceptional instances. Meehl admits as much: "Mostly we will use our heads, because there just isn't any formula." But he is optimistic about the prospect of developing one if clinicians will only shake off what he elsewhere calls "their dogmatic slumbers [Meehl, 1965, p. 27]." "In his daily decision-making," Meehl goes on to complain, "the clinician continues to function, usually quite unabashedly, as if no such book [as *Clinical Versus Statistical Prediction*] had ever been written." Yet nowhere does he demonstrate by specific job analysis that any large part of ordinary clinical work could be handled by formulas. Twenty years earlier, Chein (1945) argued eloquently that clinicians are mainly concerned with control, not prediction, putting the burden of proof on the critics to demonstrate the contrary. They still have not done so.

The misconception that clinical assessment is a predictive enterprise may arise partly from an overestimation of the importance of prediction in science. Some statistically minded psychologists argue that understanding does not signify anything different from predictive efficiency. The point of view presented here is that science is primarily concerned with understanding, which usually aids but is *not* identical with the ability to predict. It is easy to predict accurately that many a baby will bang his head against his crib if he awakens during the night, but it is difficult to know why. To understand such a form of behavior requires insight into its inner and outer causes, as instances of general laws or principles. Such insight will, it is true, usually lead to better prediction than could be attained without it, and also to more effective control. Yet it is not uncommon in science for prediction and even control to outstrip understanding. In medicine, for example, most of the effective drugs in use (at least until a few years ago) were discovered by trial and error and were put into use simply because they worked, long before the mechanism of their action was understood. That is still the case with aspirin, the most widely used and effective drug of all.

The expectation that clinical assessment ought to be reducible to a routine operation for clerks and computers may grow from a misconception of the nature of psychodiagnosis: Doesn't the clinical psychologist or psychiatrist simply check the diagnostic data on any new patient against a memorized list of the signs of each mental illness, to find the one that best fits the case?

In medicine, such an approach is actually being developed by collaborating teams of diagnosticians and computer experts. The computer's memory can store descriptions of thousands of diseases, many more than a physician can keep in his head and more than any single doctor can ever have personally seen in a patient. But its main usefulness is precisely in suggesting possibilities that might otherwise be overlooked, *not* in reaching a final diagnosis. Even in the field of internal medicine, where there are such relatively clear-cut conditions as measles, with a known germ, typical symptoms, and standard therapy, diagnosis remains an art. A computer is equipped with neither common sense nor judgment, and its program is no better than the human intelligence that produced it.

In the field of "mental illness" there are very few true diseases after the model of measles. Instead, there are people with problems. True, both the people and the problems may be sorted into categories of various kinds; there are types of personalities, and there are recurring types of difficulties they have in living satisfactory and socially constructive lives. Some clinicians object to the very idea of psychodiagnosis because they are so impressed with the rarity with which they encounter textbook cases of manic-depressive psychosis or psychopathic personality or hypochondriasis. To abandon diagnostic concepts would be like discarding the compass because one's city did not contain any streets running precisely north or west. True, as orienting points, the standard psychiatric diagnostic groups are a great deal less clear-cut and simple than geographic directions; they are more like the church steeple and big red barn pointed out by the farmer giving directions to a traveler. Nevertheless, landmarks have served mankind well in helping people to get about, and generations of psychiatrists and clinical psychologists have found diagnostic ideal types useful in much the same way.

To use diagnostic conceptions like hysteria as orienting points, not as boxes into which to drop people, means to describe *in what ways* and *to what extent* a person is hysterical. Any other such diagnostic landmark that may locate the particular subject under consideration is then used in a similar way. Clinical assessment of normal people also very often finds the diagnostic typologies helpful, as was demonstrated in the case of Morris Brown.

In the best psychodiagnostic practice, the psychologist describes the person's ingrained pattern of coping with his impulses and with environmental pressures, which developed from the interaction of constitution and formative influences during his childhood. Then the clinician judges how far (if at all) this style of adaptation has broken down and relates it to the kinds of symptoms that have emerged. A good diagnostic report for clinical use will describe as many aspects of personality as seem relevant to understanding and helping the person—in the end putting the pieces together in a dual diagnostic formulation of the sort just described.

The "cookbook" approach of Halbower (see Chapter 8, page 171) was advocated by Meehl (1956) not as a way of putting patients into pigeonholes but as a means of arriving at general descriptions of their personalities. Nevertheless, this ingenious approach has two serious drawbacks. First, it is applicable only to persons whose test scores fall into a common type, or pattern. Yet *in most clinical contexts, the only cases referred for testing are the atypical ones, the diagnostic puzzles.* It would thus be inherently quite difficult to extend Halbower's cookbook approach enough to make it helpful in everyday practice. Second, the output or result of this essentially statistical method is a Q sort—a rehash of a set of statements made about other patients. To submit such a list of standard sentences, hierarchically organized though it is, as a report on every patient would be a sure recipe for getting the psychologist's contribution disregarded. For a diagnostic report is a *communication* to someone who has therapeutic or administrative responsibility, and it will be worthless, no matter how valid it may be, unless the information is transmitted in readily usable, intelligible form.

Other statistical enthusiasts have developed computer programs that write test reports when given an input of test scores. The process is actually a simple one: A sentence written by a psychologist expressing a primary inference in terms that therapists use is stored by the computer for each possible test score; the machine prints out as many such sentences as it is fed scores. Not surprisingly, the result sounds as if it was written by a machine, and it is a pretty good simulation of the unimaginative reports turned out by a conscientious but plodding novice who knows just enough to copy out sentences from books on testing. It is hardly any better than a Q sort as a substitute for a lively, individualized picture of a person, with causal hypotheses about genetic and other relationships among trends and traits, which a good diagnostic tester can turn out.

Nevertheless, these forms of automated test analysis may have a limited role in the preliminary processing of objective tests—an extension of machine scoring, as it were. The best-fitting Q sort can be used as a source of hypotheses and formulations for the final report, but not as a substitute for it.

Assessment Assessed

How shall we evaluate personality assessment, if not by the methods suggested so far? Let us make clear what we are evaluating: We can look at assessment as the work of a number of people at particular times and places or as a body of knowledge and technique. Taking the first of these standpoints, we can say that the situation is much the same as with any kind of professional practice. For example, despite the dramatic advances of medical science and technology, there is no way a person can know what level of care he will get if he consults a physician chosen at random from the telephone book. There are probably many more mediocre dentists than expert ones; surely the same is true of personality assessors. From society's standpoint it is very important to measure the general level of any professional practice and then to try to raise it; but in many ways it makes more sense to investigate the scientific underpinnings of a profession, as embodied in its best practitioners.

Viewing it from this vantage point, then, we can say in retrospect that the field of personality assessment is undergoing a good deal of needed development and improvement through research. Not very much is firmly established and universally accepted, yet much is known. At its best, the technology can be extremely useful; multiform, intensive assessment is the best available ultimate criterion of what a person truly is and remains the best way of gaining a deep understanding of him. Yet there is still a gap between understanding a person and understanding personality, a gap that is not likely to be filled by accumulating case studies. By such means one may learn wisdom about human nature, but science demands explicit hypotheses and their verification. Many psychologists of personality believe that significant research on personality, which will ultimately lead to a body of laws, can be done only by people who have some degree of such wisdom and unformulated (or poorly articulated), intuitive insight.

Progress in this field will depend both on improving assessors and on strengthening their science. That is, we must first select better people and give them more thorough training than has been generally available so far. Personality assessment needs people with a variety of gifts: Ideally, they should be capable of rigorous scientific research and should have a humanistic and humane outlook. In examining a projective test protocol, for example, the interpreter should be free to draw on intuitive insights from thorough self-knowledge and from a rich literary culture, but he should also be stern in testing his hunches and ruthless in discarding them if they cannot be supported by evidence. In short, the best assessor is capable of both tough-mindedness and tender-mindedness.

Clinical assessment can be greatly aided by sympathetically informed but relentless inquiry into all of its aspects. We need to know much more about the base rates of all the relevant variables in the populations most frequently studied, not just diagnostic syndromes but all their constituent elements. As new forms of psychotherapy and other ways of helping people with problems are invented, there must be systematic study of the kinds of people who are helped and not helped by each. Much research could be usefully focused on collecting statistics to convert hunch-based inferential rules to statistical inferences. An inference may be based on a fairly good theory, but we can never know how far to trust it until actual experience has been tabulated. Thus, clinical assessment will be advanced by first explicating and then testing out all kinds of inferential rules, whether they are applied to life-history data, objective test scores, projective techniques, or whatever.

Likewise, objective assessment can learn from the clinical tradition. Progress in the use of inventories will depend less on complex statistical manipulation of scores than on a clear understanding of what the basic data are and how they can be improved. There is no bypassing judgment; in an objective test, the examiner relies on the subject to observe and report on his own behavioral patterns. Objective measurement will be advanced, therefore, when the subject is helped to do as good a job as possible. That can be accomplished, first, by earning his trust and confidence (not just by "building rapport") so that his defensiveness will be minimal. This means *not* trying to trick the subject or pry into his inner life without his consent; it means respecting his confidence meticulously and being completely candid about how the results are used. The next step is to make the test items clear, interesting, and unambiguous. The format and instructions of tests need more work so that taking them will be less burdensome and more attractive and so that a set, or orientation, may be created in the subject that will aid him in taking the test seriously and reporting or rating accurately.

Many techniques of assessment exist that have not been adequately covered in this book. It may well be that some of the best methods of future assessment lie in the area between tests and interviews. Most workers in the field agree, however, that progress depends less on the invention of more ingenious methods than on the development of a better theory of personality. To be sure, in the testing of any theory or method, there must be ultimately a resort to statistics, as Meehl (1954) has insisted. Just as inevitably, however, there is no escape from the necessity of interpreting the results of any test, whether the word is used in the sense of an objective or projective test of personality or a statistical test of a theory-generated hypothesis. Any way we look at it, then, the future of personality assessment belongs to those who can combine the best from the objective and the clinical traditions.

REFERENCES

Citations in the text are made by author and date of publication.

ADCOCK, C. J. A factorial examination of Sheldon's types. *Journal of Personality,* 1948, *16,* 312–19.

ADORNO, T. W., FRENKEL-BRUNSWIK, E., LEVINSON, D. J., & SANFORD, R. N. *The authoritarian personality.* New York: Harper & Row, 1950.

ALLPORT, G. W. *Personality: A psychological interpretation.* New York: Holt, Rinehart and Winston, 1937.

ALLPORT, G. W. *The use of personal documents in psychological science.* New York: Social Science Research Council, 1942 (Bulletin 49).

ALLPORT, G. W. *Pattern and growth in personality.* New York: Holt, Rinehart and Winston, 1961.

ALLPORT, G. W. (Ed.) *Letters from Jenny.* New York: Harcourt Brace Jovanovich, 1965.

ALLPORT, G. W., & ALLPORT, F. H. *A-S reaction study.* Boston: Houghton Mifflin, 1928.

ALLPORT, G. W., & ODBERT, H. S. Trait-names: A psycho-lexical study. *Psychological Monographs,* 1936, 47(1, Whole No. 211).

ALLPORT, G. W., & VERNON, P. E. *The study of values.* Boston: Houghton Mifflin, 1931.

ALLPORT, G. W., VERNON, P. E., & LINDZEY, G. *The study of values.* Boston: Houghton Mifflin, 1951.

ALLPORT, F. H., *see* Allport & Allport (1928).

BAILEY, D. E., *see* Sarbin, Taft, & Bailey (1960).

BARRON, F. Some personality correlates of independence of judgment. *Journal of Personality,* 1952, *21,* 287–97.

BARRON, F. An ego-strength scale which predicts response to psychotherapy. *Journal of Consulting Psychology,* 1953, *17,* 327–33.

BELLAK, L., & HOLT, R. R. Somatotypes in relation to dementia praecox. *American Journal of Psychiatry,* 1948, *104,* 713–24.

BIRCH, H. G., see Clark & Birch (1945).

BLOCK, J. *The Q-sort method in personality assessment and psychiatric research.* Springfield, Ill.: Charles C Thomas, 1961.

BLOCK, J. *The challenge of response sets.* New York: Appleton-Century-Crofts, 1965.

BRUNER, J. S., & TAGIURI, R. The perception of people. In G. Lindzey (Ed.), *Handbook of social psychology*, Vol. 2. Reading, Mass.: Addison-Wesley, 1954. Pp. 634–54.

BURGESS, E. W. Factors determining success or failure on parole. In A. A. Bruce (Ed.), *The workings of the indeterminate sentence law and the parole system in Illinois.* Springfield, Ill.: Illinois State Board of Parole, 1928. Pp. 205–49.

BUROS, O. K. (Ed.) *The sixth mental measurements yearbook.* Highland Park, N.J.: Gryphon Press, 1965.

CAMPBELL, E. H. Effects of mothers' anxiety on infants' behavior. Unpublished doctoral dissertation, Yale University, 1957.

CARROLL, J. B. Ratings on traits measured by a factored personality inventory. *Journal of Abnormal and Social Psychology*, 1952, 47, 626–32.

CARTWRIGHT, D. P., & FRENCH, J. R. P., JR. The reliability of life-history studies. *Character and Personality*, 1939, 8, 110–19.

CATTELL, R. B. *Description and measurement of personality.* Yonkers, N.Y.: World Book Co., 1946.

CATTELL, R. B. *Personality and motivation structure and measurement.* New York: Harcourt Brace Jovanovich, 1957.

CATTELL, R. B. Validity and reliability: A proposed more basic set of concepts. *Journal of Educational Psychology*, 1964, 55, 1–22.

CHEIN, I. The logic of prediction: Some observations on Dr. Sarbin's exposition. *Psychological Review*, 1945, 52, 175–79.

CLARK, G., & BIRCH, H. G. Hormonal modifications of social behavior, 1: The effect of sex-hormone administration on the social status of a male-castrate chimpanzee. *Psychosomatic Medicine*, 1945, 7, 321–29.

COMREY, A. L. A factor analysis of items on the MMPI Hypochondriasis Scale. *Educational and Psychological Measurement*, 1957, 17, 568–77.

COMREY, A. L. A factor analysis of items on the MMPI Psychopathic Deviate Scale. *Educational and Psychological Measurement*, 1958, 18, 91–98.

COUCH, A. S., see Kassebaum, Couch, & Slater (1959).

COUCH, A. S., & KENISTON, K. Yeasayers and naysayers: Agreeing response set as a personality variable. *Journal of Abnormal and Social Psychology*, 1960, 60, 151–74.

CRONBACH, L. J. Assessment of individual differences. In P. R. Farnsworth & Q. McNemar (Eds.), *Annual review of psychology*, Vol. 7. Palo Alto, Calif.: Annual Reviews, 1956. Pp. 173–96.

CRONBACH, L. J. *Essentials of psychological testing.* (2nd ed.) New York: Harper & Row, 1960.

DAHLSTROM, W. G., see Meehl & Dahlstrom (1960).

DAHLSTROM, W. G., & WELSH, G. S. *An MMPI handbook: A guide to use in clinical practice and research.* Minneapolis: University of Minnesota Press, 1960.

DAVITZ, J. R., et al. *The communication of emotional meaning.* New York: McGraw-Hill, 1964.

DELGADO, J. M. R. Aggressive behavior evoked by radio stimulation in monkey colonies. *American Zoologist*, 1966, 6, 669–81.

DEMPSEY, P. A unidimensional depression scale for the MMPI. *Journal of Consulting Psychology*, 1964, 28, 364–70.

DIMITROVSKY, L. The ability to identify the emotional meaning of vocal expressions at successive age levels. In J. R. Davitz et al., *The communication of emotional meaning.* New York: McGraw-Hill, 1964. Pp. 69–86.

DU BOIS, P. H. (Ed.) *The classification program.* AAF Aviation Psychology Program Research Reports, No. 2. Washington, D.C.: U.S. Government Printing Office, 1947.

EBEL, R. L. Must all tests be valid? *American Psychologist*, 1961, 16, 640–47.

EDWARDS, A. L., & HEATHERS, L. B. The first factor of the MMPI: Social desirability or ego-strength? *Journal of Consulting Psychology*, 1962, 26, 99–100.

ERIKSON, E. H. Identity and the life cycle. *Psychological Issues*, 1959, 1, Monograph No. 1.

ERIKSON, E. H. *Childhood and society.* (2nd ed.) New York: Norton, 1963.

ESTES, S. G. Judging personality from expressive behavior. *Journal of Abnormal and Social Psychology*, 1938, *33*, 217–36.

EYSENCK, H. J. The effects of psychotherapy: An evaluation. *Journal of Consulting Psychology*, 1952, *16*, 319–24.

EYSENCK, H. J. *The structure of human personality.* (2nd ed.) New York: Barnes & Noble, 1960.

EYSENCK, H. J. *Maudsley Personality Inventory.* San Diego, Calif.: Educational and Industrial Testing Service, 1962.

EYSENCK, H. J., & EYSENCK, S. B. G. *Eysenck Personality Inventory.* San Diego, Calif.: Educational and Industrial Testing Service, 1963.

EYSENCK, S. B. G., *see* Eysenck & Eysenck (1963).

FELEKY, A. M. The expression of the emotions. *Psychological Review*, 1914, *21*, 33–44.

FISS, H. Physiognomic effects of subliminal stimulation. *Perceptual and Motor Skills*, 1966, *22*, 365–66.

FLANAGAN, J. C. *Factor analysis in the study of personality.* Stanford, Calif.: Stanford University Press, 1935.

FRENCH, J. R. P., JR., *see* Cartwright & French (1939).

FRENKEL-BRUNSWIK, E. Intolerance of ambiguity as an emotional and perceptual personality variable. *Journal of Personality*, 1949, *18*, 108–43.

FRENKEL-BRUNSWIK, E., *see also* Adorno, Frenkel-Brunswik, Levinson, & Sanford (1950).

FREUD, A. Adolescence. *Psychoanalytic Study of the Child*, 1958, *13*, 255–78.

FREUD, S. (1887–1902) *The origins of psycho-analysis: Letters to Wilhelm Fliess, drafts and notes: 1887–1902.* London: Imago, 1954.

FREUD, S. (1916) Some character-types met with in psycho-analytic work. *Standard edition*, Vol. 14. London: Hogarth Press, 1957. Pp. 309–33.

FRIJDA, N. H. The understanding of facial expression of emotion. *Acta Psychologica*, 1953, *9*, 294–362.

GARDNER, R. W., HOLZMAN, P. S., KLEIN, G. S., LINTON, H. B., & SPENCE, D. P. Cognitive control: A study of individual consistencies in cognitive behavior. *Psychological Issues*, 1959, *1*(4).

GATES, G. S. An experimental study of the growth of social perception. *Journal of Educational Psychology*, 1923, *14*, 449–61.

GILL, M. M., *see* Rapaport, Gill, & Schafer (1945) (1968).

GLUECK, E., *see* Glueck & Glueck (1950).

GLUECK, S., & GLUECK, E. *Unraveling juvenile delinquency.* Cambridge, Mass.: Harvard University Press, 1950.

GLUECK, B. C., MEEHL, P. E., SCHOFIELD, W., & CLYDE, D. J. The quantitative assessment of personality. *Comprehensive Psychiatry*, 1964, *5*, 15–23.

GOLDBERG, L. R. Simple models or simple processes? Some research on clinical judgments. *American Psychologist*, 1968, *23*, 483–96.

GOLDBERG, L. R., *see also* Hase & Goldberg (1967).

GOTTSCHALDT, K. Über den Einfluss der Erfahrung auf die Wahrnehmung von Figuren [On the influence of experience on the perception of figures], 2. *Psychologische Forschung*, 1929, *12*, 1–87.

GOUGH, H. G. *Manual for the California Psychological Inventory.* Palo Alto, Calif.: Consulting Psychologists Press, 1957.

GOUGH, H. G. The Adjective Check List as a personality assessment research technique. *Psychological Reports*, 1960, *6*, 107–22.

GOUGH, H. G. Clinical versus statistical prediction in psychology. In L. Postman (Ed.), *Psychology in the making: Histories of selected research problems.* New York: Knopf, 1962. Pp. 526–84.

GOUGH, H. G. *Adjective Check List manual.* Palo Alto, Calif.: Consulting Psychologists Press, 1965.

GROSS, M. *The brain watchers.* New York: Random House, 1962.

GRUEN, A. A critique and re-evaluation of Witkin's perception and perception-personality work. *Journal of General Psychology*, 1957, *56*, 73–93.

GUILFORD, J. P. *The nature of human intelligence.* New York: McGraw-Hill, 1967.

HARLOW, H. F. The heterosexual affectional system in monkeys. *American Psychologist*, 1962, *17*, 1–9.

HASE, H. D., & GOLDBERG, L. R. Comparative validity of different strategies of constructing personality inventory scales. *Psychological Bulletin*, 1967, *67*, 231–48.

HATHAWAY, S. R., *see* Meehl & Hathaway (1946).

HATHAWAY, S. R., & MC KINLEY, J. C. *The Minnesota Multiphasic Personality Inventory*. New York: Psychological Corporation, 1943.

HEATHERS, L. B., *see* Edwards & Heathers (1962).

HOFFMAN, P. J. The paramorphic representation of clinical judgment. *Psychological Bulletin*, 1960, 57, 116–31.

HOLT, R. R. The accuracy of self-evaluations: Its measurement and some of its personological correlates. *Journal of Consulting Psychology*, 1951, 15, 95–101.

HOLT, R. R. Clinical *and* statistical prediction: A reformulation and some new data. *Journal of Abnormal and Social Psychology*, 1958, 56, 1–12.

HOLT, R. R. Clinical judgment as a disciplined inquiry. *Journal of Nervous and Mental Disease*, 1961, 133, 369–82.

HOLT, R. R. Forcible indoctrination and personality change. In P. Worchel & D. Byrne (Eds.), *Personality change*. New York: Wiley, 1964. Pp. 289–318.

HOLT, R. R. Individuality and generalization in the psychology of personality. In R. S. Lazarus & E. M. Opton, Jr. (Eds.), *Personality: Selected readings*. Baltimore: Penguin Books, 1967. Pp. 38–65.

HOLT, R. R., *see also* Bellak & Holt (1948).

HOLT, R. R., & LUBORSKY, L. *Personality patterns of psychiatrists*. New York: Basic Books, 1958. 2 vols.

HOLZBERG, J. D., *see* Wittenborn & Holzberg (1951).

HOLZMAN, P. S., *see* Gardner et al. (1959).

HOLZMAN, P. S., & KLEIN, G. S. Cognitive system-principles of leveling and sharpening: Individual differences in assimilation effects in visual time-errors. *Journal of Psychology*, 1954, 37, 105–22.

JACKSON, D. N., *see* Messick & Jackson (1961).

JACKSON, D. N., & MESSICK, S. Content and style in personality assessment. *Psychological Bulletin*, 1958, 55, 243–52.

JENKINS, T. N. *How well do you know yourself?* New York: Executive Analysis Corp., 1959.

JENKINS, T. N. Measurement of the primary factors of the total personality. *Journal of Psychology*, 1962, 54, 417–42.

JONES, E. *The life and work of Sigmund Freud*, Vol. 1. New York: Basic Books, 1953.

JUNG, C. J. (1921) *Psychological types*. New York: Harcourt Brace Jovanovich, 1923.

KALINA, W. Badania nad rozpoznawaniem wrazow mimicznych uczuc u ludzi [A study of the recognition of mimic expressions in people]. *Przeglad Psychologiczny*, 1960, 4, 177–85.

KASSEBAUM, G. G., COUCH, A. S., & SLATER, P. E. The factorial dimensions of the MMPI. *Journal of Consulting Psychology*, 1959, 23, 226–36.

KELLEY, H. H. The warm-cold variable in first impressions of persons. *Journal of Personality*, 1950, 18, 431–39.

KENISTON, K., *see* Couch & Keniston (1960).

KLEIN, G. S. The personal world through perception. In R. R. Blake & G. V. Ramsey (Eds.), *Perception: An approach to personality*. New York: Ronald Press, 1951. Pp. 328–55.

KLEIN, G. S., *see also* Gardner et al. (1959); Holzman & Klein (1954).

KLEINER, R. J. The effects of threat reduction upon interpersonal attractiveness. *Journal of Personality*, 1960, 28, 145–55.

KRETSCHMER, E. (1921) *Physique and character*. New York: Harcourt Brace Jovanovich, 1925.

KUDER, G. F. *Kuder Preference Record—Vocational*. Chicago: Science Research Associates, 1948.

KVALE, S., *see* Rommetveit & Kvale (1965).

LACEY, J. I. Psychophysiological approaches to the evaluation of psychotherapeutic process and outcome. In E. A. Rubinstein & M. B. Parloff (Eds.), *Research in psychotherapy*. Washington, D.C.: American Psychological Association, 1959.

LEVINSON, D. J., *see* Adorno, Frenkel-Brunswik, Levinson, & Sanford (1950).

LEVITT, E. A. The relationship between abilities to express emotional meanings vocally and facially. In J. R. Davitz *et al.*, *The communication of emotional meaning*. New York: McGraw-Hill, 1964. Pp. 87–100.

LEVY, I., ORR, T. B., & ROSENZWEIG, S. Judgments of emotion from facial expressions by college students, mental retardates, and mental hospital patients. *Journal of Personality*, 1960, 28, 342–49.

LINDZEY, G. Thematic Apperception Test: Interpretative assumptions and related

234   *References*

empirical evidence. *Psychological Bulletin*, 1952, *49*, 1–25.

LINDZEY, G. Seer versus sign. *Journal of Experimental Research in Personality*, 1965, *1*, 17–26.

LINDZEY, G., *see also* Allport, Vernon, & Lindzey (1951).

LINTON, H. B. Dependence on external influence: Correlates in perception, attitudes, and judgment. *Journal of Abnormal and Social Psychology*, 1955, *51*, 502–07.

LINTON, H. B., *see also* Gardner et al. (1959).

LORENZ, K. *King Solomon's ring.* New York: T. Y. Crowell, 1952.

LORR, M., O'CONNOR, J. P., & STAFFORD, J. W. Confirmation of nine psychotic symptom patterns. *Journal of Clinical Psychology*, 1957, *13*, 252–57.

LOVELL, V. R. The human use of personality tests: A dissenting view. *American Psychologist*, 1967, *22*, 383–93.

LUBORSKY, L., *see* Holt & Luborsky (1958).

MACHOVER, K. *Personality projection in the drawing of the human figure.* Springfield, Ill.: Charles C Thomas, 1949.

MAHL, G. *Psychological conflict and defense.* New York: Harcourt Brace Jovanovich, 1971.

MASLING, J. Role-related behavior of the subject and psychologist and its effects upon psychological data. In D. Levine (Ed.), *Nebraska symposium on motivation*, Vol. 14. Lincoln: University of Nebraska Press, 1966. Pp. 67–103.

MAY, H. S. A study of emotional expression among Chinese and Americans. Unpublished Master's essay, Columbia University, 1938.

MC KINLEY, J. C., *see* Hathaway & McKinley (1948).

MEAD, G. H. *Mind, self, and society.* Chicago: University of Chicago Press, 1934.

MEEHL, P. E. *Clinical versus statistical prediction.* Minneapolis: University of Minnesota Press, 1954.

MEEHL, P. E. Wanted—A good cookbook. *American Psychologist*, 1956, *11*, 263–72.

MEEHL, P. E. When shall we use our heads instead of the formula? *Journal of Counseling Psychology*, 1957, *4*, 268–73.

MEEHL, P. E. Seer over sign: The first good example. *Journal of Experimental Research in Personality*, 1965, *1*, 27–32.

MEEHL, P. E., *see also* Glueck, Meehl, Schofield, & Clyde (1964).

MEEHL, P. E., & DAHLSTROM, W. G. Objective configural rules for discriminating psychotic from neurotic MMPI profiles. *Journal of Consulting Psychology*, 1960, *24*, 375–87.

MEEHL, P. E., & HATHAWAY, S. R. The K factor as a suppressor variable in the MMPI. *Journal of Applied Psychology*, 1946, *30*, 525–64.

MEEHL, P. E., & ROSEN, A. Antecedent probability and the efficiency of psychometric signs, patterns, or cutting scores. *Psychological Bulletin*, 1955, *52*, 194–216.

MELTZER, L., *see* Thompson & Meltzer (1964).

MERRILL, M. A., *see* Terman & Merrill (1937).

MESSICK, S. *Hidden Figures Test-cf-1.* Developed under NIMH Contract M-4186. Princeton, N.J.: Educational Testing Service, 1962.

MESSICK, S., *see also* Jackson & Messick (1958).

MESSICK, S., & JACKSON, D. N. Acquiescence and the factorial interpretation of the MMPI. *Psychological Bulletin*, 1961, *58*, 299–304.

MILLER, R. E., MURPHY, J. V., & MIRSKY, I. A. Relevance of facial expression and posture as cues in communication of affect between monkeys. *AMA Archives of General Psychiatry*, 1959, *1*, 480–88.

MIRSKY, I. A., *see* Miller, Murphy, & Mirsky (1959).

MORENO, J. L. *Who shall survive?* (Rev. ed.) Beacon, N.Y.: Beacon House, 1953.

MORGAN, C. D., & MURRAY, H. A. A method for investigating fantasies: The Thematic Apperception Test. *Archives of Neurology and Psychiatry*, 1935, *34*, 289–306.

MUNN, N. L. The effect of knowledge of the situation upon judgment of emotion from facial expressions. *Journal of Abnormal and Social Psychology*, 1940, *35*, 324–38.

MURPHY, G. *Personality: A biosocial approach to origins and structure.* New York: Harper & Row, 1947.

MURPHY, J. V., *see* Miller, Murphy, & Mirsky (1959).

MURRAY, H. A. The effect of fear upon estimates of the maliciousness of other personalities. *Journal of Social Psychology*, 1933, 4, 310–29.

MURRAY, H. A. *Thematic Apperception Test.* Cambridge, Mass.: Harvard University Press, 1943.

MURRAY, H. A., *see also* Morgan & Murray (1935).

MURRAY, H. A., *et al. Explorations in personality.* New York: Oxford University Press, 1938.

MUSSEN, P. H., *see* Scodel & Mussen (1953).

NORMAN, W. T. Toward an adequate taxonomy of personality attributes: Replicated factor structure in peer nomination personality ratings. *Journal of Abnormal and Social Psychology*, 1963a, 66, 574–83.

NORMAN, W. T. Personality measurement, faking, and detection: An assessment method for use in personnel selection. *Journal of Applied Psychology*, 1963b, 47, 225–41.

O'CONNOR, J. P., *see* Lorr, O'Connor, & Stafford (1957).

ODBERT, H. S., *see* Allport & Odbert (1936).

ODEN, M. H., *see* Terman & Oden (1947).

ORR, T. B., *see* Levy, Orr, & Rosenzweig (1960).

OSS ASSESSMENT STAFF (Office of Strategic Services). *Assessment of men.* New York: Holt, Rinehart and Winston, 1948.

PACKARD, V. *The naked society.* New York: McKay, 1964.

PETERSON, D. R. Scope and generality of verbally defined personality factors. *Psychological Review*, 1965, 72, 48–59.

PIAGET, J. *The language and thought of the child.* New York: Harcourt Brace Jovanovich, 1926.

POLANYI, M. *Personal knowledge: Towards a post-critical philosophy.* New York: Harper & Row, 1964.

POSTMAN, L. Review of H. A. Witkin *et al., Personality through perception* (1954). *Psychological Bulletin*, 1955, 52, 79–83.

RAPAPORT, D., GILL, M. M., & SCHAFER, R. *Diagnostic psychological testing*, Vol. 1. Chicago: Yearbook Publishers, 1945.

RAPAPORT, D., GILL, M. M., & SCHAFER, R. *Diagnostic psychological testing.* (Rev. ed., edited by R. R. Holt.) New York: International Universities Press, 1968.

REDL, F. *When we deal with children.* New York: Free Press, 1966.

ROMMETVEIT, R., & KVALE, S. Stages in concept formation. *Scandinavian Journal of Psychology*, 1965, 6, 59–79.

RORSCHACH, H. (1921) *Psychodiagnostics.* New York: Grune & Stratton, 1949.

ROSEN, A., *see* Meehl & Rosen (1955).

ROSENZWEIG, S., *see* Levy, Orr, & Rosenzweig (1960).

SACKETT, G. P. Monkeys reared in isolation with pictures as visual input: Evidence for an innate releasing mechanism. *Science*, 1966, 154, 1468–73.

SANFORD, N. (Ed.) *The American college.* New York: Wiley, 1962.

SANFORD, R. N., *see* Adorno, Frenkel-Brunswik, Levinson, & Sanford (1950).

SARBIN, T. R. A contribution to the study of actuarial and individual methods of prediction. *American Journal of Sociology*, 1943, 48, 593–602.

SARBIN, T. R., TAFT, R., & BAILEY, D. E. *Clinical inference and cognitive theory.* New York: Holt, Rinehart and Winston, 1960.

SAWYER, J. Measurement *and* prediction, clinical *and* statistical. *Psychological Bulletin*, 1966, 66, 178–200.

SCHAFER, R. Generative empathy in the treatment situation. *Psychoanalytic Quarterly*, 1959, 28, 342–73.

SCHAFER, R., *see also* Rapaport, Gill, & Schafer (1945) (1968).

SCHOFIELD, W., *see* Glueck, Meehl, Schofield, & Clyde (1964).

SCHONBAR, R. A. Some manifest characteristics of recallers and nonrecallers of dreams. *Journal of Consulting Psychology*, 1959, 23, 414–18.

SCHWARTZ, M. S., *see* Stanton & Schwartz (1954).

SCODEL, A., & MUSSEN, P. H. Social perceptions of authoritarians and nonauthoritarians. *Journal of Abnormal and Social Psychology*, 1953, 48, 181–84.

SHELDON, W. H., *et al. The varieties of human physique.* New York: Harper & Row, 1940.

SHELDON, W. H., & STEVENS, S. S. *The varieties of temperament.* New York: Harper & Row, 1942.

SHELDON, W. H., *et al. Varieties of delinquent youth.* New York: Harper & Row, 1949.

SIEGEL, L. A biographical inventory for students. *Journal of Applied Psychology*, 1956, *40*, 5–10, 122–26.

SINGER, J. L. *Daydreaming*. New York: Random House, 1966.

SPENCE, D. P., *see* Gardner et al. (1959).

SPRANGER, E. *Types of men: The psychology and ethics of personality*. New York: Johnson Reprint Corp., 1928.

STAFFORD, J. W., *see* Lorr, O'Connor, & Stafford (1957).

STANTON, A. H., & SCHWARTZ, M. S. *The mental hospital: A study of institutional participation in psychiatric illness and treatment*. New York: Basic Books, 1954.

STAR, S. A. The screening of psychoneurotics. In S. A. Stouffer, L. Guttman, E. A. Suchman, P. F. Lazarsfeld, S. A. Star, & J. A. Clausen, *Measurement and prediction*. Princeton, N.J.: Princeton University Press, 1950. Pp. 486–567.

STEVENS, S. S., *see* Sheldon & Stevens (1942).

STRONG, E. K., JR. *Vocational interests of men and women*. Stanford, Calif.: Stanford University Press, 1943.

STRONG, E. K., JR., & TUCKER, A. C. The use of vocational interest scales in planning a medical career. *Psychological Monographs*, 1952, *66*(9, Whole No. 341).

SZASZ, T. S. *The myth of mental illness*. New York: Harper & Row, 1961.

TAFT, R. The ability to judge people. *Psychological Bulletin*, 1955, *52*, 1–23.

TAFT, R., *see also* Sarbin, Taft, & Bailey (1960).

TAGIURI, R., *see* Bruner & Tagiuri (1954).

TERMAN, L. M., & MERRILL, M. A. *Measuring intelligence: A guide to the administration of the new revised Stanford-Binet tests of intelligence*. Boston: Houghton Mifflin, 1937.

TERMAN, L. M., & ODEN, M. H. *Genetic studies of genius*. Vol. 4. *The gifted child grows up*. Stanford, Calif.: Stanford University Press, 1947.

THOMPSON, D. F., & MELTZER, L. Communication of emotional intent by facial expression. *Journal of Abnormal and Social Psychology*, 1964, *68*, 129–35.

TUCKER, A. C., *see* Strong & Tucker (1952).

TYLER, F. T. A factorial analysis of fifteen MMPI scales. *Journal of Consulting Psychology*, 1951, *15*, 541–46.

VERNON, P. E. *Personality assessment: A critical survey*. New York: Wiley, 1964.

VERNON, P. E., *see also* Allport & Vernon (1931); Allport, Vernon, & Lindzey (1951).

WECHSLER, D. *Wechsler Adult Intelligence Scale*. New York: Psychological Corp., 1955.

WELSH, G. S. Factor dimensions A and R. In G. S. Welsh & W. G. Dahlstrom (Eds.), *Basic readings on the MMPI in psychology and medicine*. Minneapolis: University of Minnesota Press, 1956. Pp. 264–81.

WELSH, G. S., *see also* Dahlstrom & Welsh (1960).

WHITE, R. W. *Lives in progress*. (2nd ed.) New York: Holt, Rinehart and Winston, 1966.

WHYTE, W. H., JR. *The organization man*. New York: Simon & Schuster, 1956.

WITKIN, H. A. Individual differences in ease of perception of embedded figures. *Journal of Personality*, 1950, *19*, 1–15.

WITKIN, H. A., et al. *Personality through perception*. New York: Harper & Row, 1954.

WITKIN, H. A., et al. *Psychological differentiation: Studies of development*. New York: Wiley, 1962.

WITTENBORN, J. R., & HOLZBERG, J. D. The generality of psychiatric syndromes. *Journal of Consulting Psychology*, 1951, *15*, 372–80.

WITTMAN, M. P. A scale for measuring prognosis in schizophrenic patients. *Elgin Papers*, 1941, *4*, 20–33.

YOUNG, K. (1940) *Personality and problems of adjustment*. (2nd ed.) New York: Appleton-Century-Crofts, 1952.

INDEX

Page numbers in *italics* refer to illustrations.

Behavior (*Cont.*)
structural determinants of, 6, 7
"total," and personality assessment, 52–53
Behaviorism, 13
Bender Gestalt Test, 55
Bernreuter Personality Inventory, 66
Binet, Alfred, and intelligence testing, 62, 63, 121, 208
Biochemistry, 80
Biographical inventory, 49–50
Block, Jack, and personality assessment, 73, 172, 183
Brain, 6, 7
Brown, Morris, case study of, 90, 92, 95, 96, 97, 117, 166, 188, 189, 191, 199–200, 205, 227
adolescence of, 107–09
adult years of, early, 111–15
affects and impulses of, 160
and California Q Set, 181–85, *182*, 182 (table), 184 (table)
castration anxiety of, 133, 134, 144
childhood of, 104–07
clinical assessment of, 99–115, 101 (table), 191–95
cognitive style of, 160, 186
criticism of assessment of, 98
diagnostic formulation of, 162–63
direct observation of, 97–98
family background of, 154–57, 161–62, 163
formal assessment of, 117–49
and free association, 146–48
and Hidden Figures Test, 187
homosexual activity of, 107, 108, 111, 112, 158, 162, 195
impulses and affects of, 160
infancy of, 102–04
informal assessment of, 90, 93–115
I.Q. of, 121, 153, 177
maturation of, 194, 196–98
and MMPI, 167, *168*, 169, 170, 171, 172, 185
motives of, 100, 113–15, 123, 160–61
objective assessment of, comment on, 123–24
parental relationships of, 154, 155–57, 161–63, 192–93, 198
personality pattern of, 158–63
projective assessment of, comment on, 148–49
and Q-sorting method, 181–85, *182*, 182 (table), 184 (table)
results of 1966 clinical assessment of, 191–95
and Rorschach Test, 139–41, 143–45, 163, 198
sense of identity of, 136, 162, 197–98

Brown, Morris (*Cont.*)
sexual behavior of, summary of, 157–58, 195
and TAT, 124, 125–30, 132–39, 143, 145, 147, 155, 198
values of, profile of, 119–20, *120*, 161, 175, 176
and WAIS, 176, 177
Brown, Thomas, quoted, 18
Burgess experience table, 209–11

c

California F-Test, 89
California Psychological Inventory, 173
California Q Set, 181–85, *182*, 182 (table), 184 (table)
Carlyle, Thomas, quoted, 91
Case study of Morris Brown, *see* Brown, Morris
Castration anxiety, of Morris Brown, 133, 134, 144
Central nervous system, 6
Cerebrotonia, 122
Chesterfield, Lord, quoted, 164
Clinical personality assessment, 14–15, 45, 59, 229
autobiographies in, 49–50
diaries in, 50
direct methods of, 46–51
free association in, 46, 47–48
indirect methods of, 51–56
interpretation in, 56–57
interview in, 46–48
letters in, 50–51
multiform, 57
observation in, 49
personal documents in, 49–51
prediction in, *see* Clinical prediction
projective techniques for, *see* Projective personality tests
tests in, 48, 57
Clinical prediction:
achievements of, 217–19
naive, 215 (table), 217–18
sophisticated, 216, 217–19
versus statistical prediction, 206–28, 215 (table)
Clinical Versus Statistical Prediction (Meehl), 212, 225
Code of Ethics, of American Psychological Association, 74, 75
Cognitive style, objective measures of, 81–84, 146, 160, 185–89
Collective monologues (Piaget), 39
Communication and mature empathy, 39
Computers, 10
Conflict(s):
individual differences in, 93

Conflict(s) (*Cont.*)
   resolution of, process of, 194, 196–98
   See also Anxiety; Defense(s)
Conscience, 135, 137
   See also Superego
Contagion, emotional, 12, 35, 36–37, 38
Correlation, statistical method of, 64
Crime and Punishment (Dostoevsky), 9
Critical score, in personality inventory, 66, 67
Cultural standards, for emotional expression, 32–33
Cultural tradition and personality, 153–54
Cycloid personality, 153

D

Defense(s), 23–24, 93, 158–60
   of avoidance, 138, 159
   of denial, 160, 199
   of identification, *see* Identification
   in personality assessment, 23–24, 99
   of projection, 24, 28
   See also Anxiety; Conflict(s)
Delinquency, juvenile, 78, 79
Denial, 160, 199
Diaries, in clinical personality assessment, 50
Diderot, Denis, quoted, 190
Digit-span test, 61
Draw-a-Man Test, 56
Dreams and indirect personality assessment, 51
Dyplastic body build (Kretschmer), 77
Dysplasia, 122

E

Ebel's critique of validity, in personality testing, 204, 205
Ectomorphy, 77, 78, 79, 79 (table), 121
Educational guidance, 15–16
Educational selection, 16
Educational Testing Service, 187
Ego control (Block), 73, 172
Ego identity, *see* Identity
Ego resiliency (Block), 73, 172
Ego strength, 76, 171, 172
Ego structure, 138, 144, 158–60
Electroencephalograph (EEG), 15
Embedded Figures Test, 187
Emotion(s):
   ability to experience, 40–41
   perception of, in face and voice, 29–33
   See also Affect(s); Empathy
Emotional contagion, 12, 35, 36–37, 38
Empathy, 11–12, 13, 24, 33–41, 97, 130, 218
   esthetic, 33

Empathy (*Cont.*)
   mature, 34, 37–41, 97
   See also Affect(s); Emotion(s)
Empirical keying, in personality testing, 68, 70, 75, 171, 174
Endocrinology, 80
Endomorphy, 77, 78, 79 (table), 121, 122
Epistemological issue, in clinical-versus-statistical controversy, 222
Erikson, E. H., 163
   on moratorium period, 196
   on postadolescent identity crisis, 162
Ethics of personality testing, 74–75
Euphoria, 80
Existentialism, 224
Experience table, Burgess, 209 (table), 209–11
Explorations in Personality (Murray), 101
Extroversion, 174, 175 (table)
Eysenck Personality Inventory, 48, 165, 174–75, 175 (table)

F

Factor analysis, 87, 172–73, 186
   of Bernreuter Personality Inventory, 66
   of intelligence tests, 64–65
Fantasies:
   of Morris Brown, 124–30, 147
   unconscious, *see* Unconscious fantasies
Fear, *see* Anxiety; Defense(s)
Field articulation (field dependence–independence), 82–84, 83, 84, 187–88, 188
Fliess, Wilhelm, Freud's letters to, 50
Free association, 46, 47–48, 146–48
Freud, Anna, 163
Freud, Sigmund, 13, 27, 46
   on free association, 146
   and indirect personality assessment, 51
   interview developed by, 47, 48
   letters of, to Fliess, 50
   on overdetermination, 53
   on projection, 24

G

Galton, Francis, and mental testing, 62, 64
Galvanic skin response (GSR), 80, 81
Gestalt, in informal personality assessment, 20, 29
Gottschaldt Test, 83
Gough, Harrison, and nonprojective personality assessment, 165, 173, 178, 179
Guilt, 137
   See also Anxiety
Gynandromorphy, 122

H

Halo effect, in informal personality assessment, 21, 28
Harvard Psychological Clinic, 89, 124
Hatred, see Aggression; Anger
Hawthorne, Nathaniel, quoted, 44
Hidden Figures Test, 187, *188*
Holtzman Inkblot Test, 55
Homogeneous keying, of Kuder Preference Record, 68
Homosexuality, 107, 108, 111, 112, 133, 135–36, 158, 162, 169, 195, 217
Hostility, see Aggression; Anger
House-Tree-Person Test, 56
Humm-Wadsworth Temperament Scale, 123

I

Identification, 136, 162, 197–98
Identity, secure sense of, 38–39, 198
Incest, taboos against, 133, 197
Informal personality assessment:
  of Brown, Morris, see Brown, Morris
  conversation in, 41–42
  empathy in, see Empathy
  errors in, 20–28, 42, 99
  Gestalt in, 20, 29
  mechanisms of, 11–12
  methods of, 41–42
  of nonconformity, 9
  observation in, 41
  through perception of emotions in face and voice, 28–34
  place of, in modern psychology, 12–13
  projection in, 24, 28
  of self, 10
  systematization of, 43
  tolerance for ambiguity in, 25
  uses of, 8–13
Institute for Personality Assessment and Research, 178, 179
Integrative synthesis, in personality assessment, 94
Intelligence quotient (I.Q.), 29, 48, 63, 120, 121, 176, 177, 219
Intelligence tests, 48, 53, 120–21, 176–78, 208
  factor analysis of, 64–65
  and psychometric tradition, 62–65
  uses of, 63–64
Interview, in clinical personality assessment, 46–48
Intraceptive judgment, 89
Intuition, 13, 56
Inventories:
  biographical, 49–50
  personality, see Personality inventories

Ipsative scaling, in personality assessment, 181, 183

J

Jones's biography of Freud, 50
Joyce, James, quoted, 150

K

Kraepelin's assessment methods, 45
Kretschmer's body types, 77
Kuder Preference Record, 68, 69

L

Learning in childhood, 7, 33–34, 39
Leniency effect, in informal personality assessment, 21
Letters from Jenny (Allport), 51
Leveling-sharpening, in cognitive style, 82–83, 185–87
Locke, John, quoted, 201

M

Masturbation, 107, 108, 113
Maturation, 194, 196
Maudsley Personality Inventory, 174
Maugham, W. Somerset, quoted, 2
Meehl, Paul E., on clinical versus statistical prediction, 212–14
Menninger Foundation, 217
Menninger School of Psychiatry, 218
Merton's concept of "self-fulfulling prophecies," 22
Mesomorphy, 77, 78, 79, 79 (table), 121
Minnesota Multiphasic Personality Inventory (MMPI), 70–75 *passim*, 131, 165, 166, 167, *168*, 177, 178, 213
  of Brown, Morris, 167, *168*, 169, 170, 171, 172, 185
  interpretation of, 170–74
Monkeys:
  innate ability of, to recognize emotion, 32, 35
  socially deprived, 36, 37
Monologues, collective (Piaget), 39
Moratorium period (Erikson), 196
Motives, assessment of, 47–48, 51–56, 70–72, 93
Multiple determinants of behavior, 53–55
Multiple regression, prediction by, 211–12
Murray, H. A., on personality assessment, 72, 89, 101, 127, 173

N

Nervous system:
  autonomic, 80–81
  central, 6

Neuropsychiatric Screening Adjunct
(NSA), 67, 68 (table)
Nonconformity, assessment of, 9
Normative rating, 181

O

Objective Analytic Tests, 76
Obsessive-compulsive personality, characteristics of, 138, 143, 158–60, 197
Oedipal complex, 133
See also Castration anxiety
Office of Strategic Services (OSS), 221
Overdetermination (Freud), 53

P

Paranoia, 24, 80
Paranoid scale, 172
Paresis, 79, 79 (table)
Peace Corps, 16, 72
Perception, 81
Person:
distinguished from personality, 8
perception of, in informal personality assessment, 20
Personal Data Sheet, 65
Personality:
assessment of, *see* Personality assessment
authoritarian, 25, 26
cycloid, 153
defined, 5, 6
development of, *see* Personality development
genetic method of studying, 6
judgments of, as objective measures, 84–90
nature of, 5–8
as pattern of traits, 5
person distinguished from, 8
psychopathic, 40
synthesis of data on, 151–52
Personality and Problems of Adjustment (Young), 101
Personality assessment, 4, 5–8
biochemical measures in, 80
of Brown, Morris, *see* Brown, Morris
clinical, *see* Clinical personality assessment
cognitive style in, 81–84, 185–89
as descriptive discipline, 6–8
diagnostic, 14, 15
direct approach to, 65–69
errors in, sources of, 20–28, 42, 99
ethics of, 74–75
evaluation of, 202–29
formal, uses of, 14–17
ideal, specifications for, 93–95
indirect approach to, 69–76

Personality assessment (*Cont.*)
informal, *see* Informal personality assessment
integrative synthesis in, 94
ipsative scaling in, 181, 183
and judgments of personality as objective measures, 84–90
in legal settings, 15
nonverbal tests in, 75–76
normative rating in, 181
and objective measures of cognitive style, 81–84
and objective measures from physical anthropology and biology, 77–81
objective tests in, 67–76, 117–24
and personality inventories, *see* Personality inventories
projective personality tests in, *see* Projective personality tests
psychophysiological measures in, 80–81
reliability of techniques of, 60–62, 203, 204, 205
in research settings, 16–17
self-rating devices in, 178–85
somatotypes in, 77, 77–80, 78, 79, 79 (table), 121–22
and statistical versus clinical prediction, 206–28
temperament typing in, 122–23
validity of techniques of, 60–62, 203, 204, 205
variables in, 93–94
and vocational interest tests, 68–69, 69 (table)
Personality inventories, 65–67, 68 (table), 70–75
ethics of, 74–75
and problem of response sets, 72–74
Philanthropy, 175
Physique:
behavior influenced by, 6
and personality assessment, 77, 77–80, 78, 79 (table)
Piaget, Jean, on personality development, 39, 42
Picture Completion subtest of WAIS, 177, 187, 188
Pleasure principle (Freud), 39
Portrait of the Artist as a Young Man, A (Joyce), 158
Postadolescent identity crisis (Erikson), 162
Prediction in personality assessment:
actuarial approach to, 214, 215 (table), 219; *see also* Statistical prediction
clinical, *see* Clinical prediction
statistical, *see* Statistical prediction
Privacy, invasion of, and personality testing, 74–75

Trait(s), 59
  defined, 5, 6
  paired, 86–87, 88 (table)
  pattern of, 5
  vocabulary of, 86–88, 87, 88 (table)
Types of Men (Spranger), 118

U

Unconscious fantasies, 134, 136, 156

V

Values, assessment of, 93, 118–20, 144, 161, 165, 175, 175–76
Veterans Administration Mental Hygiene Clinic, 171
Viscerotonia, 122
Vocational guidance, 15–16, 69, 118

Vocational interest tests, 68–69, 69 (table)
Vocational selection, 16, 118

W

Wechsler Adult Intelligence Scale (WAIS), 48, 120, 165, 176–78, 187
Wechsler-Bellevue Scale, 176, 218, 219
Wechsler Intelligence Scale for Children (WISC), 48
Witkin's concept of field independence, 83, 187
Woodworth, R. S., and personality inventories, 65, 66
Word Association Test, 55, 218
World Test, 55
World War I, 63, 65, 174
World War II, 16, 56, 67, 163, 166, 196, 211
Wrightstone Test of Civic Beliefs, 124

D
E
F 6
G 7
H 8
I 9
J 0